RUTGERS SERIES IN Accounting Information SYSTEMS

CAPEX: A Knowledge-Based Expert System

for Substantive Audit Planning

By

J. EFRIM BORITZ
School of Accountancy, University of Waterloo

ANTHONY K. P. WENSLEY
Faculty of Management, University of Toronto

Markus Wiener Publishers
Princeton

For information write to:
Markus Wiener Publishers
114 Jefferson Road, Princeton, NJ 08540

Library of Congress Cataloging-in-Publication Data
Boritz, J. Efrim.
CAPEX: a knowledge-based expert system for subsantive audit planning/ by J. Efrim Boritz, Anthony K.P. Wensley.
(Rutgers series in accounting information systems: 5)
Includes bibliographical references
ISBN 1-55876-056-3
1. CAPEX (Computer file) 2. Auditiong—Computer programs.
I. Wensley, Anthony K. II. Title. III. Series..
HF5667.12.B67 1995 95-34466
657'.45'02855369—dc20 CIP

Printed in the United States of America on acid-free paper.

TABLE OF CONTENTS

APPENDICES

The following appendices are numbered to correspond
to the chapters with which they are associated.

ACKNOWLEDGEMENTS

Major funding for the project was provided by Peat Marwick, Canada and the Ontario Government through its University Research Incentive Func (URIF) matching grant program.

We would like to thank many partners and managers of Peat Marwick, Canada and Peat Marwick, Maine who provided substantial support in the construction of the system and its subsequent testing: Dennis Hogarth, David Knight, Julia Lelik, John Willingham, Richard Webb, Reinhard Dotzlaw, Garth Pudwell, Brian Reel, Al Schope, Tim Gunther and several managers in Montvale, New Jersey who provided invaluable assistance in testing CAPEX in its many incarnations.

In addition, Jerry Whelan and Jeff Trost of Price Waterhouse, Canada, assisted in some of the validation experiments.

We also wish to acknowledge the research assistance provided by Cindy Ditner and Michelle Lynch and, in particular, the outstanding technical assistance provided by Glenn Wettlaufer and Nick Favron.

Chapter 1

AN OVERVIEW OF CAPEX

INTRODUCTION

CAPEX is a research prototype expert system designed to generate substantive audit program plans using an assertion-oriented risk-based approach to structuring audit objectives and the assessment of audit evidence. This type of approach is advocated by the American Institute of Certified Public Accountants and the Canadian Institute of Chartered Accountants and is being increasingly used by major audit firms both in North America and around the world. The assertion-based approach considers that, in presenting a set of financial statements, a client is making a variety of implicit or explicit assertions concerning those statements. It is the task of the auditor to assess the appropriateness of these assertions by gathering sufficient appropriate evidence and forming a reasoned judgment. This type of approach is described in more detail later on in this chapter.

The principal objective of this research was to evaluate the feasibility of developing a computational model and an associated knowledge-base for constructing valid substantive audit program plans using an assertion-based approach. The computational model and the knowledge-base, referred to by the acronym CAPEX (Canadian Audit Planning Expert), were developed and validated using techniques and tools derived from expert systems methodology, with particular attention being paid to the elicitation/acquisition, structuring, representation and validation of knowledge.

CAPEX is a computer program written in Prolog with a user interface written in C for the X windows environment. CAPEX encodes a considerable body of knowledge about audit evidence gathering procedures, including both tests of detail and analytical procedures, obtained from practicing auditors. In its present implementation it can generate audit plans for the revenue, receipts, receivable cycle for banking, retail and manufacturing clients and the inventory, purchases, payables, and cost of sales cycle for manufacturing clients. Uncertainty is represented in terms of probability values which are revised using Bayesian revision.

Both the computational model and the knowledge-base are composed of a number of components. Some of these components are amenable to direct validation by practicing auditors. Other components, particularly the heuristics which are used by the computational model in the construction of audit program plans, can best be validated by comparing the performance of the system to the performance of practicing auditors. A full discussion of approaches to validating the components of the knowledge-base and the computational model may be found in Chapter 4. CAPEX has been evaluated using cases developed by experienced auditors. These evaluations indicate that the system operates at a modest level of "expertise".

A prototype computational model and knowledge-base of the type developed in this research can be utilized in a number of different ways. First, it can be used to further refine the structure of the assertion-based approach to audit planning. From a policy stand-point, the explicit representation and processing of evidence provided by audit procedures within an assertion-based structure may highlight ambiguities, inconsistencies, and omissions from the structure as it is presently articulated by various professional bodies, the accounting firms participating in the research, and the research literature.

Second, the computational model and the knowledge-base can be used to test hypotheses concerning the nature of audit program planning and audit program planning expertise.

Third, the knowledge-base can provide a basis for the development of future expert systems.

This chapter will present an overview of CAPEX and the methodology which was used to develop its computational model and the associated knowledge-base. In addition, this chapter provides an overview of the system by describing the user interface.

Chapter 2 will provide details of the knowledge representation used in CAPEX.

Chapter 3 will describe the knowledge acquisition process.

Chapter 4 will describe the evaluation of the system.

Chapter 5 will discuss future research opportunities.

RESEARCH OBJECTIVES

As noted earlier, the overall objective of this research was to establish the feasibility of developing a computational model and an associated knowledge-base which could be used to generate valid audit program plans. Although many features of the computational model and knowledge base were developed as a result of extensive interaction with practicing auditors, it was not intended that the computational model developed in this research be an isomorph of the process by which practicing auditors actually construct audit program plans; rather, our objective was to use computational techniques to produce acceptable audit plans.

To determine whether the overall objective of the research had been achieved it was necessary to perform a variety of validation tests. As Bailey *et al.*(1987) indicate, such tests are not "critical" tests in the sense that they distinguish between correct or incorrect computational models. They often involve comparisons of the performance of the computational model under controlled conditions with some type of reference performance. These comparisons may lead to revisions being made to the computational model but will rarely result in its outright rejection. Thus, in this research, validation tests were designed to identify weaknesses in the computational model and provide information which could be useful in refining the model to improve its performance.

This research does not represent the first time that expert systems methodology has been applied in the domain of auditing. Prior research in this area is briefly summarized in the following section.

PREVIOUS AUDITING RESEARCH UTILIZING EXPERT SYSTEMS METHODOLOGY

Table 1.1 summarizes previous academic research involving the use of expert systems in auditing.

Table 1.1 Previous Academic Auditing Research Utilizing Expert System Methodology

System	Area	Researchers
Auditplanner	Materiality	Steinbart
Auditor	Allowance for Doubtful Accounts	Chandler, Dungan, Braun
	Allowance for Doubtful Accounts	Gal
EDP-Expert	EDP Controls	Hansen & Messier
TICOM	Internal Control	Bailey, Duke, Gerlach, Ko, Meservy, Winston
ICE	Internal Control	Kelly
Inherent Risk	Inherent Risk	Boritz, Kielstra & Albuquerque
CAPEX	Audit Programming	Boritz & Wensley
APX	Audit Planning	Bharadwaj, Mahapatra, Karan, Murthy
GCX	Going Concern	Biggs & Selfridge
FCEX	Financial Condition, Risk of Business Failure, Validity of Going Concern Assumption	Boritz

Steinbart (1984, 1987) developed an expert system, AUDITPLANNER, for making materiality judgements. The knowledge-base consisted of 75 rules. The system was validated by six auditors and judged to have "a general level of competence for making planning stage materiality judgments."

Chandler, Dungan, Braun (Dungan, 1983) developed an expert system AUDITOR to assist the auditor in assessing the appropriateness of the allowance provided for doubtful accounts by a client. AUDITOR is a rule-based system. Cues were initially identified by a number of experts and rules developed. The rules linked the cues to an hypothesis stating that a reserve for the delinquent portion of an account should specifically be provided for in the allowance for doubtful accounts.

The strength of each rule was assessed by a number of auditors. Subsequent to constructing the initial prototype Dungan refined the system (both in terms of rule weights and new rules) with the help of experts.

Validation consisted of two phases. In the first phase an audit manager examined the workpapers relating to the determination of the appropriateness of the provision for doubtful accounts for five separate accounts for each of two clients. In 9 out of the 10 cases AUDITOR was in agreement with the workpapers. That is, it recommended the appropriate reserve with a high probability. In the 10th case AUDITOR recommended a reserve of twice that which was recommended in the work papers with a high probability.

The second validation phase involved one auditor analyzing 11 invoices owing to a particular client with AUDITOR. Another auditor was then provided with the information which had been typed into AUDITOR by the first auditor, his assessment and the one made by AUDITOR. The second validator was asked to assess the competence of the two "other" auditors. He was not made aware that one of the auditors was, in fact, AUDITOR. AUDITOR was judged to have performed as well as the first auditor in all eleven cases.

Gal (1985) also developed an expert system for determining the allowance for bad debts.

Hansen and Messier (1982, 1984, 1986a, 1986b, 1988) developed an expert system, EDP-EXPERT, to assist computer audit specialists make judgments on the reliability of controls in advanced computer environments. The prototype system had 60 rules which were refined and expanded through interaction with experts to 133 rules. The system has been extensively validated over the years and is probably the most validated system of its type in existence.

Bailey, Duke, Gerlach, Ko, Meservy, Winston (1985) developed TICOM, a computer-based analytical tool for modelling a client's internal controls and subsequently querying the model to evaluate the adequacy of those internal controls. Kelly also developed an internal control system (ICE).

Meservy, Bailey, and Johnson (1986) developed a computational model of the process by which an auditor assesses a client's internal controls. The system, which was developed using a variety of sources of knowledge, consisted of over 300 rules. The system was validated from two different perspectives:

1. the quality of the process used by the system, and

2. the sufficiency and adequacy of the model outcomes.

Boritz, Kielstra and Albuquerque (1989, 1991) developed an inherent risk assessment system using an expert system shell. The system was subsequently used as a basis for Price Waterhouse's PLANET (Delisio, McGowan and Hamscher, 1993).

Selfridge and Biggs (1986, 1988) and Biggs and Selfridge (1991) have developed a system for modeling going concern judgments, GCX, in ways that are qualitatively similar to the ways in which an expert auditor performs the judgment. It is a very complex and sophisticated system that encodes the following knowledge:

- financial knowledge in a financial reasoning network
- financial knowledge in a financial model
- operational knowledge in an operational model
- an event memory about the relationships between the financial model and the operations model
- entity, mental activity knowledge and action knowledge
- inference knowledge

Boritz (1993) has developed a knowledge-based system for supporting the auditor's evaluation of a client's financial condition, assessing the risk of business failure and the validity of the going concern assumption.

The CAPEX system described in this book has served as the model for Grant Thornton's ADAPT system (Gillett, 1993). Bharadwaj, Karan, Mahaptra, Murthy (1992) and Vinze, Karan, Murthy (1991) also outline the design of a comprehensive audit planning system similar to CAPEX; however, only a small part of the system has actually been developed.

A number of accounting firms have developed expert system-based decision aids (see Boritz, 1992; Brown and Murphy, 1990). For example, LOANPROBE was developed by the accounting firm of Peat Marwick Mitchell (Willingham, Kelly, and Ribar, 1986). The LOANPROBE system is extremely comprehensive and contains in excess of 7,000 rules. Other systems developed by accounting firms include Expertax (Shpilberg and Graham, 1986), Risk Advisor (Graham, Damens and Van Ness, 1991) and PLANET (Delisio, McGowan and Hamscher, 1993). A number of accounting firms have also been working on systems which utilize an assertion-based approach for assisting in the construction of audit program plans (e.g., EY Decision Support and Grant Thornton's ADAPT). However, due to the proprietary nature of these systems, little information about their internal operation is available.

Some of the above mentioned systems were designed to reproduce expert judgments by modeling expert knowledge and the process used by experts in making judgments based on their knowledge. Other systems neither model expert knowledge nor the process used by experts in reaching judgments. Intermediate systems may use a combination of expert knowledge and knowledge derived from other sources. In these systems knowledge may also be processed in a manner which is different from the way experts are believed to process knowledge.

CAPEX is an example of an intermediate type of system. Some features of CAPEX are descriptive of particular auditors' judgments. For instance, the system requires that audit evidence-gathering procedures be selected based on their relevance to the objectives of a particular audit and the reliability of the audit evidence they provide. Assessments of the relevance and reliability of audit evidence-gathering procedures were provided by practicing auditors.

Other features of CAPEX are essentially normative. For example, uncertainties were modeled using a Bayesian probability revision approach. The overall approach adopted to uncertainty modeling and methods used for its combination and revision are discussed briefly in this chapter and in more detail in Chapter 2.

FEATURES OF CAPEX

At the present time CAPEX can perform the following functions for manufacturing, retail and banking clients:

- Given details of a particular client, CAPEX can generate a substantive audit program plan for that client to achieve pre-defined risk objectives at the financial statement item assertion level.

- Given details of a particular client, it is possible to investigate a number of different substantive audit program plans to determine both their individual costs and the extent to which each achieves pre-defined risk objectives at the financial statement item assertion level.

- Given details of a particular client, it is possible to investigate the impact of a variety of different policy decisions on the types of audit procedures selected, extent to which risk levels are reduced, etc.

In the future it is expected that the capabilities of CAPEX will be extended to expand the knowledge-bases used by CAPEX to allow the system to:

- Plan for a larger variety of industries, to reflect alternative approaches to the determination of the reliability of evidence provided by audit procedures and the costs of performing those procedures.

- Construct substantive audit program plans for all cycles for a particular client.

- Provide different approaches to modeling uncertainty. With relatively little additional programming it is possible to adapt the system to make use of other types of uncertainty modeling approaches (such as Dempster-Shafer belief functions).

SYSTEM INPUTS

The present implementation of CAPEX enables the user to provide information about both the client for which an audit is being constructed and the audit evidence gathering procedures which are available. It is also possible for the user to specify a number of parameters which will guide the manner in which audit program plans are constructed by the system.

An example of the type of information provided to CAPEX is given in Figures 1.15a and 1.15b.

SYSTEM OUTPUTS

At the present time the system generates the following outputs:

Reasoning Process:
CAPEX produces a step by step summary of its reasoning process to provide a trace of the way in which it satisfies the planning requirements.

Figure 1.1 Sample of Capex Output - Reasoning Process

{SECTION 1}

Should we directly apply procedure 361 to accounts_receivable completeness under?

Procedure applies to	accounts_receivable
Procedure gives	0.475
need	0.8932412
Sampling confidence factor	1.0
use	0.475

.

{SECTION 2}

Directly applying procedure 361 to accounts_receivable completeness under

Achieved is	0.91356301
Direct is	0.91356301
New achieved is	0.95267764

.

{SECTION 3}

accounts receivable feeds back to cash_receipts_on_account and sales_on_account

Indirectly applying procedure 361 to cash_receipts_on_account occurrence over

Achieved is	0.88816271
Direct is	0.8682
Indirect is	0.17053418
New achieved is	0.89154013
Indirect is	0.19863099
Additional indirect assurance is	0.17053418
Indirect assurance used is	0.17053418

Achieved Assurances by Financial Statement Item and Assertion:
Each procedure which is chosen to be included in a given audit program plan is recorded along with the confidence level to which the procedure is to be performed and the assertion to which it is directed. An example of such a set of procedures for a particular audit program plan is provided in Figure 1.2.

Figure 1.2 Sample of CAPEX Output of Achieved Assurances by Item and Assertion

ns_accounts receivable_gross

	CU	**EXO**	**VHO**	**VHU**
Initial assurance	0.95	0.95	0.95	0.95
Indirect				
Initial indirect assurance	0.00	0.00	0.00	0.00
40m	0.69		0.68	0.69
41m	0.68	0.67	0.67	0.67
42m	0.67	0.66	0.66	0.67
43m	0.67	0.66	0.66	0.67
55m	0.67	0.66	0.66	0.67
Achieved indirect assurance	0.86	0.85	0.86	0.86
Applied indirect assurance	0.87	0.85	0.86	0.87
Target indirect assurance	0.00	0.00	0.00	0.00
Direct				
Initial direct assurance	0.95	0.95	0.95	0.95
Achieved direct assurance	0.95	0.95	0.95	0.95
Achieved assurance	0.99	0.99	0.99	0.99
Target assurance	0.99	0.99	0.99	0.99

Note: CU=Completeness under(statement), EXO=Existence over, VHO=Valuation hard over, VHU=Valuation hard under

Summary Audit Program Plan:
Each procedure which is chosen to be included in a given audit program plan is recorded along with the sample size and relative cost. An example of such a set of procedures for a particular audit program plan is provided in Figure 1.3.

Figure 1.3 Sample of CAPEX Output - Audit Program Plan

Procedure	**N**	**Cost**
Positive confirmation of accounts receivable Type A	40	1200
Positive confirmation of accounts receivable Type B	40	1200
Review of subsequent receipts - Type A accounts receivable	1	400

At the present time CAPEX does not construct a log detailing alterations which have been made to the main knowledge bases. This is clearly a desirable feature for a "delivery" system.

AUDIT PLAN CONSTRUCTION PROCESS

As mentioned earlier, CAPEX generates substantive audit program plans using an assertion-based approach. One of the features of this approach is that it decomposes the task of generating an audit program plan into a set of sub-tasks. The decomposition is achieved by decomposing the overall goal associated with the complete audit program plan into a set of sub-goals for the system to solve.

The overall goal associated with conducting an external audit is to gather sufficient appropriate evidence to be able to render an opinion concerning the fairness of the presentation of a client's financial statements taken as a whole. This overall goal is then decomposed into a set of sub-goals. Each sub-goal relates to the gathering of sufficient evidence to have a reasonable level of assurance concerning the propriety of each of the components of a client's financial statements. These sub-goals are decomposed further to yield sub-sub goals associated with assertions. Each sub-sub goal relates to the gathering of sufficient evidence to provide a reasonable level of assurance that a particular type of error, in excess of a certain size, has not occurred in the recording or processing of information concerning a particular component of the client's financial statements.

Assertions stating that specific types of mis-statements are not present in specific financial statement items are referred to as *financial statement item assertions*. An example of the decomposition of an overall goal into a set of sub-sub goals is presented in Figure 1.4.

Figure 1.4 Audit Planning Goal Decomposition Using an Assertion-based Approach

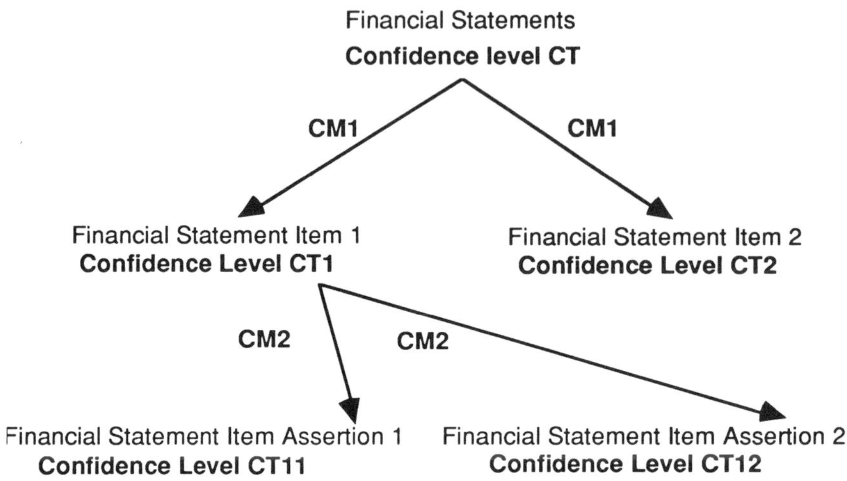

Notes: Arrows indicate mapping of confidence levels from the financial statement level to the financial statement item assertion level.

CM1 = Confidence mapping function from the financial statement level to the financial statement item level.

CM2 = Confidence mapping function from the financial statement item level to the financial statement item assertion level.

Thus, an assertion-based approach requires identifying all the financial statement item assertions which have been made implicitly or explicitly in a client's financial statements and establishing required levels of assurance or their complement, the maximum level of risk permissible with respect to each financial statement item assertion. These required levels of assurance may either be provided directly by the planner or may be obtained by mapping the required assurance from the financial statement item, or financial statement level, to the financial statement item assertion level as illustrated in Figure 1.4.

The conceptual stages involved in the generation of an audit program plan are summarized in Figure 1.5.

Figure 1.5 The Structure of the System

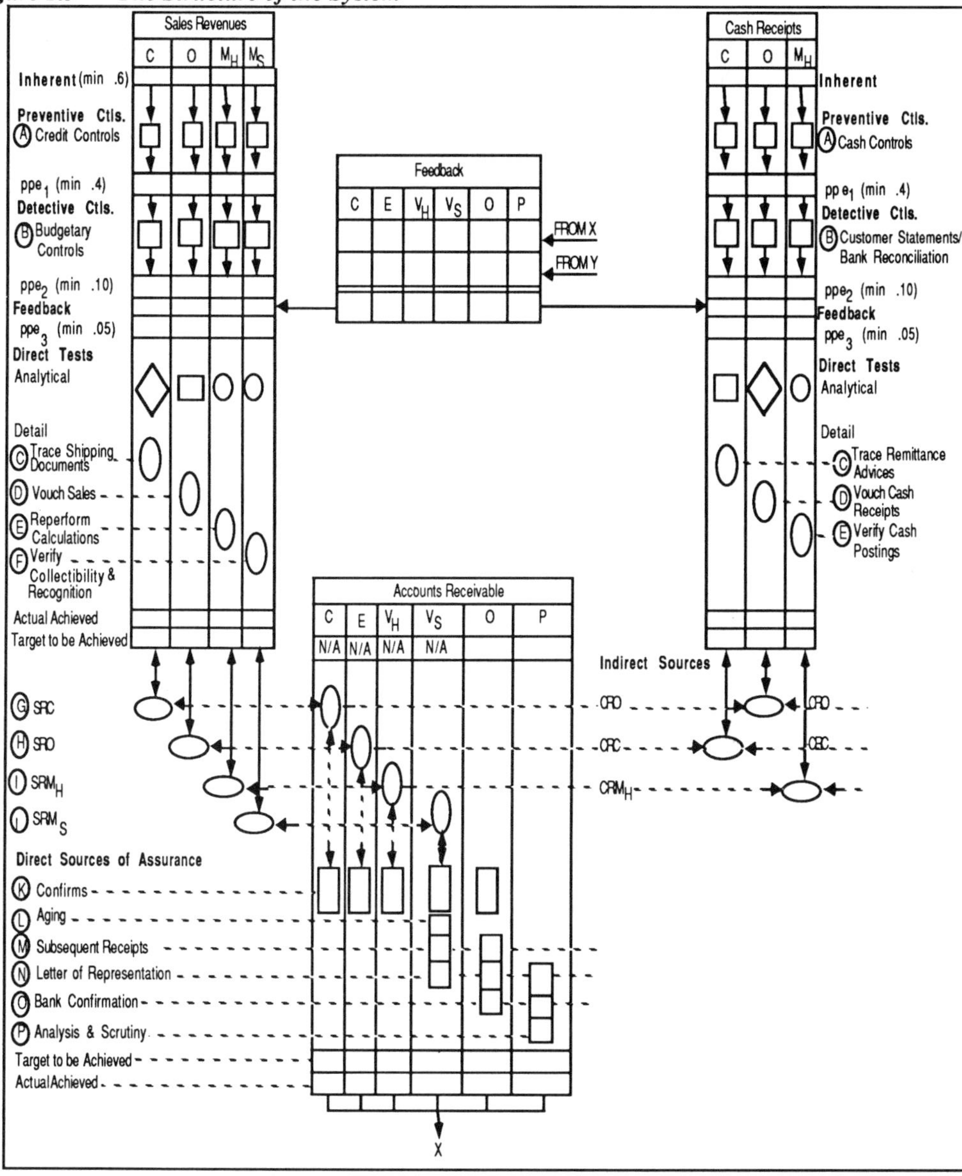

As Figure 1.5 indicates, a plan to gather evidence about the financial statement item accounts receivable can be decomposed into sub-plans to gather evidence about six specific accounts receivable assertions — Completeness (C), Existence (E), Valuation Hard (V_H), Valuation Soft (V_S), Ownership (O) and Presentation (P). The following relationships in an assertion-based approach to constructing a substantive audit program plan for the sales/receivables/receipts cycle are identified by Figure 1.5.

ARC	=	f(Direct, Indirect)	(1)
Direct	=	$f(DT_1, DT_2, ..., DT_n)$	(2)
Indirect	=	f(SR, CR)	(3)
SR	=	$f(PPE3_{(SR)}, DT(AP, TD))$	(4)
CR	=	$f(PPE3_{(CR)}, DT(AP, TD))$	(5)
$PPE3_{(.)}$	=	$f(PPE2_{(.)}, Feedback(.))$	(6)
$PPE2_{(.)}$	=	$f(PPE1_{(.)}, DCR_{(.)})$	(7)
Feedback(.)	=	$f(DT_m(AR))$	(8)
$PPE1_{(.)}$	=	$f(IR, PCR_{(.)})$	(9)

1. As Figure 1.5 indicates, evidence about Accounts Receivable is a function of both Direct and Indirect sources of evidence.

2. *Direct* evidence comes from specific direct tests aimed at a particular assertion. For audit procedures to qualify as direct tests of given assertions, they must be judged *Relevant* to those assertions (as will be discussed later).

3. *Indirect* evidence about Accounts Receivable is a function of evidence about both Sales Revenues and Cash Receipts. In our model, Sales Revenues involves four assertions — Completeness (C), Occurrence or Validity (O), Measurement Hard or Accuracy (M_H) and Measurement Soft or Valuation (M_S). Cash receipts involves three assertions (there is no Valuation assertion involved). These transaction flow assertions combine to accounts receivable assertions. For example, evidence about Accounts Receivable Completeness (ARC), is a function of the evidence about Sales Revenue Completeness (SRC) and Cash Receipts Occurrence (CRO). The precise relationships among various assertions are detailed in Chapter 2.

4. The evidence obtained about the component transaction flows that generate financial statement items is derived from a combination of evidential sources, including the Prior Probability of Error (PPE3) and Direct Tests of assertions by means of Analytic Procedures (AP) or Tests of Detail (TD). PPE3 is the probability of error prior to direct tests of related assertions.

5. Evidence flowing from Cash Receipts transactions is structurally similar to that flowing from Sales Revenue transactions, but the parameters used will differ to reflect differences in prior probabilities of error and differences in direct tests applied. Thus, $PPE3_{(SR)}$ is the prior probability of error prior to direct tests of Sales Revenue, while $PPE3_{(CR)}$ is the corresponding prior probability of error in the Cash Receipts stream.

6. $PPE3_{(.)}$ is computed by combining the prior probability of error prior to any direct tests of the generating transaction stream assertions (PPE2) with the prior probability of error based on direct tests already carried out on assertions of derived financial statement items (Feedback (AR).

7. Feedback is a function of the evidence that flows to generating items from direct tests of derived financial statement items already carried out. In the case of SR and CR, the evidence

already carried out. In the case of SR and CR, the evidence will flow from direct tests of related Accounts Receivable assertions ($DT_{m(AR)}$). For example, tests of Accounts Receivable Completeness will provide feedback to Sales Revenue Completeness and Cash Receipts Occurrence, as will be detailed in Chapter 2.

8. PPE_1 and PPE_2 incorporate any previous assessments, at the assertion level, of the risks associated with preventive and detective controls over Sales Revenue and Cash Receipts. PPE_2 is a combination of PPE_1 and Detective Control Risk for the relevant assertion ($DCR_{(.)}$).

9. $PPE_{1(.)}$ is a combination of the Inherent Risk (IR) and Preventive Control Risk for the relevant assertion ($PCR_{(.)}$).

Once a set of financial statement assertions and their associated required assurance levels have been identified, an overall audit program plan is constructed by dealing with individual sub-plans to achieve the required assurances with respect to each financial statement item assertion separately. Each plan consists of a set of audit evidence-gathering procedures. Figure 1.6 summarizes the plan generation process.

Figure 1.6 The Plan Generation Process

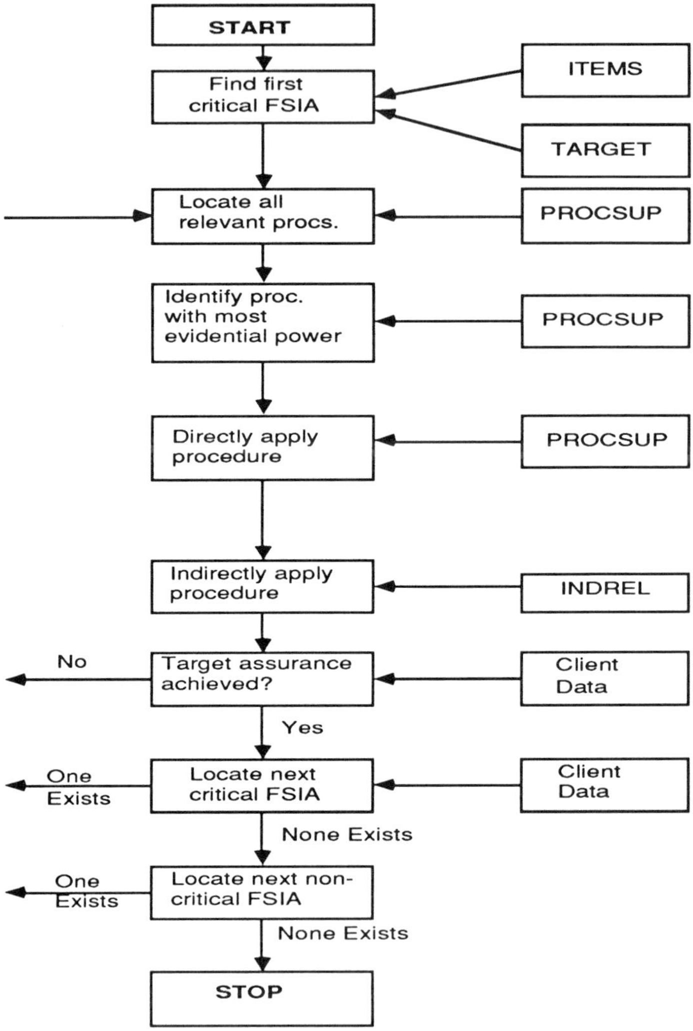

Note: FSIA= Financial Statement Item Assertion

As illustrated in Figure 1.6 all the relevant financial statement item assertions are ordered and sub-plans are constructed sequentially as follows:

- The user specifies both a target level of desired assurance and an entry level of achieved assurance for every financial statement item assertion which he/she wishes to address in a particular consultation. Currently, the entry level achieved assurance corresponds to the assurance the user has that no material mis-statements are present following inherent risk assessment and internal control review and compliance testing. In terms of the probabilities discussed earlier, the entry level achieved assurance in the current version of CAPEX corresponds to PPE_2.

- CAPEX currently provides for the specification of one of two global strategies governing the selection of financial statement item assertions for planning purposes. One strategy, referred to as *transaction stream oriented,* results in CAPEX constructing sub-plans to address all transaction stream item assertions before it constructs any sub-plans to address balance sheet item assertions. In contrast, the *balance sheet oriented* approach results in CAPEX constructing sub-plans to address all balance sheet item assertions before it constructs any sub-plans to address transaction stream item assertions.

- For each financial statement item balance it is possible to specify one or more critical assertions. If these are specified, sub-plans will be constructed by CAPEX for all critical assertions relating to a particular financial statement item before constructing any sub-plans for non-critical assertions. If more than one critical assertions are specified for a particular financial statement item assertion, sub-plans will be constructed according to the *priority* of the relevant financial statement items specified in the data which is input into CAPEX. Once the critical assertions relevant to a particular financial statement item have been addressed, CAPEX constructs sub-plans for each non-critical assertion in order of their priorities.

- After having selected a financial statement item assertion, CAPEX tests to determine whether the target assurance has already been achieved. It is possible that for some financial statement item assertions a combination of inherent risk assessment and internal control review will provide sufficient evidence to achieve the target assurance. Additionally, if other financial statement item assertions have been addressed already, it is possible that audit evidence-gathering procedures which have been selected already will provide sufficient support, either directly or indirectly, for the financial statement item in question. CAPEX continuously updates and monitors the levels of achieved assurance by assertion.

- If the target assurance for the financial statement item in question has not been achieved, CAPEX identifies *all* the audit evidence-gathering procedures which potentially provide evidence *relevant* to establishing the "truth" of the assertion selected. These procedures are identified through a search of the ***proc_support*** predicate.

- CAPEX attempts to achieve the target level of assurance by applying procedures which give direct evidence concerning the propriety of the assertion in question. With respect to each Accounts Receivable assertion, a procedure is selected to achieve the target risk starting with the direct tests of the existence assertion. In this case, the system will plan for the application of accounts receivable confirmations. If the target level of assurance can be achieved through the application of these procedures, the system will proceed to planning for the next balance sheet item assertion. If, however, the target level of assurance cannot be achieved through the application of directly relevant procedures, the remaining assurance must be obtained indirectly, as will be described briefly below and in more detail in Chapter 2.

- The *evidential power* of each of the *relevant* procedures is then determined, using an heuristic, and the procedure with the greatest evidential power is selected to be the initial or next component of the appropriate sub-plan. The *evidential power* heuristic trades off the overall contribution of the evidence provided by a particular audit procedure and the cost of applying the procedure.

  $$\textbf{Evidential Power} = \frac{\textbf{Assurances obtainable for all assertions}}{\textbf{Cost of obtaining the assurances}}$$

  This heuristic is designed to take into account the fact that the evidence provided by some audit procedure will furnish support for a variety of financial statement item assertions. Such procedures may be significantly more costly than other procedures which provide evidence which only supports one financial statement item assertion. The heuristic calculates a weighted sum of the maximum derivable assurances associated with all financial statement item assertions for which the procedure in question provides relevant evidence. This weighted sum is then divided by the total cost of performing the procedure.

- Once the preferred procedure to apply next has been selected, it is necessary to determine the extent to which it will be performed. This first requires the determination of the maximum possible contribution of assurance by the evidence provided by the procedure. CAPEX compares the prior achieved assurance with respect to the financial statement item assertion with its pre-defined target assurance. Using its uncertainty modeling approach, CAPEX determines the additional assurance needed to reach the target assurance. The *maximum derivable assurance* from the selected procedure is then compared to the assurance required, and the following decision rule invoked:

  1. If the *maximum derivable assurance* is less than the required assurance, then plan to apply the procedure to its maximum extent.

  2. If the *maximum derivable assurance* is greater than the required assurance, and if sampling is appropriate, then the extent to which the procedure will be applied is determined using the following formula:

     $$\textbf{Sampling Confidence} = \frac{\textbf{Required Assurance}}{\textbf{Maximum Derivable Assurance}}$$

     The sample size factor is then determined by the use of a "lookup table". The entries of this table assume monetary unit sampling based on a Poisson distribution assuming 0 errors and the given sampling confidence level as calculated above. The actual sample size is determined using the standard formula:

     $$\textbf{Monetary Unit Sample Size} = \frac{\textbf{Account Balance}}{\textbf{Basic Precision}} * \textbf{SSF}$$

     where Basic precision ≤ Materiality and the abbreviation SSF stands for Sample Size Factor associated with the sampling confidence factor.

  3. If the *maximum derivable assurance* is greater than the required assurance, and if sampling is not appropriate for the selected procedure, then the procedure will be applied without sampling. This will result in an assurance being achieved which is greater than the target assurance.

  Once the testing extent has been determined, CAPEX "applies" the procedure. This entails revising the achieved assurances for all of the financial statement item assertions for which the procedure provides relevant evidence. This is a two-step process. First, CAPEX takes account of the **direct** evidential support provided by the procedure. Next, CAPEX identifies the financial statement item assertions which are **indirectly** supported by evidence provided by the procedure and revises the achieved indirect and total assurances of these financial statement item assertions. The details of this process will be provided in the next chapter.

- If the target assurance has not been achieved for the financial statement item assertion in question, the above steps are repeated. Otherwise, the next financial statement item assertion in order of priority is selected and then the above steps are repeated. This iterative process continues until sub-plans have been constructed for all the relevant financial statement item assertions or the set of uncompleted procedures has been exhausted.

- Typically it will be necessary to obtain some level of indirect support for the target assurance to be reached. The remaining assurance which must be obtained indirectly is calculated using Bayes' formula. Thus, if the target assurance is 98% and direct procedures provide 80% assurance, then the remaining assurance to be derived indirectly is 92%.

- The required level of indirect support is mapped back using accounting relationships into levels of assurance which need to be achieved with respect to Cash Receipts and Sales Revenue transaction streams. For example, with respect to Accounts Receivable Existence, audit procedures should be selected for both the Sales Revenue Occurrence and the Cash Receipts Completeness assertions to provide $\sqrt{.92}$ which is about .96 assurance.

- The system then selects procedures, if necessary, to achieve the derived target assurance for the generating transaction stream assertion; for example, Sales Revenue Occurrence and Cash Receipts Completeness, taking into account feedback relationships. That is, the direct tests which provide evidence concerning Accounts Receivable Existence also provide some evidence with respect to the SRO and CRC assertions. This evidence is taken into account in the revision of PPE_2, which results in PPE_3.

The "balance sheet approach" policy described above can easily be modified to reflect either a "transactions stream approach", or, a mixed approach. In the "transactions stream approach", an auditor sets transaction stream assertion risks first, then solves for the remaining required assurance with respect to direct tests of balances. Mixed approaches occur when an auditor sets target risks both for balance sheet item assertions and selected transaction stream item assertions (e.g., Revenue Occurrence).

The assertion-based approach described above enables the overall task of constructing an audit program plan to be decomposed into a set of relatively simpler sub-tasks requiring the construction of sub-plans to achieve objectives at the financial statement item assertion level. There are, however, a number of important points to be recognized. First, financial statement item assertions may not be independent. This issue is the subject of considerable debate and has been discussed by Boritz and Wensley (1989) and Aldersley (1989). The fact that some very simple procedures are considered to support more than one financial statement item assertion indicates that financial statement item assertions, as they are defined by the CICA and AICPA, may not actually be completely independent. The computational model represented in CAPEX requires that financial statement item assertions be independent of each other.

Second, there is no general agreement as to how required assurances should be mapped from the financial statement level to the financial statement item assertion level. This issue is discussed in Boritz and Wensley (1989) and Kinney (1992). In its present implementation CAPEX does not provide for the automatic decomposition of required assurances. Required assurances at the financial statement item assertion level are provided to the system as input data.

UNCERTAINTY MODELING IN CAPEX

There are a number of different types of uncertainty modeling in CAPEX:

1. Uncertainty revision of direct assurances.
2. Uncertainty revision of indirect assurances.
3. Uncertainty revision of total assurances to reflect changes in direct assurances.
4. Uncertainty revision of total assurances to reflect changes in indirect assurances.
5. Uncertainty combination of direct assurances to yield indirect assurances.

CAPEX uses a modified Bayesian approach for the first four types of assurance calculations. For the fifth type, uncertainty modeling is performed using a simple "product of risks" rule.

Modified Bayesian uncertainty modeling is based on the *Extent of Audit Testing* (CICA, 1980) approach to uncertainty revision which relates Prior (risk), Testing (risk), and Target (risk) by using the following formula:

$$\textbf{Target Risk} = \frac{\textbf{Prior * Testing}}{\textbf{Prior * Testing + (1 - Prior)}}$$

The product rule is used in the following way. If two independent items of evidence indicate that the probability of a mis-statment being present is P_1 and P_2, respectively, then the risk that there is still an undetected mis-statement present, given knowledge of <u>both</u> independent items of evidence, is $P_1 * P_2$.

KNOWLEDGE IN CAPEX

CAPEX encodes a variety of different types of knowledge in a number of distinct modules which are indicated in Figure 1.7.

Figure 1.7 The Principal Knowledge Modules in CAPEX

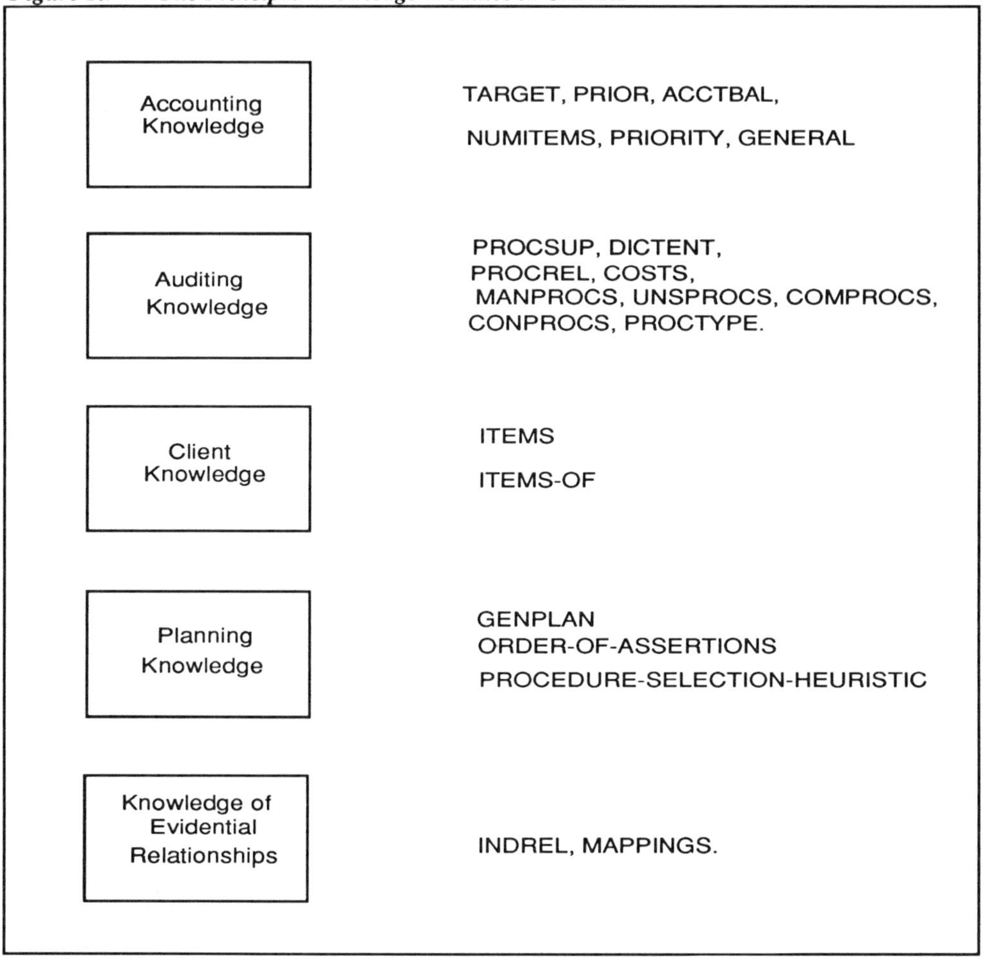

Some of the principal types of knowledge represented in the knowledge modules in Figure 1.7 are:

1. Knowledge concerning the specific client for which an audit program plan is being constructed. This knowledge includes knowledge of the relevant financial statement item assertions, the prior achieved and target assurance associated with each, the dollar value of each account balance, and a variety of other client characteristics.

2. Knowledge concerning relevant audit evidence-gathering procedures. This knowledge includes knowledge of the financial statement item assertion(s) supported by each procedure, the strength of this support, the reliability and cost of each procedure, a textual description of each procedure, and a variety of other characteristics of each procedure.

3. Knowledge of accounting. This knowledge includes knowledge of the categories of account balances, their interrelationships, and their typical sub-components.

4. Meta-knowledge concerning how the above types of knowledge are structured. The dominant structure in the case of CAPEX is derived from the assertion-based approach to auditing promulgated by the CICA. Another aspect of meta-knowledge relates to the processing of uncertainties.

5. Knowledge concerning the process of plan construction. This knowledge includes knowledge concerning how the overall planning task can be decomposed into a number of sub-tasks and knowledge concerning how each sub-task can be completed. Some items of planning knowledge are generic while other items refer specifically to audit planning. An example of the latter are the heuristics which are used to guide the selection of audit evidence-gathering procedures.

6. Knowledge of evidential relationships. This knowledge includes knowledge of direct and indirect evidential support relationships and their respective strength.

THE CAPEX USER INTERFACE

GENERAL WINDOWING TECHNIQUES

There are two input sources from which CAPEX obtains the data it requires to produce an audit plan for a client. The first is an audit management-level program which is used to record evidential characteristics of audit procedures, while the second is an auditor-level program used to record specific characteristics of a client engagement. Both of these programs are written in C for the X windowing environment. The programs also handle the translation of window-entered data to Prolog, giving users a straightforward, user-friendly means of entering data and transparent access to the Prolog-based expert system. Figure 1.8 illustrates the appearance of the Main Window.

Figure 1.8 The Main Window

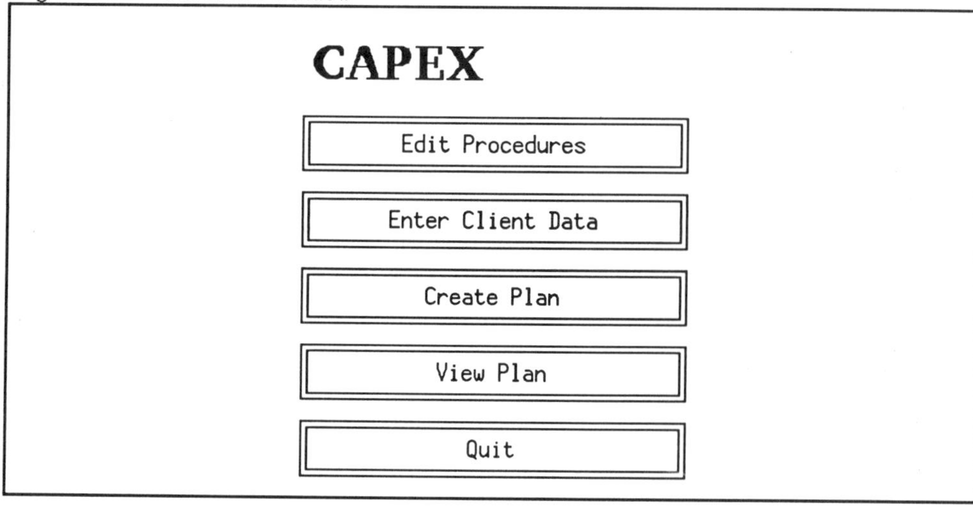

Window managers in X are clients of the X server, just as any other X application is a client of the X server. This window managing model permits the user to customize functions such as window moving, window resizing, iconification, etc. There are many different window managers; thus, users should consult their documentation for specific details concerning the particular window manager used locally.

When the user wishes to select some menu item, he or she moves the mouse on top of the desired menu. The menu window will become highlighted in black. The user presses the mouse button, and the menu items will appear below the menu window. The user selects one such item by dragging the mouse down the list of menu items, with the mouse button still depressed, and releasing the button when the mouse is over the desired menu item. The items will be highlighted as the mouse passes over them. The function corresponding to the selected item will then be performed. In CAPEX, all mouse buttons are treated indiscriminately (except in the case of scrollbars, which will be dealt with later), so mouse input can be performed by pressing any of the mouse buttons.

Most of the processing takes place in one window, but in a few particular cases, a subwindow containing the active menu is created. If the image (either graphics or text) is too large to fit in the main window, the main window is drawn with one or more scrollbars. A scrollbar is a sub-window which resides along one edge of its parent window. Inside the scrollbar is an elevator which indicates what portion of the image is currently visible in the main window.

With a three-button mouse, the user can perform absolute scrolling or relative scrolling. Absolute scrolling is accomplished by pressing the middle mouse button while the mouse is in the scrollbar. The elevator will move to the position of the mouse, and the display will be adjusted accordingly. Thus, if the user clicks the middle mouse button at the top of the scrollbar, the display will be adjusted so that the top of the image is displayed at the top of the window.

Relative scrolling is accomplished by pressing either the left or right mouse buttons in the scrollbars -- left moves forward, right moves backward. If either of these mouse buttons is pressed at the bottom of a vertical scrollbar, or at the rightmost side of a horizontal scrollbar, the display will be updated by one full page relative to where the display was positioned before the scrolling event. A right or left button press in the middle of a scrollbar would update the display by half a page.

There are many instances when the user will need to edit certain fields of text, numbers, or buttons. There are two methods of editing: alphanumeric and pop-up menu editing.

- *Alphanumeric editing* requires input from the keyboard. When the user is editing an alphanumeric field, he or she must move the mouse on top of the string which is to be edited. When the mouse is on top of the desired field, an edit window will highlight the region which is to be edited, and an edit cursor will mark the user's spot in the string. The user can then type at will, and can change locations within the string by clicking a mouse button anywhere in the edit window. Input will be accepted as long as the mouse is inside the edit window.

- *Pop-up menu editing* is the second type of editing. When there is a small number of discrete choices available to the user, these choices will be contained in a list. The user selects the desired item and clicks the mouse button.

MANAGEMENT-LEVEL PROCEDURE SPECIFICATION

CAPEX provides audit management with the opportunity to define the various available audit procedures, and determine the relevance, reliabilities, and associated costs of those procedures. Once the procedures have been fully defined, the system translates the procedure specifications into Prolog predicates, which are then written to disk, and used as input to CAPEX. Figure 1.9 illustrates the Procedure Window as it appears during procedure editing.

Figure 1.9 The Procedure Window

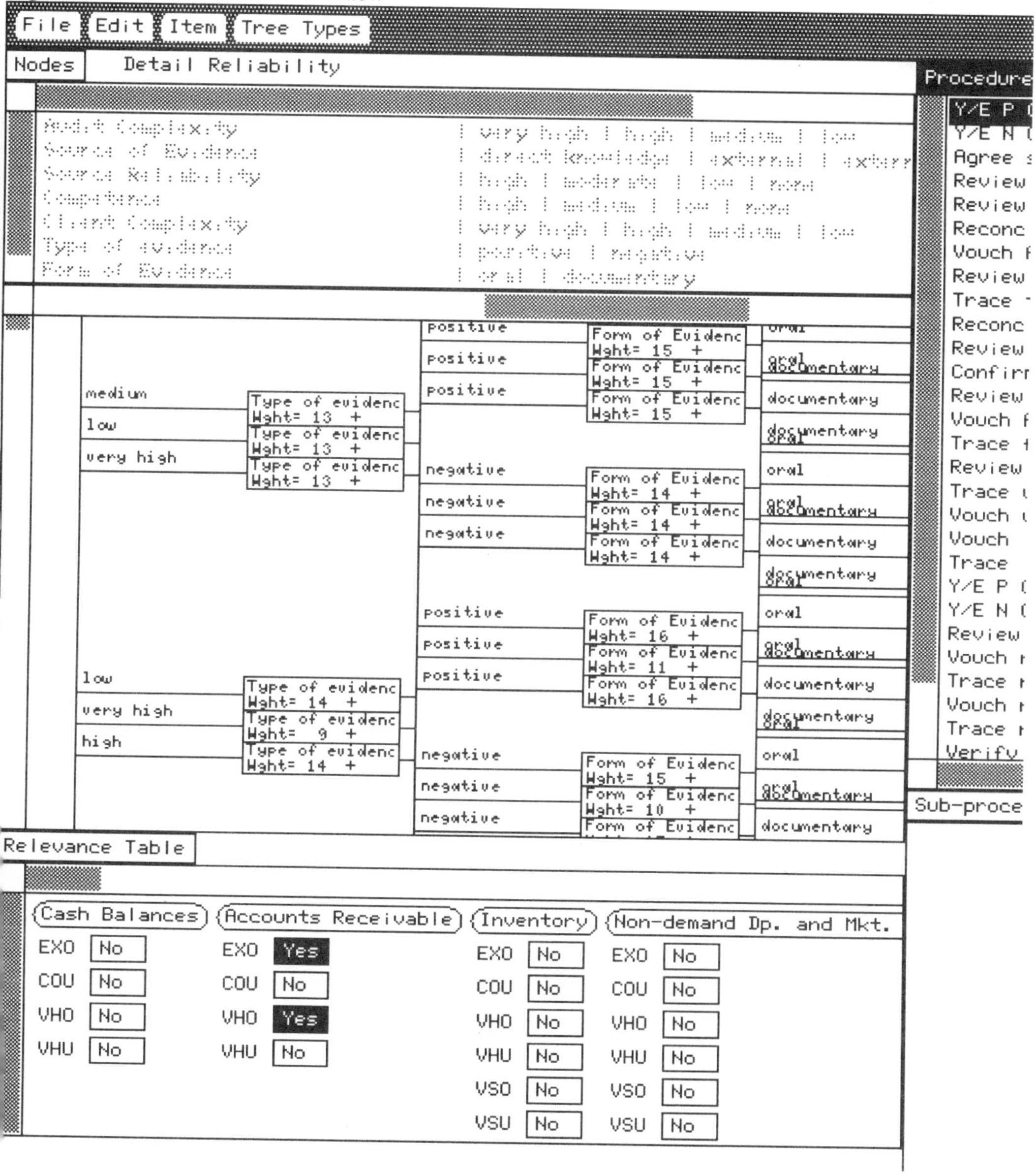

The following choices are available under each of the horizontal menu items displayed at the top of Figure 1.9: File, Edit, Item and Tree Types.

File

- **New**
- **Open**
- **Save**
- **Save As...**
- **Quit**

Edit

- **Insert**
- **Delete**
- **Change**

Item

- **Node**
- **Tree**
- **Procedure**
- **Sub-procedure**
- **Relevance**

Tree Types

- **Detail Cost**
- **Analytical Cost**
- **Detail Reliability**
- **Analytical Reliability**

Adding a procedure: Adding a procedure to the procedure list is accomplished by selecting **Procedure** from the **Item** menu and **Insert** from the **Edit** menu. Figure 1.10 illustrates the sub-window which enables the user to record some of the information required about each procedure. Because the sub-window is too wide to display horizontally in its entirety, it is illustrated here in three panels. In the actual system, the window is scrollable.

Editing a procedure: Editing a procedure is accomplished by either selecting the desired procedure and then selecting **Change** from the **Edit** menu. The sub-window shown in Figure 1.10 is displayed and the user is then free to edit this data.

Deleting a procedure: Deleting a procedure from the procedure list is accomplished by selecting the button of the procedure to be deleted from the list, and then selecting Delete Procedure from the menu. The user will then be asked if he or she really wishes to delete the specified procedure. If the user responds affirmatively, the procedure list will be redrawn without the deleted procedure.

Figure 1.10 The Maintain Procedure Information Sub-Window

Panel (a)

Maintain Procedure Information

Done | Field | Record

Name	Description	Setup Costs	Timing
/E P Confirm A/R		0	Year End

Panel (b)

Maintain Procedure Information

Done | Field | Record

Type	Class	Enable Sampling	Minimum Sample Size	Maximum Sample Size
etail	Positive Confirm	Yes	5	100

Panel (c)

Maintain Procedure Information

Done | Field | Record

Composite	Application Type	Principal Audit Document	Completion Time
No	Mandatory	AR Sub-ledger	15

Operations on sub-procedures:

Sub-procedures are treated much like procedures. The current **Item** is set to **Sub-procedure**. The selected procedure must be a composite procedure. Only cost can be recorded for a sub-procedure. Relevance and reliability are recorded at the procedure level.

The following values may be selected for the various attributes of a procedure:

Attributes	Values
Name	User Supplied
Description	User Supplied
Setup Costs	$ Figure (assumed to be 0 by default)
Timing	Interim or Year-end
Type	(Test of) Detail or Analytic
Class	Positive Confirm, Negative Confirm, etc.
Enable Sampling	Yes or No
Minimum Sample Size	Number
Maximum Sample Size	Number
Composite	Yes or No
Application Type	Mandatory, Discretionary, or Mand-Non-Credit
Principal Audit Document	User Supplied
Completion Time (per unit)	Number

Once the information in Figure 1.10 is recorded, it is necessary to record the Relevance, Reliability and Cost of the procedure.

MAINTAINING RELIABILITY AND COST TREES

Procedure Reliability and Cost are crucial factors in the definition of an audit procedure. CAPEX represents the Reliability and Cost of procedures by a hierarchical tree structure, in which every node in the tree represents some pragmatic Reliability or Cost consideration. The possible attribute values are represented by a set of arcs emanating from the node, each of which is weighted. For instance, in a Cost Tree, one of the nodes might be labeled 'Time Required', and it may have three associated arcs, 'low', 'medium', and 'high'. It follows intuitively that 'low' would have a lower weight than 'medium' and 'high', and 'medium' would have a lower weight than 'high'. This case is shown in Figure 1.11 below, where the three arcs are assumed to have weights 1, 2, and 3, respectively.

Each tree consists of a network of nodes, where nodes are connected by arcs. Each node in the tree has an associated weight. These weights will ultimately be used to evaluate the cost or reliability weight of a certain procedure, given that procedure's path from the root of the tree to a leaf node. However, the weight of a node is not defined implicitly by the node itself. Rather, the weight of a node is calculated by applying the arithmetic operation of its parent to the weight of its parent and the weight of its incoming arc. The user specifies either addition, subtraction, multiplication, or division as the arithmetic operation of a node. Figure 1.11 shows a Time Required node with addition as its arithmetic operation.

There are two types of procedures: detail and analytic, each of which require distinct Reliability and Cost Trees, necessitating four distinct trees which management must maintain. It is assumed that these trees are reasonably static (i.e., trees are only changed when management revises its policies), and apply to all procedures (i.e., the costs of all detail procedures will be evaluated on the same tree).

Figure 1.11 A Node and its Arcs

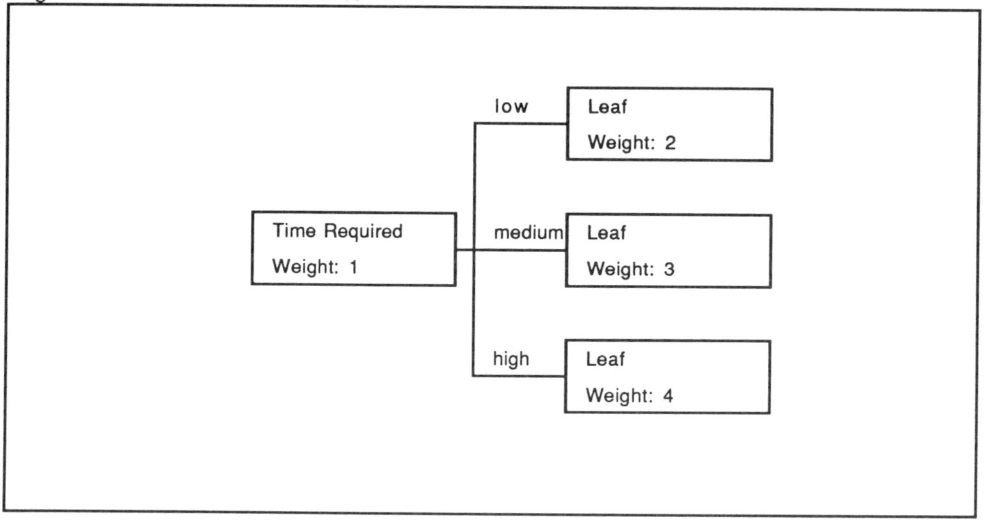

Figure 1.12 Editing a Node and its Arcs

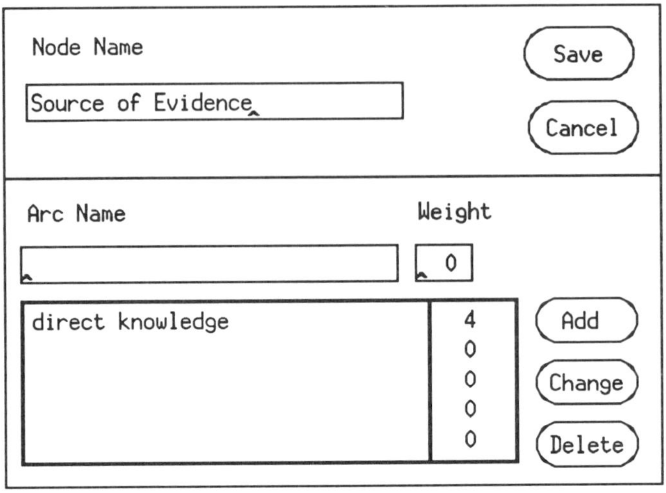

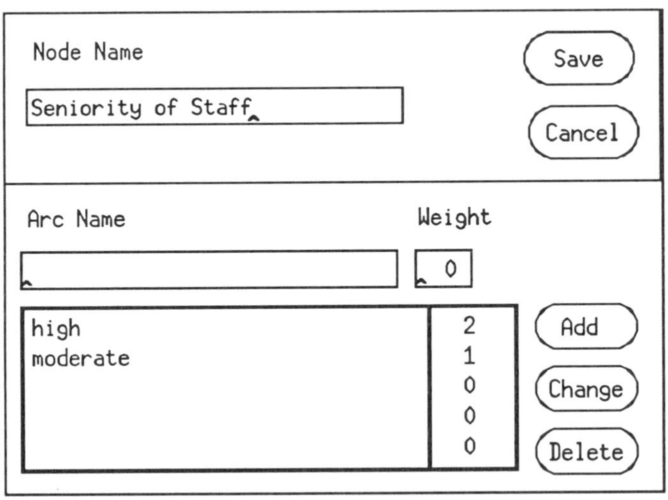

The Procedure Menu contains four tree maintenance options: one for each of the four trees discussed above. To maintain a tree, the user selects the appropriate tree maintenance option from the Main Menu. The tree is displayed on the screen. The following courses of action may then be taken:

Changing arithmetic operation: Changing the arithmetic operation of a node is accomplished by clicking on the node in question ('selecting' the node), and choosing **Change** from the **Edit** menu. A new edit window will then appear, in which all possible arithmetic operations will be displayed in buttons.

To change the arithmetic operation, the user simply selects the desired button, and then chooses either to save changes or quit, by selecting Save or Quit from the Edit menu of the edit window. The user is not allowed to perform any further operations on the tree until he or she selects Quit from the Edit menu.

If the user makes changes to the arithmetic operation of a node, and selects Quit without having saved the changes, he or she will be asked whether the changes should be saved before quitting. This verification mechanism is standard procedure for any window in which the user is performing an edit.

The weight of all descendent nodes is automatically recalculated. Recalculation of node weight is performed each time the tree is reconfigured. Once **Quit** has been selected from the **Edit** menu, the edit window is destroyed, and the user may select another option from the Tree Options menu.

Adding a node: Adding a node to the node list is accomplished by selecting **Add** from the **Edit** menu. This selection will produce a new edit window which has space for the user to enter the name of the node, the names of its arcs, and their corresponding weights.

Changing a node: Changing a node in the tree to another node is accomplished by selecting the node with the mouse, then selecting **Change** from the **Edit** menu. This selection will produce a new edit window which contains the name of the selected node, the names of its arcs, and their corresponding weights. Any or all of these fields may be edited. Arcs can be added up to the limit displayed on the screen, or can be deleted by editing out their names. Arc weights can be modified in the same way. Upon quitting, changes are applied to all occurrences of the edited node in the tree.

Deleting a node: Deleting a node from the node list is accomplished by selecting a node then selecting **Delete** from the **Edit** menu. The user will then be asked whether he or she really wishes to delete the specified node. If the user answers yes (by clicking the 'Yes' button), the node is deleted from the internal node list.

Upon completion of the tree maintenance session, the user can save changes or quit in the usual way. Quitting will clear the tree from the screen and place the user back at the Main Menu.

MAINTENANCE OF RELEVANCE TABLE

As mentioned earlier, the CAPEX system maintains client information, including details about various financial statement items. The knowledge base administrator must define the degree of relevance each audit procedure has to the audit of each financial statement item. Currently, Relevance is a binary function, so an audit procedure is either relevant to a financial statement item assertion, or it is not. Ideally, a graduated scale would be used to enable the auditor to indicate degrees of relevance.

To maintain this table, the user must select a procedure in the Procedures sub-window, then move to the Relevance Table sub-window. As Figure 1.10 illustrates, the Relevance Table sub-window is formatted with the audit assertions listed vertically and the financial statement items listed horizontally. The generating stream assertions are: OCO, COU, MHO, MHU, MSO, and MSU. The derived assertions are: EXO, COU, VHO, VHU, VSO, and VSU.

The layout of the screen is governed by two scrollbars. The vertical scrollbar along the left-hand side of the window determines which assertions are visible. Scrolling up will make visible assertions which are closer to the beginning of the procedure list, whereas scrolling down will accomplish the opposite. The horizontal scrollbar along the top is used to display the financial statement items.

The user must specify to which financial statement items and assertions a highlighted procedure is relevant. The default value is no relevance. To indicate that procedure C is relevant to financial statement item A, assertion B, the user scrolls through the list of financial statement items and assertions and clicks in the button which is horizontally aligned with assertion B, and vertically aligned with financial statement item A. Relevance is indicated in that window by means of highlighting and the word "YES" displayed in the button. Relevance between a procedure and a financial statement item assertion can be disassociated in the same way, changing the "YES" to "NO".

EVALUATING THE RELIABILITY OF A PROCEDURE

Evaluating the reliability of a procedure is accomplished by selecting **Tree Type,** then selecting the appropriate reliability tree from the menu. The reliability tree, either the "detail" or "analytic" review tree, depending on whether the selected procedure is of type "detail" or "analytic" review, is then displayed in the middle portion of the screen.

The user then steps through the tree, starting at the root. At each node, the user must indicate the attribute that best reflects the nature of the procedure (see the section entitled "The Maintenance of Trees"). The user selects the node corresponding to the correct decision by clicking on it. The node will then become highlighted. This process continues until the user has defined a path from the root of the tree to a leaf node, as shown in Figure 1.13 which illustrates a portion of a Reliability Tree.

A user does not have to proceed stepwise through the tree. Any time the user clicks on a node, the system will select all nodes implicitly falling between the root and the node which has been selected, even if the intermediate path was incompletely specified, or another path was specified.

Figure 1.13 A Portion of a Reliability Tree

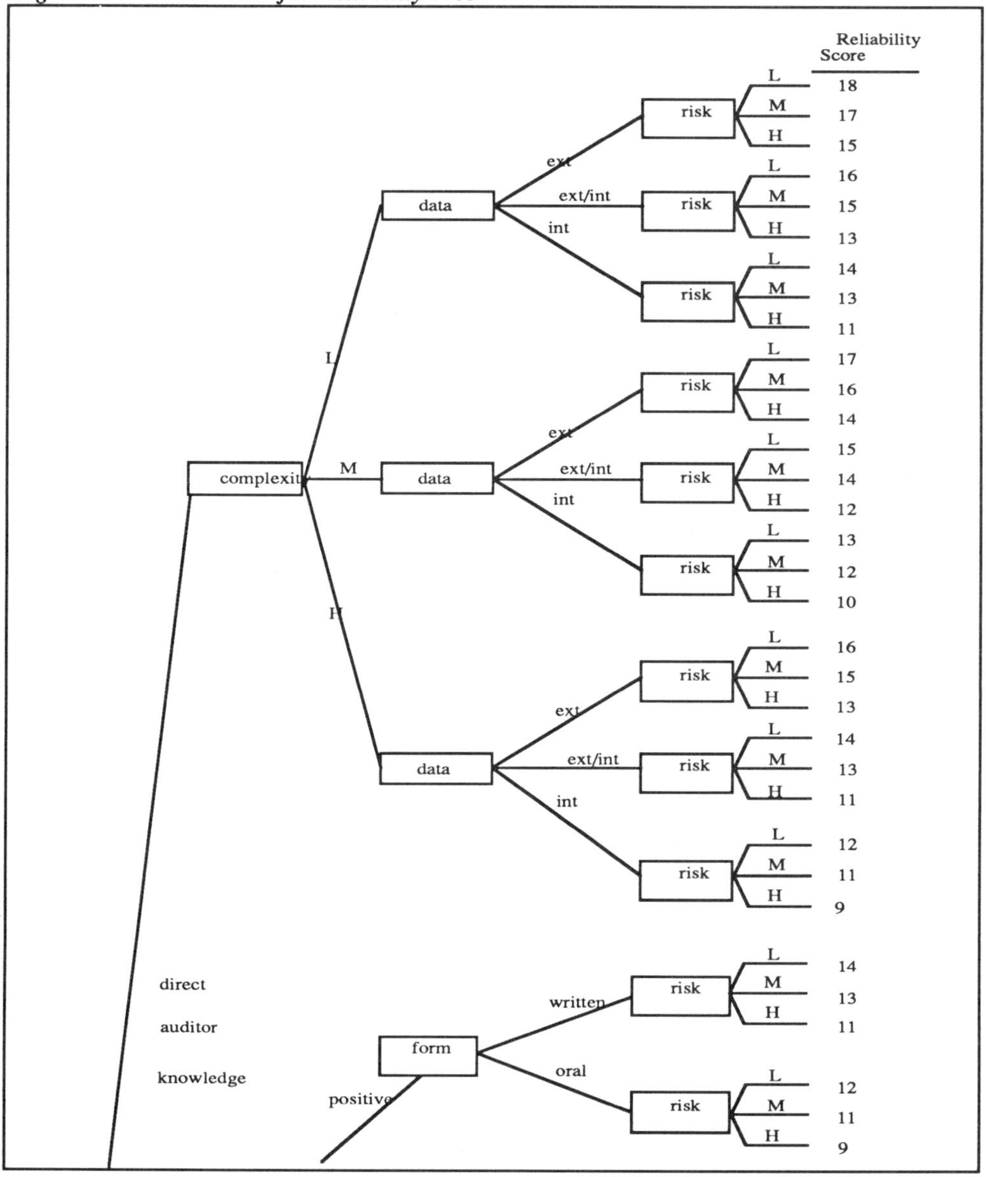

EVALUATING THE COST OF A PROCEDURE

Evaluating the Cost of a procedure is accomplished by selecting **Tree Types** and then selecting the appropriate cost tree from the menu. The relevant type of Cost Tree is then displayed: either the "detail" or "analytic" review cost tree, depending on whether the selected procedure is of the type "detail" or "analytic" review. Definition of procedure cost occurs in exactly the same way as the definition of procedure Reliability as detailed previously. Figure 1.14 illustrates an example where the user has defined the cost of a procedure for which the Time Required is low, the Staff Level is senior, and the Behavioral Cost is medium. The cost of this procedure is 4 units, as indicated by the weight of the highlighted leaf node.

If the selected procedure is not a composite (parent) procedure, then its cost is determined by its path in the Cost Tree. If the selected procedure is a parent procedure, and the user does not define a cost for it, its cost is calculated to be the sum of the costs of its sub-procedures.

Figure 1.14 A Path in a Cost Tree

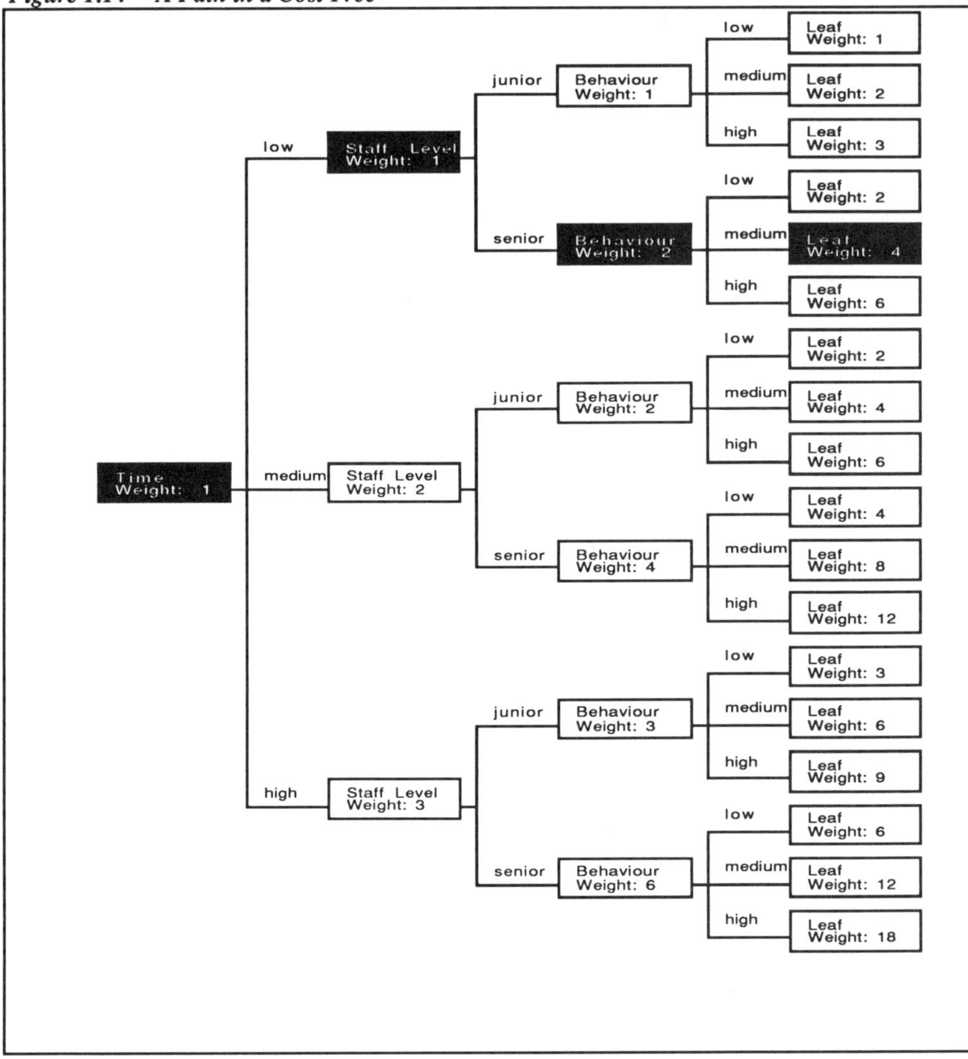

RECORDING CLIENT-SPECIFIC DATA

Client-specific data such as the client's financial statement items and various parameters pertaining to the client are recorded using the screens in Figure 1.15a and 1.15b. The data is then translated into Prolog predicates, which are used in conjunction with the procedure-related data in CAPEX to produce the audit program for the specific client.

Figure 1.15a displays the window which allows the auditor to Maintain the Client-specific data pertaining to the various Financial Statement balances.

Figure 1.15a Maintenance of Client Parameters

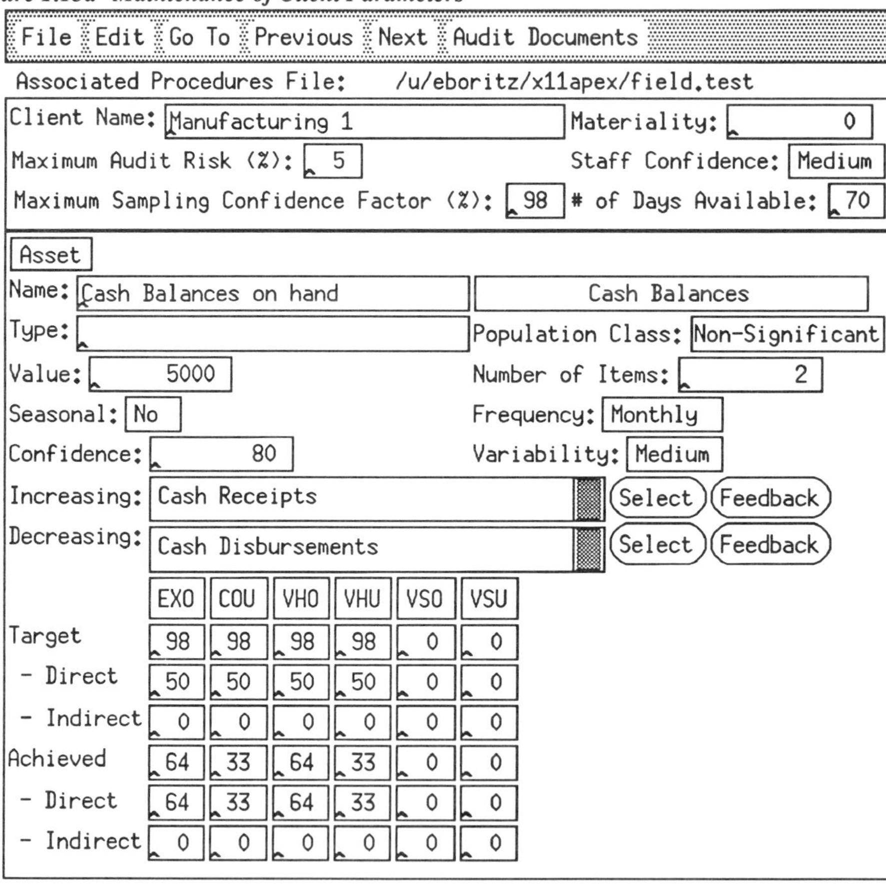

Figure 1.15b displays the window which allows the auditor to Maintain the Target Assurances of the various Financial Statement Item transaction streams.

Figure 1.15b Maintenance of Target Assurance Parameters

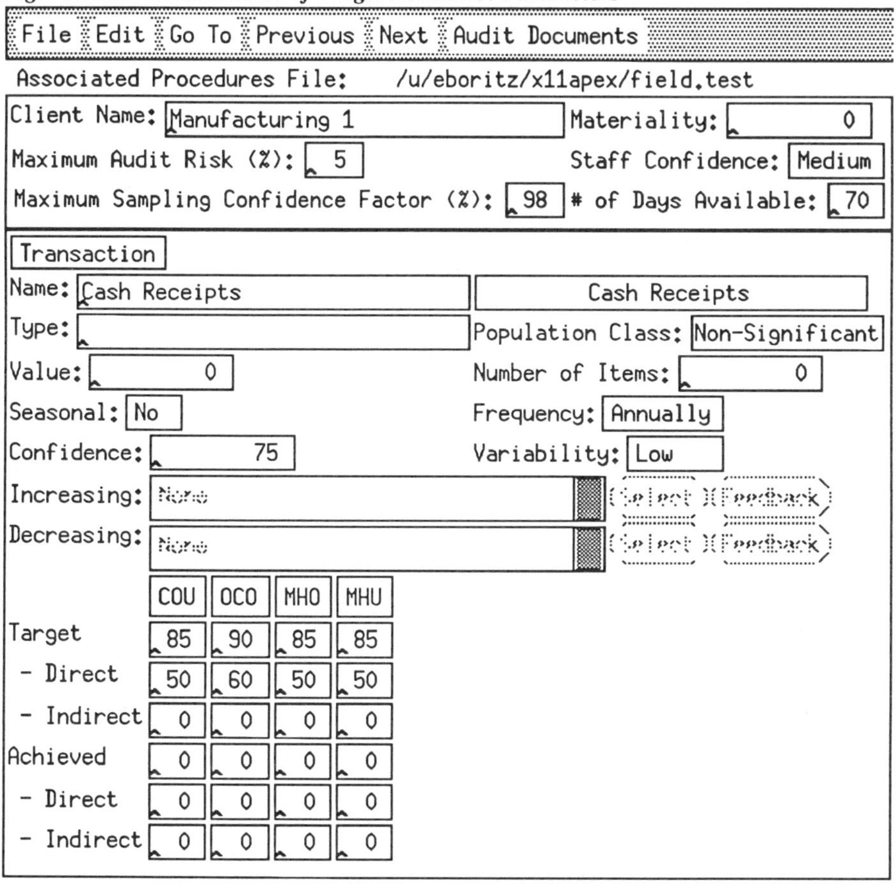

Maintaining Indirect Supporting Relationships
Figure 1.16 displays the sub-window which enables the auditor to record the strength of indirect supporting relationships between various generating and derived assertions.

Figure 1.16 Maintenance of Indirect Supporting Relationships

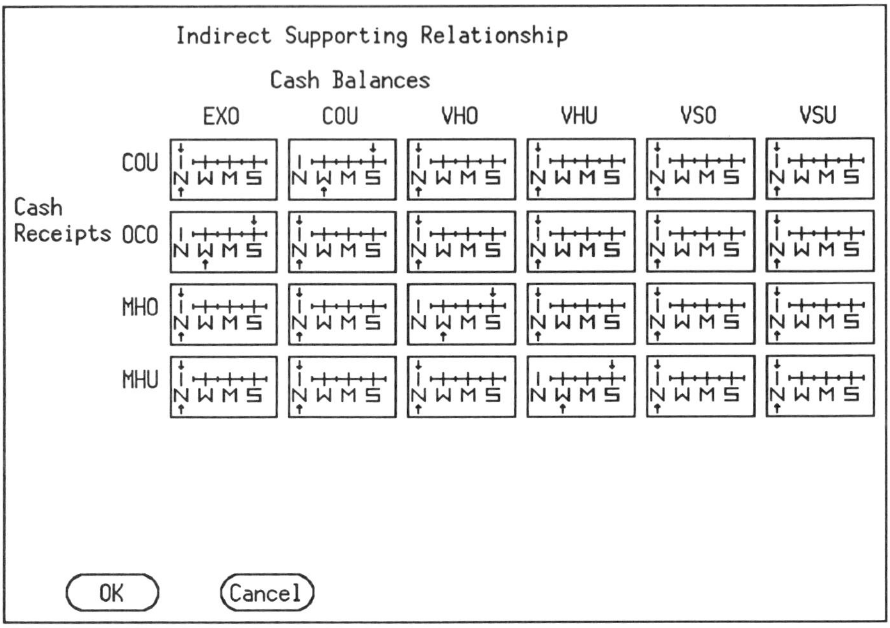

GENERATION OF INTERMEDIATE FILES

The program automatically translates procedure-related data into Prolog predicates which can then be manipulated by the expert system.

SUMMARY

This chapter has provided an overview of CAPEX, a knowledge-based system which was constructed by the authors. CAPEX was designed to construct audit program plans for firms in three different industries: banking, retailing and manufacturing. As we discuss, these plans were intended to be acceptable to practicing auditors though they might not necessarily be the type of plans they would generate themselves.

Expert systems methodology has been used to investigate a number of different areas of auditing. These areas include materiality determination, internal control assessment and going concern determination. To our knowledge there have only been two academic attempts to apply experts systems methodology to the process of generating complete audit plans - CAPEX and a system which is under development by Bharadwaj et al. (1993). The latter system does not provide for the generation of substantive audit program plan as does CAPEX.

In addition to academic applications of expert systems methodology to auditing, most of the major accounting firms have developed expert systems over the last ten years. As with the academic systems, these systems address a range of audit issues including audit program planning. Grant Thornton's ADAPT system (Gillett, 1993), can trace its parentage and many aspects of its structure and function to CAPEX.

CAPEX can be used to construct audit plans to achieve certain predefined objectives and also to evaluate audit plans which have already been completed. In addition, CAPEX can be used to investigate the impact of implementing different types of policies for developing audit plans.

The types of inputs required by CAPEX are the specifications of audit objectives, the data concerning the client being audited and parameter values for a number of variables which influence the manner in which any audit program plan is constructed. The chapter also deals with the X-WIndows-based user interface that we have designed for CAPEX.

In addition to introducing the nature of the inputs required by CAPEX, we also review the types of output generated by CAPEX. For example, CAPEX generates a trace which details every stage of the planning process. Further, having constructed a complete plan or, at least, a plan which comes closest to achieving pre-specified audit objectives, CAPEX provides an output which details how close it has come to achieving each objective.

One of the key characteristics of CAPEX is that it uses an assertion-oriented risk-based approach to constructing audit plans. Audit knowledge, relevant to the construction of audit plans is structured consistently to provide evidence which is relevant to the assertion-based approach to auditing. We provide a detailed discussion of this approach as well as a presentation of how an assertion-based approach is implemented in CAPEX. One of the central concerns with respect to implementing the approach relates to the selection of audit procedures to apply. We have developed an heuristic which we refer to as *evidential power*. We introduce and discuss the application of this heuristic at some length.

As we chose to structure both the knowledge available to CAPEX and its predefined objectives in terms of financial statement assertions *and risk* we provide a brief discussion of the uncertainty modeling approach that we have adopted in CAPEX. This area is of increasing relevance as many researchers are exploring alternative approaches to modeling and processing uncertain information.

Different types of knowledge are represented in CAPEX as relatively independent modules. These modules are introduced and briefly discussed.

One feature which is often missing, or underdeveloped, in academic expert systems is the user interface. Although we consider that CAPEX is primarily a research tool of considerable power and flexibility, we worked hard to develop a user interface for the system in X-Windows. Our review of the user-interface for CAPEX details the types of data which can be input into the system through the user interface.

Chapter 2

KNOWLEDGE REPRESENTATION IN CAPEX

THE STRUCTURE OF KNOWLEDGE IN CAPEX

Audit planning knowledge may be classified as being either *strategic* or *factual* knowledge. Broadly speaking, factual knowledge concerns "knowns" and assumptions about the domain, while strategic knowledge concerns knowledge of how such factual knowledge should be utilized in problem solving.

Factual knowledge is knowledge of accounting relationships, auditing procedures and client-specific facts.

- **Accounting relationships:** Knowledge of financial statement items and related assertions. This includes knowledge of the characteristics of sub-components of financial statement items which are relevant to the selection of audit evidence-gathering procedures and the specification of achieved and target assurances for financial statement item assertions and the related indirect supporting relationships. This knowledge is particularly complex in the case of banking audits.

- **Auditing procedures:** Knowledge of evidence-gathering procedures and their characteristics. Some of these procedures may only apply to one particular type of industry, say, manufacturing, but they are considered to be applicable to all clients in the industry.

- **Knowledge about the client being audited:** This includes knowledge of client characteristics, of its key financial items, and fundamental accounting processes. This knowledge can be further subdivided into two types:

  - **Knowledge which does not change as the audit plan is generated:** An example of this type of knowledge is client-specific data including the client's financial statements, the client's history, etc.

  - **Knowledge which is continually updated as the audit plan is generated:** This type of knowledge is exemplified by the assurance achieved to date for each relevant financial statement item assertion at any stage of the development of the audit plan.

Strategic knowledge concerns knowledge of how factual knowledge such as that outlined above should be utilized in problem solving.

- **Planning heuristics:** An overall plan is developed by constructing a set of sub-plans. Each sub-plan is directed towards obtaining sufficient evidence to achieve a pre-defined level of assurance with respect to each relevant financial statement item assertion.

- **Audit program planning rules and heuristics:** Knowledge concerning various evidence-gathering procedures and rules or "heuristics" for combining procedures so as to achieve overall audit objectives with respect to target levels of audit assurance in the most economical way, including knowledge of the extent-assurance relationships for procedures.

CAPEX contains components corresponding to these knowledge sets: a computational model which implements the strategic knowledge of planning rules and heuristics and a number of associated data-bases containing problem-relevant knowledge sets. The computational model and the knowledge sets are, collectively, the CAPEX knowledge base. A schematic diagram which summarizes the interaction of the computational model and the principal knowledge sets is presented in Figure 2.1.

Figure 2.1 The Structure of CAPEX

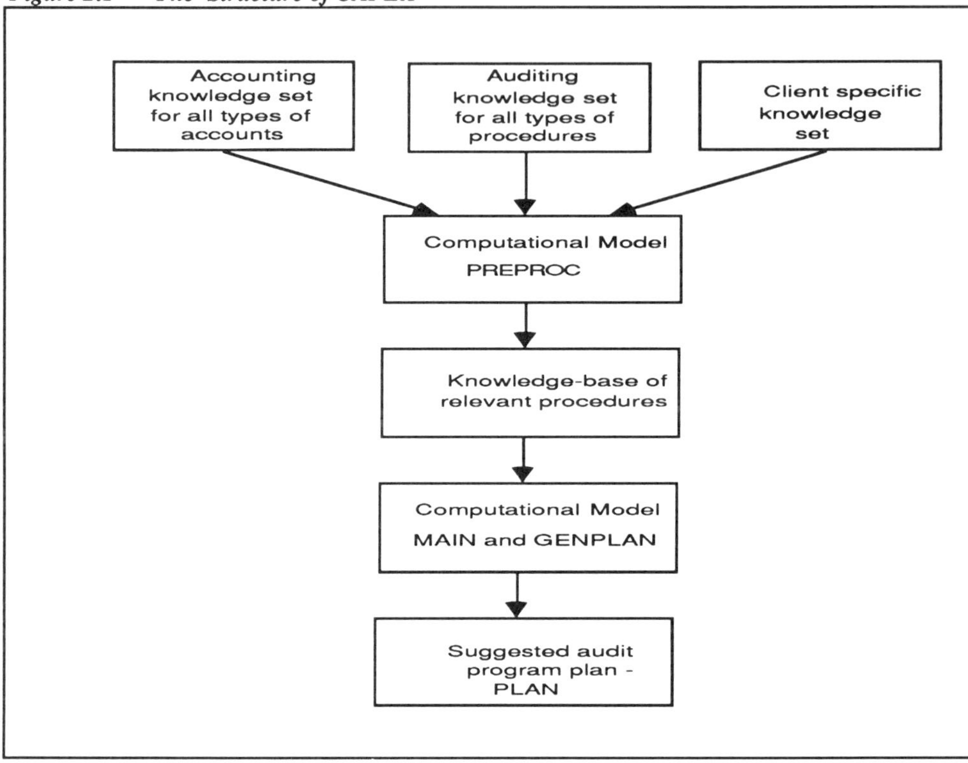

This chapter will first describe, in detail, the audit planning knowledge sets, followed by a discussion of the computational model.

ACCOUNTING KNOWLEDGE

THE ACCOUNTING MODEL

Perhaps the most fundamental type of knowledge encoded in CAPEX relates to the accounting model. This knowledge is so fundamental that, in many instances, a practicing auditor may be unaware of making use of it. An example of part of this model is represented by the following relationship:

$$\textbf{A/R end} = \textbf{A/R begin} + \textbf{Sales} - \textbf{Cash Receipts} - \textbf{Credit Notes} - \textbf{Writeoffs} \qquad \textbf{(1)}$$

Thus, the overall assurance achieved with respect to Accounts Receivable is a function of the assurances achieved for the beginning balance of accounts receivable, sales, cash receipts, credit notes, and writeoffs.

Leslie et al. [1986] define a framework for thinking about indirect evidential support relationships arising from the accounting model. They refer to Accounts Receivable (A/R end) as a **derived** item, while they refer to the other items in the equation as **generating** items. Derived items result from the netting out of generating items, and "indirect supporting relationships" among evidence-gathering procedures are a result of the accounting model. These relationships will be discussed in a subsequent section.

The predicate **ITEM** in CAPEX identifies all the possible types of financial statement items that may be valid for the types of audit clients addressed by the system. Each financial statement item is classified as being an asset, a liability, revenue, expense or a some other accounting category.

The predicate also represents all the component/sub-component relationships which exist between different financial statement items. For instance, *cash balances* may be comprised of *cash balances on hand* and *cash balances on deposit*. All the possible component/sub-component relationships are identified. When CAPEX accesses the knowledge in this module it only makes use of those component/sub-component relationships which are relevant to the client and the financial statement item assertions for which it is planning.

The Composition of Accounting Balances: Significant and Insignificant Items

In the preceding section, accounting balances were viewed as the resolution of transaction streams. Another set of possible component/sub-component relationships arise if some of the items which comprise an account balance, or sub-population of an account balance, are individually significant. In this case, the account balance, or sub-population of the account balance is divided further into a population of individually significant items and a population of individually non-significant items.

The criteria used to determine whether a given item is significant or non-significant may be quantitative and/or qualitative. For example, all individual sales transactions which exceed some pre-defined dollar value may be considered to be significant or all individual accounts receivable which are judged to be high risk, from the stand-point of subsequent collectibility, may be considered to be significant.

Apart from the need to distinguish significant items from non-significant items there are a number of other reasons for dividing up the items which constitute an account balance into a number of different categories:

- Different types of items within the account balance may exhibit different susceptibilities to error. For example, it is possible that the auditor considers that the client's staff exercises far more care over recording the details of sales to other businesses than over recording the details of sales to individuals. This relationship may be reversed, however, if it is considered that individuals are more likely to complain about errors than business customers.

- Different procedures may be appropriate for obtaining evidence with respect to the different types of items. For example, in evaluating a loan to a business, procedures may be applied to evaluate the customer's financial position, these procedures may not be appropriate for the assessment of loans to individuals. Similarly, in assessing the accuracy of a recorded loan balance for a loan which has been outstanding since the prior period, which was audited, the previous audited balance may be inspected. This source of evidence is not available in the case of a loan extended during the current period being audited.

- The reliability of evidence obtained through the application of the same procedure may vary significantly depending on the type of item to which the procedure is being applied. For example, positive confirmations sent to individuals are considered to provide less reliable evidence with respect to the valuation of accounts receivable than confirmations sent to businesses.

The accurate specification of relevant sub-components of account balances is important for identifying appropriate evidence-gathering procedures and also for ensuring that the appropriate indirect supporting relationships are represented and used. These relationships are discussed next.

Indirect Support Relationships in the Accounting Model

As mentioned previously, evidential flows may be related to the flows inherent in the accounting model. Thus, using the relationship between derived financial balances and their generating financial streams, it is possible to link the assurance obtained with respect to a financial stream to the assurance required with respect to the balance the financial stream generates, and vice versa.

Indirect supporting relationships may be classified into three types: feedforward relationships, feedback relationships, and singular feedback relationships. Feedforward relationships represent the flow of evidential support from transaction stream financial statement item assertions to balance sheet financial statement item assertions. Feedback relationships represent the flow of evidential support in the opposite direction - from balance sheet financial statement item assertions to transaction stream financial statement item assertions. The third category of relation, the singular feedback relationships are only of importance in banking audits. For example, audit evidence-gathering procedures which provide evidence relating to the overstatement of the existence assertion concerning outstanding loan balances at the end of a period provides indirect support for the occurrence of interest income relating to these loans.

CAPEX identifies all the possible indirect supporting relationships between all possible financial statement items for the three types of industries CAPEX can handle. Table 2.1 summarizes relationships existing between direct and indirect evidential support.

Table 2.1 Indirect Supporting Relationships (adapted from Leslie et al., 1986, p. 10).

DERIVED	RELATED
BALANCE SHEET ITEM ASSERTION	TRANSACTION STREAM ASSERTIONS
1. Valuation	Measurement
2. Existence	Occurrence if transaction increases balance sheet account.
	Completeness if transaction decreases balance sheet account.
3. Completeness	Completeness if transaction increases balance sheet account.
	Occurrence if transaction decreases balance sheet account.

Indirect Support from Sub-Components of Accounting Balances

When financial statement items are divided up into sub-components it is sometimes a relatively straightforward matter to identify indirect supporting relationships. For instance, in the case of a merchandising client the following indirect supporting relationships may link financial statement item assertions indirectly:

- Assurance with respect to wholesale credit sales occurrence overstatement provides indirect assurance with respect to wholesale accounts receivable existence overstatement.
- Assurance with respect to wholesale credit sales completeness understatement provides indirect assurance with respect to wholesale accounts receivable completeness understatement.

If financial statement items are divided up into significant and non-significant items it may be necessary to identify separate indirect supporting relationship modules for each separate client. For example, an auditor divides up the accounts receivable, sales on account, and cash payments on account balances for a particular client into separate sub-populations, one containing significant items, and the other containing non-significant items.

Normally, evidence providing direct support for the *accounts receivable existence* assertion would provide indirect support for *cash receipts completeness* and *sales on account occurrence* assertions. It is not necessarily the case, however, that evidence providing direct support for the *significant accounts receivable existence* assertion would provide indirect support for *significant cash receipts completeness* and *significant sales on account occurrence* assertions. Non-significant sales on account may result in significant accounts receivable and significant cash receipts need not necessarily be applied to significant accounts receivable. In these cases the assurance with respect to the significant items is mapped to a higher level of generality, in this case the accounts receivable level and then the indirect supporting relationship is brought into play at this level. This is achieved because the indirect support provided by audit evidence-gathering procedures directed towards a particular financial statement item assertion is recalculated every time new evidence is obtained.

Strength of Evidential Support Relationships

Each indirect supporting relationship has a strength associated with it which corresponds to the confidence that the auditor has in the inference about a derived item drawn from evidence about a generating item, and vice versa. **Feedforward** strength is the strength of the supporting relationship between evidence from generating items and evidence for derived items. **Feedback** strength is the strength of the inverse of this relationship, relating evidence in support of derived items as support for generating items. A diagram illustrating a specific example of these relationships is given in Figure 2.2. Assuming that FF1, the feedforward strength for G1 to D, was .75 and FF2, for G2 to D, was .80, and that the direct evidence in hand about G1 and G2 was .90 and .95, respectively, the calculation of indirect evidential support would be made as follows:

Additional Indirect Evidential Support to D from G1 and G2

$$= (.75*.90) * (.80*.95)$$
$$= .513 \qquad (2)$$

The reason that the product function is used rather than a sum is that a simultaneous conclusion is being drawn from two independent sources of evidence linked by an AND condition. That is, both G1 and G2 must be true for D to be true. Conversely, the risk that D is false is the probability that either G1 or G2 is false or that both are false. The uncertainty modelling in CAPEX will be discussed in more detail in a subsequent section.

The default assessments for these levels of confidence are strong for feedforward, weak for feedback, and strong for singular indirect feedback. Strong maps to a numerical value of 0.95, whereas weak maps to a numerical value of 0.65. These default values were agreed to by the two subjects who provided the majority of the reliability and cost assessments which have been encoded in the CAPEX.

Figure 2.2 An Example of Indirect Supporting Relationships

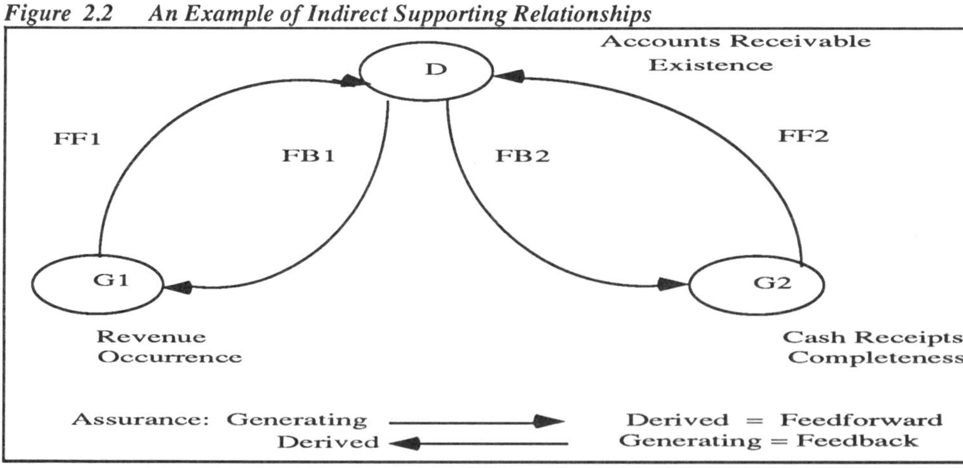

At the present time the knowledge base represents all feedback and feedforward relationships explicitly rather than inferring them from the accounting model. This is because it is not clear whether general statements of the following type can be made with any precision:

The feedforward coefficient for any procedure providing evidence with respect to the existence of a generating item is 0.8.

Feedforward and feedback strengths may vary with respect to particular client characteristics. Thus, care must be taken in the conclusions that are drawn which make use of knowledge of the accounting model. This model is not necessarily an accurate description of relationships which actually **exist** in the actual accounting system being audited, but rather, inferences that might be drawn in the absence of overriding internal control weaknesses. The auditor must assess the extent to which the client has properly implemented the accounting model and use this knowledge to modify the strength of relationships to reflect the evidence actually available.

It may be necessary to modify the default values for one or other of the indirect support relationships between specific financial statement item assertions. For example, a number of experienced auditors indicated that the indirect supporting relationships from assertions relating to cash balances to assertions relating to cash disbursements or cash receipts are particularly strong. Similarly, in the case of financial institutions, they indicated that the feedback from loan balance assertions to interest payments/loan advances is generally strong.

In other situations, an indirect supporting relationship might have its strength modified to take into account unusual client circumstances. For instance, if a large proportion of a year's sales is represented by the accounts receivable balance, tests of items in that balance are tests of a significant proportion of the sales transactions for the period. Hence the feedback from assertions relating to accounts receivable to assertions relating to sales on account would be relatively strong.

The Prolog encoding of the accounting model is presented in Appendix 2.1 in the predicates named:

- **item**
- **priority**
- **indirect supporting relationship**

THE AUDIT PROCEDURES KNOWLEDGE MODULE

The second type of knowledge contained in CAPEX's knowledge-base relates to all the substantive procedures which may be used to gather audit evidence. Substantive audit evidence-gathering procedures are divided into two types: tests of detail, and analytic procedures. This knowledge is comprised of the characteristics of all available evidence gathering procedures (reliability and cost), the financial statement item assertions which the evidence supports (relevance), and the strength of that support. In addition a variety of other characteristics such as the timing of the procedure, nature of the procedure, population to which the procedure is applied, etc. are encoded.

For each new procedure, relevance, reliability and cost scores must be determined. The relevance mapping function represents the maximum assurance that could be obtained from a particular procedure assuming that the evidence it provided was perfectly reliable. The reliability mapping function modifies this maximum attainable assurance taking into account the actual reliability of the procedure in question. The cost mapping reflects the relative cost of each procedure.

Since knowledge is represented explicitly, the user may enter new procedures or investigate the impact of modifying the various scoring rules and assurance mapping functions.

TESTS OF DETAIL

Test of detail procedures are directed towards the investigation of individual items which are accumulated in account balances, whereas substantive analysis procedures analyse either the balances themselves or some sub-category of the balances.

Test of detail procedures may be categorized in a number of different ways. The most common categorization identifies the following generic types of substantive test of detail procedures:

- Physical examination.
- Observation.
- Inquiry.
- Confirmation.
- Review.
- Vouching.
- Tracing.
- Recomputation.

These categories are useful for determining, in general terms, the type of evidence provided by different procedures. For instance, physical examination potentially provides evidence with respect to the existence of physical assets and some non-physical assets and liabilities.

In addition to determining the generic category to which a particular substantive test of detail procedure belongs, the relevance, reliability and cost of any test of details procedure need to be specified. These factors will be considered in more detail in the following sections.

The Prolog encoding of the procedures is presented in Appendix 2.2 in the predicates named:

- **dictionary entry**

- **procType**

- **unsampled procedure**
- **conflicting procedure**
- **fixed extent procedure**

Relevance of Tests of Detail

Relevance refers to the informativeness of the evidence provided by each procedure. Since CAPEX is designed to generate assertion-based audit program plans, the evidence provided by particular procedures is assessed in terms of the information it provides concerning the truth (or falsity) of financial statement item assertions. Thus, vouching items in the accounts receivable balance to supporting documents provides evidence which is relevant to the accounts receivable existence overstatement and valuation-hard overstatement and understatement assertions.

The above can be stated more precisely in the following manner:

Evidence provided by a particular procedure is relevant to establishing the appropriateness of a particular financial statement item assertion if the receipt of such evidence would lead to a revision of the previously assessed probability that the assertion expresses an actual state of affairs.

As discussed earlier in connection with the description of the CAPEX user interface in Chapter 1, the relevance relations are represented by the relevance matrix. An entry must be made for every financial statement item assertion which is supported by evidence available through the application of the procedure. The relevance of a particular procedure to the understatement or overstatement of a particular financial statement item assertion is expressed on a scale from strong to weak_limited with intermediate values of: strong_limited, moderate, and weak.[1] At the present time these relevance terms are mapped to numerical assurance values using the following mapping function:

Table 2.2 ***Correspondence Between Verbal and Quantitative Expressions of Evidential Strength***

absolute	= 1.00
strong	= 0.95
strong_limited	= 0.90
moderate	= 0.80
weak	= 0.65
weak_limited	= 0.50
none	= 0.00

[1] One of the drawbacks of this approach is that the modifier "limited" carries more meaning than simply indicating a reduction in the relevance. As an example, examination of subsequent payments provides strong_limited evidence with respect to accounts receivable existence - the evidence is limited because it only relates to a subset of the accounts receivable balance. Ideally, this richer meaning should be represented in the system.

Figure 2.3 Graphical Representation of Relationship Between Verbal and Quantitative Expressions of Evidential Strength

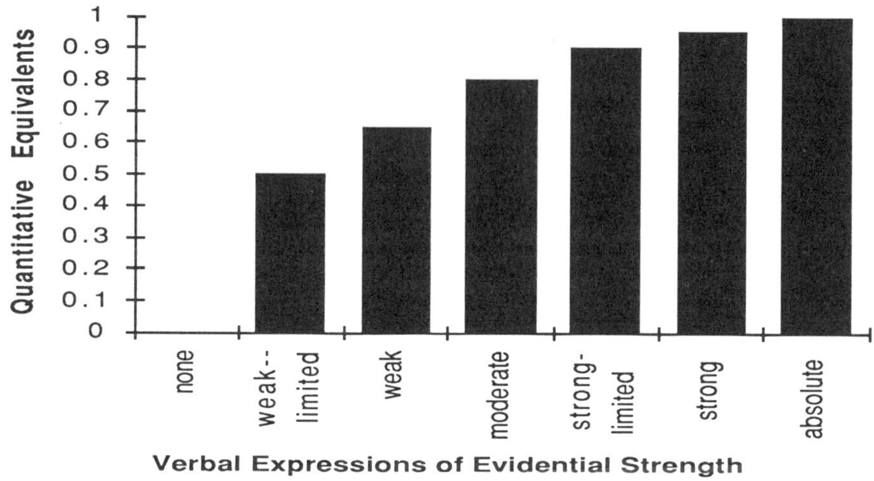

The values to which relevance terms are mapped may be considered to represent the **maximum** assurance which may be obtained through the application of a particular procedure. The less relevant a procedure is to the understatement or overstatement of a particular financial statement item assertion, the less informative is the evidence provided by the procedure and hence the lower is the assurance which can be derived. The relevance of the evidence provided by a particular procedure therefore determines the upper bound for derived assurance if the evidence is perfectly reliable. However, most procedures are unreliable to some extent.

In the present implementation of the system it is assumed that relevance is a binary variable. That is, a procedure either provides strong evidence which supports the truth of a particular financial statement item assertion or it provides none. Although theoretically a procedure could establish the truth of a particular financial statement item assertion with certainty, messages provided by actual audit evidence-gathering procedures are less than 100% reliable. It is therefore necessary to find some way of determining the reliability of the audit evidence provided by these procedures.

In the current research the reliability of the evidence provided by a particular audit evidence-gathering procedure is considered to be a function of a number of different factors. Some of these factors relate to the population to which the procedure is applied, some relate to the type of evidence provided by the procedure, and some relate to the individual applying the procedure. All of these factors are discussed in detail in the following section.

The relevance matrix for all the procedures available to CAPEX, encoded in Prolog, is presented in Appendix 2.3 in the predicate named **proc support**.

Reliability of Tests of Detail

Reliability is "the extent to which a procedure provides a correct message about some underlying state". It is a measure of the strength of support for the truth of a particular financial statement item assertion-based on the evidence provided by a particular audit evidence-gathering procedure. It is possible to argue that the reliability of the evidence provided by an audit evidence-gathering procedure depends on the exact nature of the evidence; i.e., taking into account both the procedure and the assertion being audited. This would require individual assessments of all procedures by the assertion to which they were applied. However, in the current implementation of CAPEX, the reliability of the evidence provided by a particular audit evidence-gathering procedure is considered to be a function of the procedure alone, omitting any potential interaction between a procedure and a given assertion.

One way of accommodating these varying reliabilities into the present knowledge structure is to consider that audit evidence-gathering procedures of this type are actually composite procedures. For instance, positive confirmation can be thought of as a set of procedures where each individual procedure corresponds to a single question. One procedure requests that the client confirms the existence of the asset, another procedure requests that the client confirms the valuation of the asset, and so on. Currently audit procedures are not analyzed at this level of detail. It is implicitly assumed that the reliability of the various messages provided by a particular procedure does not depend on the type of message.

The reliability of a procedure depends on a variety of different factors. Some of these factors affect the reliability of the information provided by the procedure in a known, and fairly specific way. Other factors are known to have an impact but the extent, and in some cases the nature, of that impact may be only vaguely understood. For instance, if a procedure makes use of sampling, it is possible, given a variety of assumptions, to make relatively precise statements about the characteristics of the underlying population given the characteristics of a sample of that population. In contrast, it is generally accepted by auditors that the competence of the individual carrying out a procedure and interpreting the evidence obtained is directly related to the reliability of the evidence. However, the vagueness, and complexity, of the term "competence" does not allow for a precise specification of the relationship.

Auditors have considerable difficulty in assessing the reliability of audit evidence provided by audit evidence-gathering procedures. This finding is consistent with the findings that even experts have difficulty in providing consistent weighting for factors which have been identified as influencing the reliability of audit evidence-gathering procedures.

The auditors who participated in this research were in general agreement concerning the types of factors which influenced the reliability of audit evidence-gathering procedures. These factors were originally identified by Ditner (1986) as a result of an extensive survey of the academic and professional literature on audit evidence. There was also agreement, though to a lesser extent, concerning the directional impact of reliability factor levels. For instance, one auditor who participated in one of the early validation tests indicated that, in his opinion, direct auditor knowledge was significantly less reliable than evidence provided by an external source even if the auditor were assumed to be competent in observing the item(s) in question. Subsequent questioning revealed a number of past experiences which formed the basis of this judgment.

The factors which the participating auditors judged to be relevant for determining the reliability of evidence obtained from test of detail procedures were different from those judged to be relevant for substantive analysis (analytic review) procedures. The factors which impact on the reliability of the evidence provided by test of detail procedures are considered in the section on analytical procedures.

Reliability Factors - Tests of Detail Procedures: The principal factors which were judged to be relevant, by experienced auditors, to the determination of the reliability of the audit evidence provided by a particular test of detail procedure, and their associated factor levels are summarized in Table 2.3 (adapted from Ditner, 1986).

Table 2.3 Relationships Between Reliability Factor Levels and Reliability of Evidence

Reliability Factor	Factor Level Relationships
Complexity of audit issue: very high, high, medium, low	The greater the complexity of the audit issue, the lower the reliability of the information provided.
Source of evidence: direct auditor knowledge, external, external/internal internal	Direct auditor knowledge > External source > External/Internal source > Internal source.
Reliability of the source: high, moderate, low	The greater the reliability of the source of audit information, the greater the reliability of the information
Competence of the performer:	The greater the competence of the procedure performer, the greater the reliability of the information provided.
Complexity of client's records:	The greater the complexity of the client's records, the lower the reliability of the information available.
Type of evidence: positive, negative	Positive evidence is more reliable than negative evidence.
Form of the evidence: oral, documentary	Documentary evidence is more reliable than oral evidence
Timing of the procedure: interim, year-end	Procedures performed at year-end provide more reliable information concerning the constituents of *year-end* financial statement item balances than the same procedures performed at some interim date.
Procedural extent: complete population, sample	The greater the extent to which a procedure is performed, i.e. the greater the proportion of items making up a particular financial statement item balance which are sampled, the more reliable is the information provided about the financial statement item balance.

The impact and interpretation of each of these factors will now be considered in more detail.

Complexity of the audit issue: The factor is a composite factor. The complexity of audit issue is related to the extent to which the auditor has to exercise judgment to interpret the evidence provided by a particular audit evidence-gathering procedure. The exercise of judgment reduces the reliability of the information provided by a particular procedure even if the auditor is judged to be very competent. Complexity may also refer to mathematical complexity of determining a particular characteristic. For instance, computing the outstanding balance on a loan with blended payments is a relatively non-trivial task.

Another source of complexity derives from the fact that some characteristics of a population may be inherently easier to establish with confidence than others. The existence or non-existence of accounts receivable is, generally speaking, easier to determine than their value. Thus, information provided by positive confirmations is more reliable when that information pertains to the existence of the accounts receivable than when it pertains to the "hard" valuation of those accounts receivable.

Source of the evidence: Evidence which is generated by persons outside a client's enterprise is believed to be more reliable than that generated internally. It is assumed that the external party is objective and competent, thus improving the reliability of the information, unless of course, the external party is a "related party". Evidence that is externally-generated but is in a client's possession (for example, bank statements) is considered to be more reliable than internal data, but less reliable than purely external data because the opportunity exists for the client to manipulate the evidence.

Reliability of source: In the context of audit evidence-gathering procedures which use internal or internal/external information, the reliability of the source refers to the auditor's assessment of the overall reliability of the client's records. This involves an assessment of the client's internal control environment. The higher the quality of the client's internal control system, generally speaking, the more reliable the information contained in the client's records. This assessment of the strength of the internal control environment should not be confused with the detailed assessment of the assurance (risk reduction) with respect to specific financial statement item assertions provided by compliance testing of specific controls.

With respect to procedures which rely on external information, the reliability of the source refers to the reliability of the provider of the information. For instance, if the provider is a business, the information provided is generally considered to be more reliable than if the provider is a private individual. When information is provided by direct auditor knowledge, the reliability of the source refers to the reliability of the auditor.

Competence of procedure performer: Competence may be considered to be a function of general and specific experience. The more competent the individual, the more reliable the information provided by that individual. He or she is better able both to perform procedures to collect audit evidence and interpret the audit evidence once it is collected.

Complexity of client's records: The greater the complexity of the client's records, the more documents which have to be inspected and the longer the chains of reasoning which have to be followed in order to reach relevant conclusions. The longer a chain of reasoning, the less reliable the conclusion which may be drawn if each step is less than completely reliable. It may also be noted that the more complex a client's records, the more likely it is that the individuals performing the audit will skip stages and "assume" results.

Type of evidence: If a procedure provides positive evidence, then it provides identifiable evidence. Positive confirmation of accounts receivable yields evidence in the form of confirmations (or otherwise) of accounts receivable balances by customers.

On the other hand, "negative evidence is the absence of evidence, after reasonable searching for it, contradicting the assertion" (Anderson, 1984, p. 170). Negative evidence is inherently less reliable than positive evidence because not finding a problem could be the result of an incomplete search by the auditor, or, failure to recognize the problem as well as the absence of a problem. Research studies on negative confirmations (Hubbard, Ballington, 1972; Warren, 1975) support the hypothesis that positive evidence is more reliable than negative evidence.

Form of the evidence: Oral evidence generally has low reliability because it is difficult to substantiate at a later date. Also, oral evidence may contain ambiguous terms which are interpreted differently by the parties involved. On the other hand, written evidence has a higher reliability rating because presumably people will take more care in preparing written evidence, especially if it is signed.

Timing of the procedure: In some cases it may be possible to perform procedures prior to year end. For instance, confirmation of accounts receivable often takes place several months before year end. Performing procedures prior to year end tends to reduce the reliability of the evidence as it pertains to year end balances. It becomes necessary to determine whether there have been any significant events between the interim date and year end which would lead to significant deviations between interim balances and year end balances. Thus, it is important to carry out a set of roll forward procedures if confirmations are performed prior to year end. Performing procedures prior to year end does, however, have a number of advantages particularly in terms of cost and the availability of staff to perform the procedures.

Procedures which can be performed at interim and year end are treated as distinct procedures by CAPEX with different composite costs and reliabilities. This provides a way of modeling the tradeoffs between performing a procedure at year end and at an interimdate.

Presently the interim date is considered to be three months prior to year end and is not variable. This choice can, of course, be changed to reflect changing circumstances.

Extent to which procedure is performed: The reliability of the audit evidence provided by a given procedure may be considered to vary with the proportion of the potential population to which the procedure is applied. Information obtained from 100% confirmation of accounts receivable balances will be more reliable than information obtained from confirmation of 50% of the same balances. The relationship between the extent of sampling, expressed in terms of a sampling confidence, and the overall reliability of a procedure was modeled in the following manner:

Assurance = (Max Derivable Assurance) * (Sampling Confidence) (3)

The Maximum Derivable Assurance (MDA) is the product of a procedure's relevance and reliability. MDA may be interpreted as the upper limit of the assurance which may be derived from the evidence provided by a particular procedure if the procedure is applied to all items in the relevant population.

The reliability of any procedure is considered to be a function of a variety of factors. A tree representing all the possible combinations of these factors was presented in Chapter 1. This scoring function is an example of a numerical evaluation of various different types of endorsements, as Cohen (1985) uses the term. Biggs, Messier, and Hansen (1987) have indicated that Cohen's Endorsement Theory may be useful in modeling the decision processes of computer audit specialists. The reliability tree and scoring function that we use is, to our best knowledge, the first application of the numerical evaluation of endorsements in the field of audit planning. Once reliability scores have been determined they are mapped to assurances using the mapping function in Table 2.4.

Table 2.4 Relationship Between Reliability Scores and Assurance Levels

Reliability Score Derived from Reliability Tree	**Assurance Level/ Probability**
18	0.95
17	0.94
16	0.93
15	0.92
14	0.91
13	0.90
12	0.85
11	0.80
10	0.75
9	0.70
8	0.65
7	0.60
6	0.55
5	0.50
4	0.40
3	0.30
2	0.20
1	0.10
0	0.00

Figure 2.4 ***Graphical Representation of Relationship Between Verbal and Quantitative Expressions of Evidential Reliability***

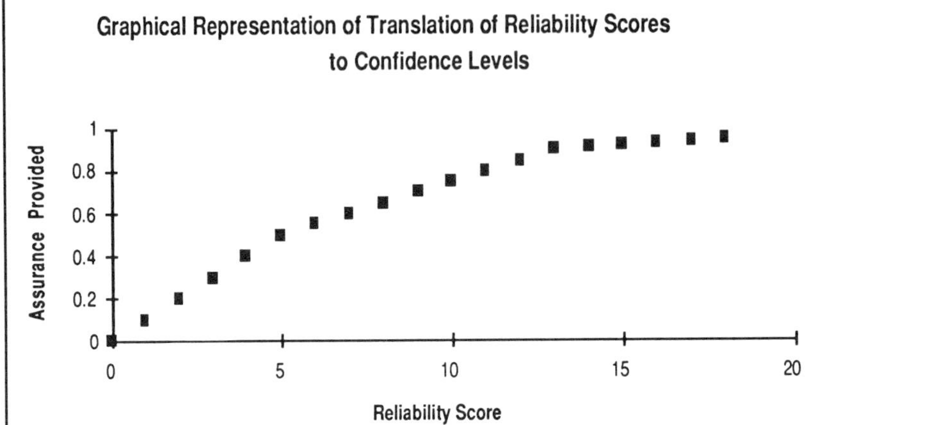

ANALYTIC PROCEDURES

The other type of audit evidence-gathering procedures which are available to the auditor for inclusion in a substantive audit program plan are analytic review, or, substantive analysis techniques.

Many auditors believe that analytic review procedures are appropriate for the preliminary planning stages of an audit to identify potential problem areas and for reviewing the results of a completed audit program plan. In adopting this position they are in broad agreement with the position that substantive analysis techniques "may be good at spotting the presence of errors, but do not reliably indicate the absence of errors" (Loebbecke and Steinbart, 1987, p. 87). Other auditors, including the subjects who participated in the construction of CAPEX, are of the opinion that some analytic procedures, particularly those which use statistical investigation rules, can be used in place of substantive tests of detail.

Analytic procedures involve generating expected values of financial statement item balances, or ratios of balances, and comparing these expected values to the actual balances, or ratios of balances, presented in the client's financial statements. Expected values may be generated in different ways. Because the information utilized by these procedures is more general than that used in tests of detail procedures, the evidence provided by substantive analysis techniques is generally less informative.[2] However, it is generally agreed that the performance of substantive

[2] This is generally true with respect to the audit evidence provided by individual substantive analysis techniques. However, the combined evidence provided by a set of related substantive analysis techniques may provide strong to very strong evidence relevant to establishing the truth of a particular financial statement item assertion. This type of evidence combination is not presently represented in CAPEX.

analysis procedures can be used to reduce or eliminate the need to conduct tests of details. For instance the AICPA states that:

> *[Substantive analysis procedures] may indicate the need for additional audit procedures, or it may indicate that the extent of other auditing procedures may be reduced [AICPA, 1979, AU 318.03]*

Substantive analysis procedures, because they rely on summary data and their reliability depends on the reliability of that data, are restricted in the assurance that they can provide. As a result, Blocher and Willingham (1985) caution that:

> *Analytical review provides a negative-type assurance rather than a positive one . . . the auditor can never rely exclusively on analytical review when risk or materiality is high [p. 10].*

Smith (1983) identified four different categories of analytic review procedures:

1. Expected values based on "reasonable" values for ratios of account balances.

2. Expected values based on prior year's results.

3. Expected values based on a combination of values of different variables.

4. Expected values based on a regression using a variety of variables.

The first set of procedures does not, according to Smith, provide any substantive assurance. He argues that the second type of procedure, because it requires the definition of what constitutes significant fluctuations and follow-up procedures to be applied to all such fluctuations, provides 30% assurance concerning the truth of relevant assertions.

The third type of approach differs from the second in that the expectations for the ratios are developed on the basis of a combination of different judgments. It is suggested by Smith that an assurance level of 50% is provided by procedures of this type. Finally, the fourth set of procedures, because they can provide statistical results, are considered to provide 70% assurance.

The above classification may be further extended, after Coakley (1982) and Knechel (1986), to reflect analytic review procedures which are actually used by the profession. These procedures are both more extensive, are actually used by the profession, and have been subjected to a variety of empirical tests in an attempt to determine their reliabilities (Kinney, 1987; Kinney and Salamon, 1982; Knechel, 1986, 1988; Loebbecke and Steinbart, 1987). Knechel (1986) investigates the following subset of analytic review procedures derived from Coakley (1982):

- Ratio Models
  - Ratio analysis - annual data.
  - Ratio analysis - monthly data.
  - Ratio analysis - seasonal monthly data.

- Random Walk Models
  - Random walk - annual data.
  - Random walk - monthly data.
  - Random walk - seasonal monthly data.

- Moving Average Models
  - Moving average - annual data.

- Moving average - monthly data.
- Moving average - seasonal monthly data.

- Regression Models
  - Univariate regression - monthly data.

Analytic procedures provide for the generation of expectations concerning the value of account balances using variables which are expected to be related to such balance values. A necessary condition for the application of a particular substantive analysis procedure is that the data which will be used to generate expectations is available and reasonably reliable. Significant deviations of actual values from expected values for the dependent variable may be the result of errors in the reporting of the actual value of the dependent variable or of errors in the reporting of the value of the independent variable. Hence, it is important that the auditor have some confidence in the reliability of the values for the variable from which expected values are to be generated.

Relevance of Analytic Procedures

Following discussions with the subjects it was established that analytic review procedures which provide no indication as to significant deviations from expected values provide evidential support for the existence/occurrence overstatement, completeness understatement and hard valuation/hard measurement[3] understatement and overstatement assertions concerning the account balance being forecast. When the data used to generate expectations with respect to a particular account balance relates only to the volume of items in the balance, more limited evidential support may be provided.

One guide to determining the relevance of a particular substantive analysis procedure is to investigate whether the client uses the variables utilized by the procedure as a means of controlling and managing the business. During the knowledge acquisition phase, one auditor indicated that she first investigates the relationships that the client uses for performance evaluation/managerial control. To the extent that a business is competently run, management will often have a well developed understanding of which variables are meaningfully related. Thus, financial institutions place considerable importance on interest spreads. Deviations from expected spreads may indicate both problems of managerial control and errors of audit significance.

If companies use external economic data to assess the performance of different units of the firm, these relationships may also provide reasonably reliable tests for detecting errors. Generally speaking, the more knowledge explicitly or implicitly represented in the relationships being used as a basis of analytic review tests, the more reliable the tests will be at detecting material error.

In the current implementation of the system it is assumed that only one type of message is provided by any particular substantive analysis procedure. This message indicates that there are no unusual deviations present in the underlying population. In addition, it is assumed that the meaning of the message provided by any substantive analysis procedure may be interpreted independently of whether specific messages have been provided by other substantive analysis procedures.

---

[3] As noted earlier a distinction is made between hard and soft valuation or measurement assertions.

The assumption that substantive analysis procedures with a particular investigation rule provide messages with an invariant meaning reduces the richness of the evidential support provided by such procedures. A number of auditors indicated that a combination of substantive analysis procedures can be used to identify specific errors and, hence, provide more precise evidential support than would be expected from the combination of the evidential support provided by each substantive analysis procedure considered individually.

At the present time CAPEX checks to see which accounting and non-accounting variables are available and enables specific substantive analysis procedures accordingly. Only that data which has been audited to some extent can be used in the generation of expectations. This requirement alerts the auditor to the need to consider, with care, the reliability of the data used in substantive analysis procedures. Biggs and Wild (1985) indicate that auditors often place undue reliance on unaudited data when evaluating substantive analysis procedures.

Analytic procedures which provide no evidence of significant deviations from the expected value of accounts receivable are considered to provide support for all accounts receivable assertions: existence overstatement, valuation hard under and over statement, and completeness understatement. The logic which supports this mapping is as follows:

> If there were any significant errors with respect to any accounts receivable assertion, then significant deviations from expected values would occur. There are no significant deviations : therefore, there are no significant errors with respect to any accounts receivable assertions.

Reliability of Analytic Procedures

The reliability of these procedures depends on a different set of factors from those discussed above. The reliability factors were identified through a review of the auditing literature, particularly, in this case, firm audit manuals and interviews with practicing auditors.

The strength of the evidence provided by a particular substantive analysis procedure also depends on the nature of the investigation rule used. That is, once forecasts have been generated, an investigation rule will be used to determine when a particular observation should be investigated. In the current implementation the decision rules which were adopted related to percentage deviations except in the case of regression analysis, where statistically-based decision rules were used.

A variety of simulation studies have investigated the power of substantive analytic techniques to identify errors. In a simulation study of the effectiveness of ratio techniques, Kinney (1988) concludes that the reliability of these techniques varies considerably with the natural variation of the accounts upon which the ratio is based and the investigation rule used. He uses the study to show that investigation rules based on simple percentages, which are common investigation rules in practice, underperform (either lead to greater Type I or greater Type II errors, or both) statistical investigation rules. He also demonstrates that investigation rules based on patterns of deviations in different ratios are potentially more powerful at detecting specific types of errors than investigation rules based on deviations of single ratios. CAPEX does not have the capability of performing the types of inferences which would allow the combination of evidence provided by a variety of different financial ratios.

In another study, Loebbecke and Steinbart (1987) investigate the effectiveness of a number of different types of analytic review procedures. They argue that tests which simply compare the value of an account balance with that for the previous year and investigate deviations of greater than a certain percentage are not very effective at detecting error. They further note that varying the cutoff percentage "simply trades off type 1 and type 2 errors" (p. 80). Most of the other methods they investigate are, in their simulations, not much more than 50% reliable. One of the reasons they cite for this result is that they use external data for their simulations. In many situations they suggest that:

There are significant behavioural dynamics involving preliminary ARP [Analytic Review Procedures], in which the auditor uses his understanding of the client's business and draws on his experience when interpreting the results of those procedures. (p. 87)

As a result:

Future research, therefore needs to be directed towards methods for more effectively utilizing the auditor's knowledge acquired through experience. (p. 87)

CAPEX takes into account client-specific information in determining whether a particular substantive analysis procedure is relevant, and in determining the reliability of the evidence provided by such a procedure.

Reliability Factors for Analytic Procedures: After extensive discussions with experienced auditors and reviews of the research literature and accounting firm manuals, the following substantive analysis reliability factors and factor levels were identified

- The variability of the data used to generate expectations - high, medium, low.
- The nature of the substantive analysis procedure - ratio, random walk, moving average, regression analysis, analytic recomputation.
- The type of investigation rule used.
- The degree of homogeneity of items in the balance - very-high, high, moderate, low.
- The frequency of the data - annual, monthly, weekly, daily.
- The competence of the performer of the substantive analysis procedure.
- The strength of the relationship used for making forecasts.

Most of the above factors are self-explanatory with the exception of the third, the investigation rule used, and the fourth, the degree of homogeneity of items in the balance. These two factors are discussed in more detail below.

The type of investigation rule used: Substantive analysis procedures generate expected values for account balances or ratios of account balances. An investigation rule is a rule which defines when the difference between the expected value and the actual value should be investigated. Generally speaking, the smaller the relative deviations allowed by the investigation rule the more likely it is that the substantive analysis procedure will detect significant errors in an account balance. However, this increased reliability comes at a price - as the probability that the procedure will correctly signal significant errors increases, so does the probability that it will signal the presence of significant errors when no errors are, in fact, present.

The degree of homogeneity of the items in the balance: This factor requires the assessment of the similarity of the items which constitute the balance. If the items constituting the balance are essentially identical then substantive analysis procedures provide very reliable estimates. If, however, the account balance contains items which are extremely diverse, this will reduce the reliability of the evidence provided by substantive analysis procedures.

Other Reliability Heuristics: In addition to identifying the above factors, a number of what may be called, "reliability heuristics", were identified which relate to the strength of evidential support provided by substantive analysis procedures.

It was found that a number of experienced auditors used heuristics when making assessments of the reliability of evidence provided by substantive analysis procedures. One heuristic is that substantive analysis procedures which use the values of balance sheet items as a basis for generating expected values for another account balance *ceteris paribus* provide less reliable evidence that those procedures which use the values of transaction-stream items. The principal rationale behind this heuristic appeared to be that balance sheet items are affected by a greater variety of events than transaction-stream items.

Another heuristic is that substantive analysis procedures which utilize data that are independent of the client's accounting information system are more reliable than procedures that use accounting information, provided that the non-accounting information is itself reasonably reliable.

A third heuristic relates to the specificity of the data being used in substantive procedures. The less client-specific the data, the less reliable is the evidence provided by substantive analysis procedures. The above heuristics are not presently implemented in CAPEX.

The full details of the Prolog implementation of the reliability assessments provided by the participating auditors are presented in Appendix 2.4 in the predicate procedure **reliability**.

COST

If the only objective of concern in constructing an audit program plan related to the achievement of a particular target assurance (set of target assurances), it would only be necessary to consider the reliability of the evidence provided by various procedures when constructing a plan. While this might lead to the construction of *effective* substantive audit program plans, they are unlikely to be *efficient*. In order to have the possibility of constructing efficient plans, the cost of performing procedures must be represented in CAPEX.

The total cost of the audit program plan generated by CAPEX is the sum of the costs of all the procedures which have been applied.

There are three components of the total cost of applying a particular procedure: the set-up cost, the variable cost per unit of work, and the number of units of work required to achieve a given level of assurance.

Cost = Set-up Cost + (Variable Cost * n) **(4)**

The first component (set-up cost) is assumed to be zero in the current version of CAPEX. The second component (variable cost) is obtained directly from the information contained in the cost tree. This component does not necessarily have an unique value since it will vary with the level of seniority of staff conducting the procedure. Unless instructed otherwise, CAPEX will select the staff allocation which will result in the lowest cost for the procedure in question. The third component (n) varies with what is termed the sampling confidence factor and the size of the population. The sampling confidence factor is a measure of the extent to which a procedure is performed and is calculated using the following formula:

$$\textbf{Sampling Confidence} = \frac{PA}{MDA} \qquad (5)$$

where PA = Planned Assurance; PA ≤ MDA; and SCF≤ max SCF
MDA = (Reliability of Procedure) * (Relevance of Procedure)

The extent is then used to calculate a numerical sample size in two stages. First, a sample size factor is obtained by inspecting Table 2.5.

Table 2.5 Relationship Between Sampling Confidence and Sample Size Factors

Sampling Confidence	Sample Size Factor[4]
Sf = 0.500	0.7
Sf > 0.500 but < 0.550	0.8
Sf ≥ 0.550 but < 0.600	0.9
Sf ≥ 0.600 but < 0.650	1.1
Sf ≥ 0.650 but < 0.700	1.2
Sf ≥ 0.700 but < 0.750	1.4
Sf ≥ 0.750 but < 0.800	1.6
Sf ≥ 0.800 but < 0.850	1.9
Sf ≥ 0.850 but < 0.900	2.3
Sf ≥ 0.900 but < 0.950	3.0
Sf ≥ 0.950 but < 0.960	3.3
Sf ≥ 0.960 but < 0.970	3.5
Sf ≥ 0.970 but < 0.975	3.7
Sf ≥ 0.975 but < 0.980	4.0
Sf ≥ 0.980 but < 0.985	4.2
Sf ≥ 0.985 but < 0.990	4.7
Sf ≥ 0.990 but < 0.995	5.5
Sf ≥ 0.995 but < 0.999	6.9
Sf ≥ 0.999 but < 1.000	9.9
Sf = 1.000	10.0

4 These confidence factors are drawn from the Poisson distribution, which is used by many auditors in making sample size decisions for various audit tests. Since monetry unit sample sizes vary directly with these factors, they can serve as a useful proxy for relative costs of various procedures when adjusted for the population size.

Figure 2.5 *Graphical Representation of Relationship Between Sampling Confidence and Sample Size*

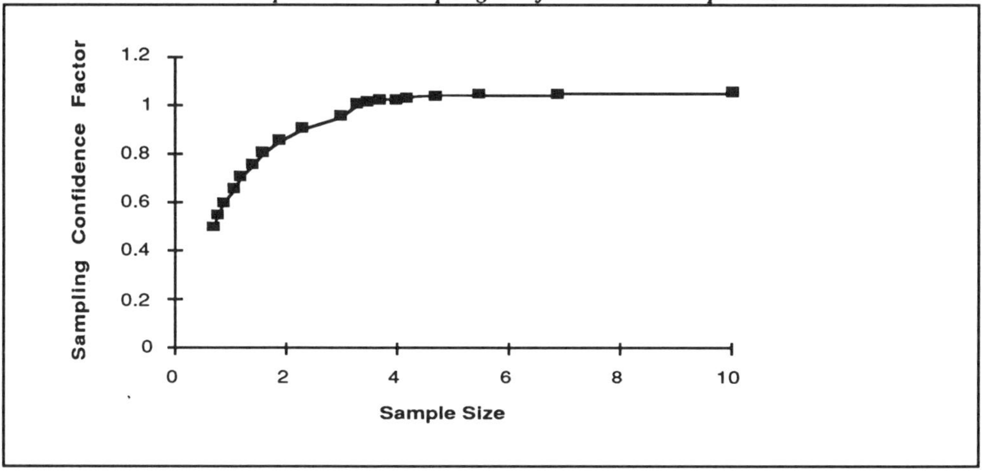

Then the actual numerical sample size, n, is calculated using the following formula:

n = (Account Total / Maximum Tolerable Error) * Sample Size Factor **(6)**

where Maximum Tolerable Error = f(Materiality)

The above approach to determining the cost of applying procedures takes into account both procedure-specific characteristics which affect the cost and the impact of sample size on the cost of applying a particular procedure.

The variable cost of each procedure is considered to be a function of a number of factors. As with the reliability factors, the relationship between the various cost factors can be represented in the form of a tree. The cost tree was described in the previous chapter in connection with the discussion of the user-interface. As indicated there, a cost scoring function is provided in CAPEX which takes into account the levels of each of the cost factors. The resulting cost figure represents the cost of performing the procedure in question on one item of the population to which it is applicable.

Cost of Performance for Test of Details Procedures

The auditors participating in the research project were first given the opportunity of revising the set of reliability factors which had been drawn up as a result of a literature search (Ditner, 1986), a review of firm manuals, and previous interviews with practicing auditors. They were then asked to make judgments with respect to the impact of different levels of the factors identified on the cost of performing a particular procedure. The factors which were identified, and the levels associated with them, were as follows:

- Seniority of staff - high, medium, or low.
- Time taken - high, medium, or low.

- Behavioural cost - high, medium, or low.
- Competence of the performer(s) - high, medium, or low.
- Complexity of the client's records - high, moderate, or low.
- Quality of the client's records - high, medium, or low.

As noted earlier, the auditors were asked to make assessments of the relative importance of the first three factors with respect to the overall cost of performing a substantive test of detail procedure. Subjects were asked to assume that the individual performing the procedure was competent, the client's records were of moderate complexity, and the client's records were of moderate quality.

Cost of Performance for Analytic Procedures

With respect to substantive analysis procedures the relative costs were initially considered to depend on the following factors and factor levels:

- Complexity of test - high, medium, low.
- Frequency of data - annual, monthly.
- Availability of data - client-generated, auditor-generated.

In discussions with the auditors who participated in the research it was established that the principal factor to be considered was the complexity of the test.

The full details of the Prolog implementation of the cost assessments provided by the participating auditors are presented in Appendix 2.5 in predicates named:

- **procedure set up cost**
- **procedure variable cost**

CLIENT-SPECIFIC KNOWLEDGE

In this section some issues with respect to client-specific knowledge will be discussed. Client-specific information may affect the construction of a substantive audit program plan in a variety of different ways. Different types of clients may :

- have different financial statement items.
- the characteristics of financial statement items may differ in terms of size, variability, and number of individual items.
- have different financial statement item assertions considered to be critical.
- involve different levels of inherent risk.
- involve different levels of control risk.

- involve different types of information with differing reliabilities and costs.
- require different audit procedures to be applied to obtain sufficient, appropriate audit evidence.
- involve different strength of feedforward and feedback relationships.
- involve special audit objectives; e.g., if the auditor is aware that items may be recorded as being sold when, in fact, they are on consignment, procedures will be performed to determine whether accounting for consigned items is appropriate.

CAPEX is designed to generate substantive audit program plans given assessments of the assurance which has already been achieved with respect to relevant financial statement item assertions based on evidence derived from considerations of inherent and control risk. These assessments are encoded in the achieved assurances module, **prior assurance**. This module is a component of the module which contains all the client specific data required by the main planning program. CAPEX can thus take into account changes in the prior probabilities of error of relevant financial statement item assertions by altering the input risk parameters. In addition to the prior achieved assurance, CAPEX encodes the following client-specific information:

- The identity of all the account balances which are greater than or equal to materiality.
- The target and actual assurances for all the relevant assertions for all the account balances.
- The total value and number of items for all the relevant account balances.
- The variability of the items in all the relevant account balances.
- Various client characteristics which lead to enabling or disabling of various procedures.

Figure 2.6 displays the window which allows the auditor to Maintain the Client-specific data pertaining to the various Financial Statement Items.

Figure 2.6 Maintenance of Client Information

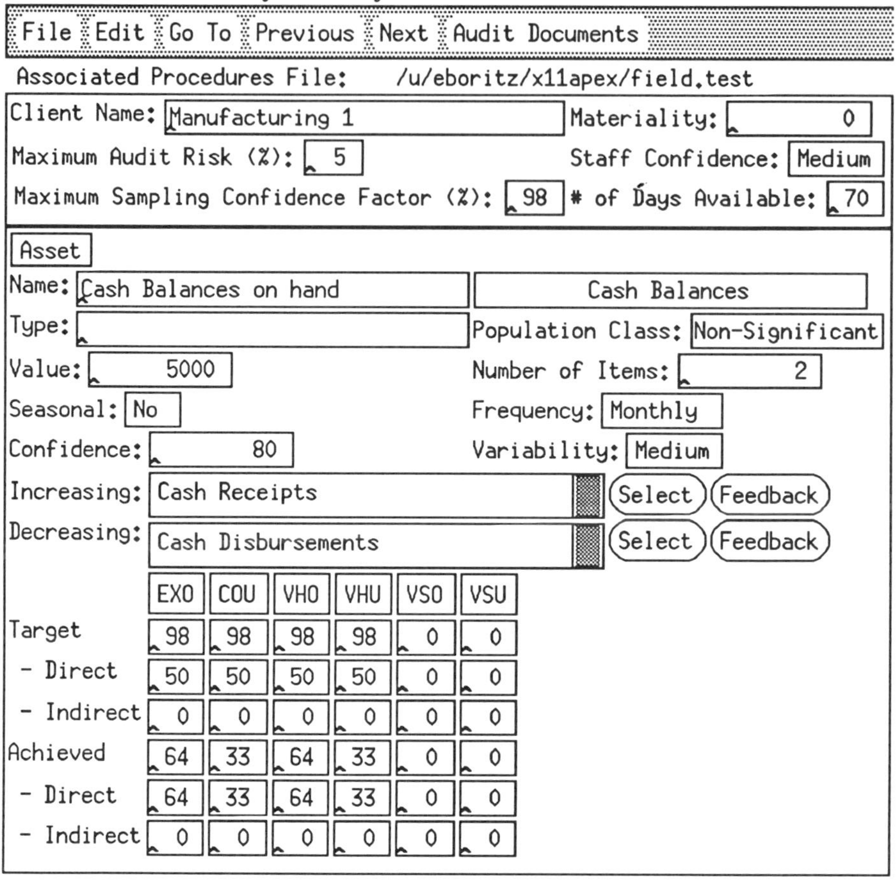

The following information is recorded.

Attributes	**Values**
Client Name:	User supplied (25 characters)
Materiality:	User supplied $ value
Maximum Audit Risk:	User supplied percentage
Staff Confidence:	High, medium, low
Maximum Sampling Confidence Factor (%):	User supplied percentage
# of Days Available:	User supplied number
For Account Balances:	
Name:	User supplied (defaults to financial statement item class)
Type:	User supplied (25 characters)
Population Class:	User supplied (Significant, Non-significant, N/A)
Value:	User supplied $ value
Number of Items:	User supplied number
Seasonal:	Yes, No
Frequency:	Daily, Weekly, Monthly, Annual
Confidence:	User supplied percentage
Variability:	High, medium, low
Name of the transaction stream which increases the asset balance:	User selected from list
Name of the transaction stream which decreases the asset balance:	User selected from list
Select	Button for choosing increasing/decreasing
Feedback	Button to modify default feedback characteristics
Target assurance for each assertion:	
Direct:	User supplied percentage
Indirect:	User supplied percentage
For Transaction Streams:	Same as above except that there are no fields for increasing/decreasing transaction streams

Figure 2.7 displays the sub-window which enables the auditor to record the strength of indirect supporting relationships between various generating and derived assertions.

Figure 2.7 Maintenance of Indirect Supporting Relationships

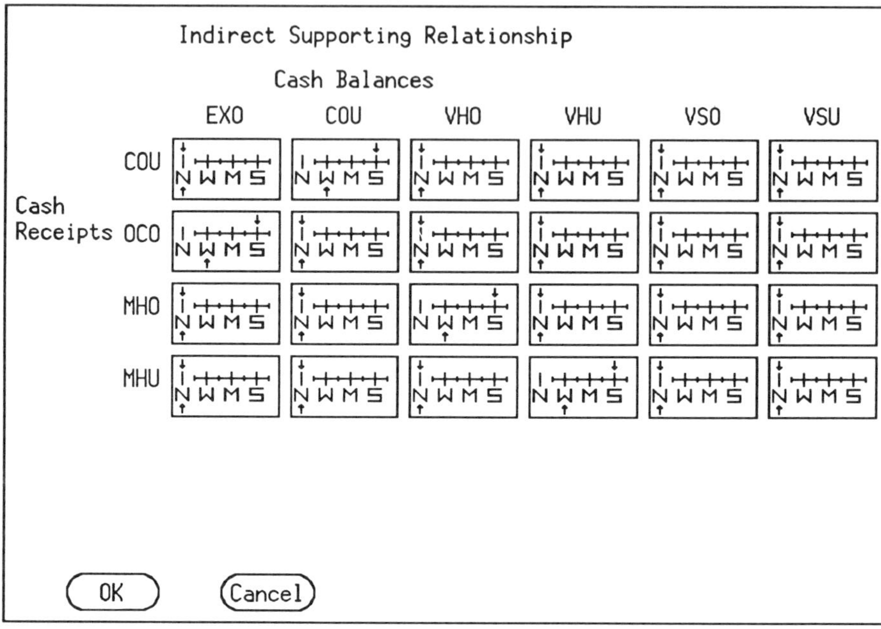

Appendix 2.6 contains Prolog predicates related to client specific knowledge, including:

- **parameters**
- **number of items**
- **target assurance**
- **prior assurance**

THE COMPUTATIONAL MODEL

The computational model first identifies the procedures which are relevant for a particular audit and which have any existing preconditions satisfied. The model then processes the knowledge in the revised knowledge-base to generate a substantive audit program plan. Figure 2.8 below summarizes the plan generation process.

Figure 2.8 The Plan Generation Process

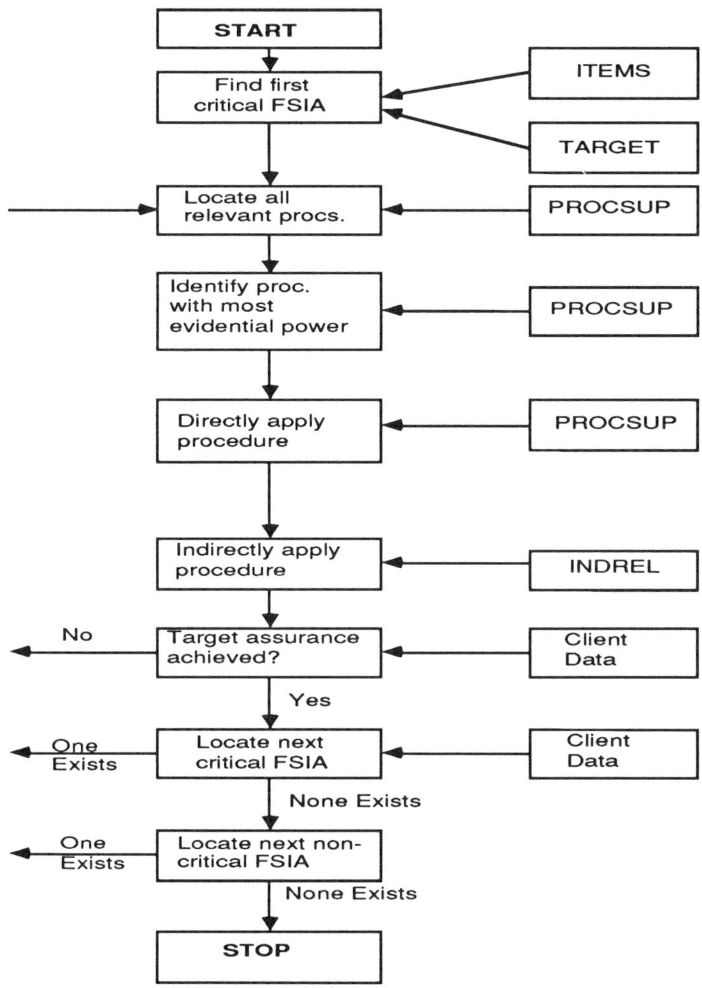

Note: FSIA= Financial Statement Item Assertion

Once a knowledge-base of procedures has been codified, including their relevances, reliabilities and costs, the plan generator can be invoked. The plan generator has two broad functions:

1. To establish the order in which the target assurances for financial statement item assertions will be sequentially planned for.

2. To construct sub-plans for each financial statement item assertion.

Planning knowledge which is necessary to construct realizable audit plans is primarily encoded in the plan generation module **generatePlan**. This knowledge is primarily procedural. It relates to the processes which must be followed in order to generate an audit plan for all the relevant assertions which satisfies, or comes closest to satisfying, the predefined objectives.

The types of planning heuristics which may be encoded in CAPEX may be expressions of overall policies with respect to audit program planning as in the following:

Balance sheet approach:

> *Audit programs are to be generated which maximize the extent of direct tests of detail with respect to balance sheet item assertions. Tests of detail will only be carried out on transaction streams to provide indirect support of the balance sheet items.*

Transaction stream approach:

> *Audit programs are to be generated which maximize the credit which may be taken for inherent risk assessment, internal control risk assessment and analytic review risk assessment. Tests of detail will be planned for balance sheet items to achieve whatever target assurance has been set to the extent that this target has not been achieved through indirect supporting relationships.*

Other planning heuristics which can be encoded describe the logic of structured planning as, for example:

> *To generate a plan for a set of financial statement item assertions {**A**} generate a plan for each element of **A**, taking into account any interactions. The overall plan will be a combination of these individual plans.*

> *To generate a plan for a set of financial statement items plan for items which represent transactions before items which represent balances.*

Yet other heuristics which can be encoded may be more specific:

> *When deciding which audit procedure to apply to achieve assurance with respect to a particular financial statement assertion, select the uncompleted audit procedure with the highest evidential power.*

Evidential power is defined as follows:

$$E_p = \frac{\sum_{i=1}^{F} \sum_{j=1}^{A} MDA_{ij}}{C_p}$$

In other words, it is the sum of all *maximum derivable assurances* (MDAs) from a procedure for all F financial items and all A assertions to which the procedure applies, divided by the cost (C_p) of applying the procedure on an appropriate number of items within the selected population as determined by applying the extent of testing algorithm described earlier. An alternative definition of evidential power is not to sum over assertions; but rather, to treat each assertion independently, to maximize the collection of independent items of evidence.

CAPEX is also able to recognize ways in which plans may not be realizable and adjust plans accordingly. For instance, in a given situation it may not be possible for two procedures to be included in the same substantive audit program plan. Some of these constraints may be global as, for example, expressed by the following rule:

Positive confirmations and negative confirmations should not be applied to the same population at the same time.

Other constraints will depend on client specific knowledge as, for example, the following:

If a client has no sales contracts then do not apply procedure "verify sales contracts".

By default, CAPEX first constructs plans for balance sheet financial statement items and then constructs plans for transaction stream financial statement items. When constructing plans for each assertion relevant to a particular financial statement item, critical assertions are addressed first, followed by non-critical assertions. Critical assertions are defined when the client data is entered and are typically financial statement item assertions which either represent a considerable exposure to the firm, for example, the occurrence of sales, or involve considerable judgment, as in the case of certain loan loss provisions.

Sub-plans for each financial statement item assertion are constructed in a number of stages:

Stage 1

A check is made to determine whether the prior assurance concerning the financial statement item assertion selected exceeds, or equals, the pre-defined target assurance. If this is the case, the plan generator proceeds to construct a sub-plan for the next financial statement item assertion. If the prior assurance is below the target assurance, the plan generator proceeds to Stage 2.

Stage 2

If there is a need to gather additional evidence to increase the assurance concerning the financial statement item assertion, the plan generator identifies all the relevant audit evidence-gathering procedures which can potentially provide evidence which will increase the assurance concerning the financial statement item assertion being considered.

Stage 3

A procedure is selected from the set of relevant procedures to be included in the sub-plan. Which procedure is selected depends on the type of selection heuristic used. Mandatory procedures are applied first, followed by discretionary procedures. In each case, the procedure with the *maximum evidential power* is selected first, and then applied to achieve the appropriate confidence factor. The revised achieved assurance (AA) from applying the procedure is compared to the target assurance (TA). If the target assurance has not been achieved, another unapplied relevant procedure is selected.

Recall that Evidential Power (EP) is defined as:

$$\textbf{EP} = \frac{\textbf{(Sum of all the } \textbf{\textit{Maximum Derivable Assurances}} \textbf{ from procedure)}}{\textbf{\textit{Cost}} \textbf{ of the procedure}}$$

Recall that the *Maximum Derivable Assurance* from a procedure (MDA) is:

MDA = (Reliability of Procedure) * (Relevance of Procedure)

Relevance is initially defined as a numerical score which is determined from the relevance table as previously described. *Reliability* is initially defined as a numerical score which is determined from the reliability tree as previously described. *Cost* is initially defined as a numerical score which is determined from the cost tree as previously described.

Stage 4

A determination is made whether sampling is appropriate and the direct and total prior assurances concerning the financial statement item assertion being planned for are revised using Bayesian revision.

The relationship between the maximum derivable assurance, the planned assurance (PA), and the sampling confidence to be derived from a procedure, if sampling is appropriate is:

If PA >= MDA
Then Sampling Confidence Factor = Maximum Sampling Confidence Factor
Else Sampling Confidence Factor = PA/MDA

If sampling is not appropriate, then the procedure is applied to all items in the appropriate population and an assurance equal to the maximum derivable assurance will be obtained.

If the selected procedure is the first procedure to be selected for the financial statement item assertion being planned for, it is only applied if it contributes assurance of more than 50%. On the other hand, for subsequent procedures the assurance cutoff value is 10%. If a selected procedure satisfies the appropriate assurance cutoff criterion, the assurance to be derived from it is used to revise the appropriate ***assertion_assurance*** entry in the dynamic database. The database is then updated to reflect the fact that many procedures provide assurance with respect to more than one assertion.

Stage 5

If the evidence available from the procedure provides support to other financial statement item assertions, the strength of this support is determined and their prior direct and total assurances are revised accordingly, using Bayesian revision, as described in more detail in the next section on Uncertainty Modeling in CAPEX.

Stage 6

If there are any indirect supporting relationships between the financial statement item being planned for and other financial statement items, these are identified. The additional indirect assurance available is determined in the manner described in the next section on Uncertainty Modeling in CAPEX and the prior indirect and total assurances of all indirectly related financial statement item assertions are revised accordingly, using Bayesian revision.

Stage 7

If the target assurance has been achieved, or the set of relevant audit evidence-gathering procedures which have not been included in the plan is empty, the plan generator iterates through the above stages for the next scheduled financial statement item assertion. Otherwise, it iterates through the above stages in an attempt to achieve the predetermined target assurance for the financial statement item being considered.

The portion of the Prolog program which implements the above process for generating plans is included, in its entirety, in Appendix 2.7.

UNCERTAINTY MODELING IN CAPEX

An auditor faces a variety of different uncertainties. Some of these uncertainties are only vaguely understood, while others are relatively well understood.

One of the principal uncertainties encountered in auditing relates to the reliability of audit evidence-gathering procedures. Hooper's work in the seventeenth century, resurrected by Shafer and Srivastava (1986), provides two models for combining reliabilities. These models are examples of a classical approach to uncertainty modeling.

An alternative approach to uncertainty modeling is presented by the Bayesian approach. The Bayesian formalism can provide an appropriate model of the sequential revision of the relevant uncertainties as evidence becomes available from audit evidence-gathering procedures.

The current implementation of CAPEX makes extensive use of both Bayesian and classical formalisms. Bayesian methods are used in situations where assurance is sequential and revised to reflect the impact of a number of different items of evidence. A classical approach is used where assurance is some combination of the assurance which has been achieved simultaneously with respect to related propositions.

The reliability of the evidence provided by a particular procedure, as represented in CAPEX, was not determined directly by the participating auditors. Each auditor was asked to identify the factors which influence the reliability of evidence provided by audit evidence gathering procedures. They were also asked to assess the relative importance of each of the factors.

The principal uncertainties modeled in CAPEX are those associated with the truth of assertions the client implicitly or explicitly makes when presenting his/her financial statements. The uncertainty associated with each financial statement item assertion is expressed in terms of *assurance*. The level of assurance associated with a particular financial statement item assertion may be interpreted as the degree of confidence in the truth of the assertion.

CAPEX models two broad ways in which evidence provided by audit evidence-gathering procedures have an impact on these assurances. First, the evidence may directly support a particular financial statement item assertion or set of financial statement item assertions. Second, the evidence may provide indirect support for a particular financial statement item or set of financial statement items.

The system maintains three achieved assurance measures for each financial statement item assertion: the total achieved assurance, the total assurance achieved as a result of the support available from evidence directly relevant to the financial statement item assertion, and the total assurance achieved as a result of the support available from evidence indirectly relevant to the financial statement item assertion.

In the current implementation, when a procedure is included in a particular plan by CAPEX, financial statement item achieved assurances are revised as follows:

Step 1

The prior achieved direct assurance in the financial statement item assertion for which the plan is being constructed is revised to take into account the direct support provided by evidence available from the audit evidence-gathering procedure selected. Revision is carried out using a Bayesian revision formula. Subsequently, the total assurance in the financial statement item assertion is also revised using a Bayesian revision formula.

Step 2

The other financial statement item assertions which are directly supported by the evidence provided by the procedure are identified and their prior achieved direct assurances and total assurances are revised to take into account the direct support provided by evidence from the procedure.

Step 3

The financial statement item assertions which are indirectly supported by the evidence provided by the procedure are identified. The actual indirect support provided is a function of the indirect support provided by the financial statement item assertion for which a plan is currently being constructed and the indirect support provided by any related financial statement item assertions. For example, as previously discussed, the accounts receivable existence overstatement assertion would obtain indirect support from direct procedures carried out to verify the sales occurrence overstatement assertion and the cash receipts completeness understatement assertion.

The marginal additional direct assurance provided by the procedure is multiplied by the appropriate indirect support coefficient to obtain a measure of the additional indirect support available from the procedure.

The total direct support in the related financial statement item assertion is then multiplied by the appropriate indirect support coefficient to obtain a measure of the indirect support available from the related financial statement item assertion.

The two indirect assurances are then multiplied together to give a combined indirect assurance in the financial statement item assertion in question. This combined indirect assurance is used to revise the prior achieved total assurance and the prior achieved total indirect assurance for the financial statement item assertion.

Example

The impact of the evidence which is expected to be provided by audit evidence-gathering procedures is represented in terms of subjective assessments of the strength of support (assurance) which it provides to financial statement item assertions. When an audit procedure is selected by one of the planning heuristics, the achieved assurances with respect to all the relevant (directly supported) financial statement item assertions are updated using a modified Bayesian revision approach based on the *Extent of Audit Testing* (CICA, 1980) approach to modeling uncertainty revision. The following formula relates Prior (risk), Testing (risk), and Target (risk):

Target = Prior * Testing / [(Prior * Testing) + (1 - Prior)]

Evidence which is expected to be provided by an audit evidence-gathering procedure also provides indirect support for a number of financial statement item assertions. Achieved assurances for the relevant financial statement item assertions are revised to reflect this support. The revised achieved assurance is determined using Bayesian revision. If the financial statement item assertion in question has more than one source of indirect support (e.g., accounts receivable existence depends upon both sales occurrence and cash receipts completeness) the combined assurance provided is determined by means of the following formula:

$$CIA = IA_1 * IA_2$$

where: CIA = Combined indirect assurance
IA_1 = Indirect assurance from procedure P_1
IA_2 = Indirect assurance from procedure P_2

Thus, if procedure P_1 provides indirect support of 0.80 and procedure P_2 provides indirect support of 0.70, then the combined indirect support of both procedures is (0.8) x (0.7) = 0.56.[5] The use of this formula may be justified on a number of grounds:

1. Indirect support is available simultaneously; hence, Bayesian revision does not seem to be appropriate.

2. The indirect supporting relationships for a derived item require that BOTH generating streams be free of material error. In constructing the plan, the goal is to obtain evidence that no material errors are present in the data to be audited; thus, the error condition is signaled if either procedure detects significant errors. Obviously, if one of them does and the other does not, then the evidence is contradictory.

3. Audit plans are constructed on the assumption that all audit evidence-gathering procedures will provide non-contradictory evidence.[6] In addition, to avoid the complication of having to

---

[5] Note that an alternative to this rule is to have Combined Assurance=1-[(1-Indirect Assurance1)*(1-Indirect Assurance2)], which would result in combined assurance of .94. The difference in assurances is obviously significant. Our rule is quite conservative, being based on the probability of both sources of support being right; whereas the alternative rule is based on the probability of both sources of assurance being wrong. This is an area of controversy which requires additional research to establish the appropriate combination approach.

[6] Of course, during the execution of the selected audit procedures it is possible that contradictory findings may be produced by different procedures. At the evaluation stage of the audit, an assessment of the net evidence supporting the assertions will need to be made, resolving any conflicting findings. While a formal approach to dealing with such conflicts would be valuable, the system described herein does not address this important issue.

program a subsystem for evaluating findings, the simplifying assumption was made that evidence-gathering procedures will not indicate the presence of a material error.

The program trace reproduced in Figure 1.1 in Chapter 1 illustrates the application of an analytic procedure. The first section of the trace demonstrates the application of rules to determine whether a procedure should be applied. CAPEX investigates the assurance which can be derived from the procedure. If no other procedures have been directly applied and the assurance available is less than 50%, the procedure will not be applied.[7] If other procedures have been directly applied and the procedure provides less than 10% assurance, then it will not be applied. In the above example, procedure 361 potentially provides 47.5% assurance[8] and other procedures have already been applied; hence it is a potential candidate for inclusion in an audit program plan.

CAPEX next determines whether all the assurance available from the procedure will be utilized. In this case, an additional 89.32412% assurance is needed to achieve the pre-defined target assurance of 99% for the financial statement item assertion accounts receivable completeness under(statement). The additional assurance required, given that 91.35601% assurance has already been obtained, is found by using the following version of the Bayesian revision approach described earlier:

$$\textbf{Testing Assurance} = \frac{\textbf{(Prior Assurance - Target Assurance)}}{\textbf{(Target Assurance * Prior Assurance - Target Assurance)}}$$

Thus:

Testing Assurance = (0.91356301 - 0.99) / ((0.99 * 0.91356301) - 0.99) = 0.8932412

In this case, since procedure 361 is an analytic procedure, it is either applied or it is not applied, sampling is not considered to be relevant; hence, the sampling confidence factor of 1.0 indicating that the complete population will be investigated.

The second section of the trace summarizes the effect of "applying" the procedure to accounts receivable completeness under. The total assurance, which has already been obtained from procedures which have already been included in the plan, is 91.356301%, all of which is direct assurance. Procedure 361 provides an additional 47.5% assurance. Under Bayesian revision, the revised assurance can be calculated using the following relationship:

$$\textbf{Revised Assurance} = \frac{\textbf{Prior Assurance}}{\textbf{(1-Testing Assurance + (Prior Assurance * Testing Assurance)}}$$

In this case:

$$\text{Revised assurance} = \frac{0.91356301}{1 - 0.475 + (0.91356301*0.475)} = 0.95267764$$

---

[7] The 50% test for the first procedure providing direct evidence in support of a financial statement item assertion is a heuristic based on the desire to avoid building up evidence based on many small degrees of assurance, none of which are individually convincing.

[8] In this section reference is made to assurance, which is expressed as a percentage. However, when assurances are used in the modified Bayesian revision formulae the decimal equivalents, representing probabilities, are used.

The third section details the effect of the indirect support provided by procedure 361. The first line in this section indicates that financial statement item "accounts receivable" is linked to both the "cash receipts on account" and the "sales on account" financial statement items, through feedback relationships. The indirect assurance, obtained through the feedback relationship, is 17.053418%.[9]

The penultimate stage of the calculation involves revising the prior indirect assurance, 17.053418%, using Bayesian revision, to reflect the effect of the additional indirect assurance of 17.053418%, which yields a revised indirect assurance of 19.863099%.[10]

The final stage of the process involves revising the achieved total assurance for "cash receipts on account occurrence over" to reflect the effect of the total indirect assurance which is now available. Since the present achieved assurance for this financial statement item assertion may reflect the effect of indirect assurance relating to previously applied procedures, it is necessary to "break out" the effect of this indirect assurance. In the above example, the total achieved assurance in "cash receipts on account occurrence over" is 88.816271%, with a contribution of 17.053418% assurance being provided indirectly. To determine the assurance which has been obtained either directly or through procedures prior to substantive work, the following approach is used:

$$\textbf{Prior Assurance} = \frac{\textbf{Achieved assurance * (1 - Indirect Assurance)}}{\textbf{1 - Achieved Assurance * Indirect Assurance}}$$

Thus:

$$\text{Prior Assurance} = \frac{0.88816271 * (1 - 0.17053418)}{1 - (0.88816271 * 0.17053418)}$$

$$= 0.8682$$

This figure corresponds to the direct assurance which has been obtained with respect to "cash receipts on account completeness over", because the prior assurance was assumed to be direct assurance for the purpose of this example.

The revised assurance for cash receipts on account completeness over is now revised to reflect the impact of the revised total indirect assurance of 19.863099%, using the following Bayesian revision approach:

---

[9] First we note that Procedure 361 provides additional direct assurance of 47.5% that there are no material errors with respect to accounts receivable completeness under. This direct support is considered to provide indirect support, through the feedback relationship, to "cash receipts on account occurrence over" and "sales on account completeness under". The amount of this indirect support is calculated as the square root of 47.5%, 68.9202438% assurance, adjusted by the "weak" feedback coefficient defined as 0.3. Thus, procedure 312 provides additional indirect support of 20.676073% to cash receipts on account occurrence over. This indirect support is further attenuated by virtue of the direct assurance which has already been obtained with respect to sales on account completeness under, 86.82%. This direct assurance feeds forward to cash receipts on account with strength 0.95. Thus, the indirect support provided is 82.479%. Finally, the additional indirect assurance is calculated by taking the product of the indirect assurance available from both sources, namely (0.20676073)*(0.82479), or 17.053418%.

[10] Revised assurance = 0.17053418 / (1 - 0.17053418 + (0.17053418*0.1753418)) = 0.19863099.

$$\text{Revised Assurance} = \frac{0.8682}{1 - 0.19863099 + (0.8682 * 0.19863099)} = 0.89154013$$

An auditor might wish to ensure that some pre-set level of assurance comes from direct testing of various assertions, and to limit the amount of indirect evidence that is obtained. CAPEX permits the auditor to set lower and upper limits, respectively, on the amount of direct and indirect assurance which will be obtained with respect to a financial statement item assertion.

Conflicting Evidence

When two different audit procedures provide conflicting evidence, it is necessary to be able to represent this conflict and suggest possible strategies for its resolution. The most direct way of representing such conflict is to allow contradictory evidence to reduce the assurance in a given assertion. In this type of approach, some evidence would be the source of negative assurance. The amount of negative assurance contributed should depend on both the source and the nature of the evidence itself in a similar way to the dependence of the assurance which can be derived from confirmatory evidence.

The occurrence of conflicting items of evidence often has a direct strategic effect which is not adequately reflected in an approach that simply modifies assurances to reflect evidential conflicts. Conflicting evidence may suggest that initial assumptions are inappropriate and that, in many cases, assessments of inherent risk, degree of evidential support etc., need to be revised. In many cases it will also be necessary to devise strategies to collect additional evidence to resolve the conflict. These issues are outside the scope of CAPEX since it is a planning expert system, rather than an evaluation expert system. We made the simplifying assumption that only corroborating evidence should be planned for. While conflicting evidence could be found during an audit, it does not appear reasonable for the planning process to attempt to obtain such evidence, except in the sense that it could serve as a "devil's advocate" approach to evidence gathering similar to the adversarial approach found in the legal system.[11]

---

[11]While a more powerful planning system would anticipate conflicts and build in robust strategies for their resolution by suggesting alternative approaches to modifying the audit plan in response to various circumstances, such as the discovery of conflicting evidence, the current version of CAPEX deals with this issue by making the simplifying assumption that no conflicting evidence will be gathered.

SUMMARY

In this chapter we discuss the structure and content of CAPEX's knowledge bases. CAPEX requires both factual knowledge relating to auditing, accounting and business, as well as strategic knowledge of how audit plans should be constructed.

CAPEX encodes both knowledge of financial statement items and, critically from the standpoint of generating efficient audit plans, knowledge of accounting relationships. These relationships provide the basis of what we term *indirect support.*

Audit evidence may be obtained as a result of applying a variety of different audit evidence gathering procedures which may be broadly classified as being either substantive tests of detail or analytic review tests or substantive analysis tests. The former, which involve tests directed to the actual components of a particular financial statement item balance, are discussed in some detail in this chapter. The evidence provided by any substantive test of detail has two key characteristics: relevance and reliability. Relevance concerns the financial statement item assertions which are supported by the evidence in question. Evidence may also be more or less reliable depending on different factors. Some factors relate to audit evidence gathering procedures while other factors concert the population to which procedures are being applied.

Whereas substantive tests of detail address individual components of financial statement item balances, analytic review procedures investigate the composition of these balances, principally longitudinally. We bring together research on analytic review procedures in order to provide an interpretation of the evidence provided by such procedure which is consistent with the assertion-based approach to audit planning.

Client specific knowledge plays an important part in the setting of objectives for audit planning and in the construction of such plans. We discuss the types of client information processed by CAPEX in order to construct audit plans. Client information is entered via X-Windows user interface which was discussed in the previous chapter.

Without some way of processing knowledge, CAPEX would be lifeless and would be unable to construct audit plans. We present the computational model which underpins CAPEX's ability to marshal and process all the different types of knowledge encoded in its various knowledge-bases. Since the processing of uncertain evidence is of particular importance to CAPEX, we have paid particular attention to this issue. In its present incarnation CAPEX is structured to process uncertainties in a Bayesian or quasi-Bayesian manner. However, as we note, it is perfectly feasible for CAPEX to process uncertainties using other approaches to uncertainty modeling such as Dempster-Shafer belief functions.

Chapter 3

KNOWLEDGE ELICITATION

INTRODUCTION

In the preceding chapter we discussed how we approached the task of knowledge representation. In the case of CAPEX, many of the decisions that were made with respect to knowledge representation were not made independently of the approaches to and outputs of the knowledge acquisition phase. Although it is often argued that knowledge representation should follow knowledge acquisition, it would appear that in domains as complex and partially pre-structured as audit planning, the two stages are intermingled to a significant extent. Knowledge acquisition takes place within a professional milieu where some degree of knowledge structuring has already taken place. This chapter details the methods which were used to gather the knowledge which is presently represented in CAPEX.

In a sense, all computer programs encode knowledge. This knowledge may be knowledge concerning the computer which is intended to process the program, the problem domain, or general or specific problem-solving strategies. The principal difference between traditional programs and knowledge-based systems is that in the latter we attempt to make the knowledge of the problem domain as explicit as possible. In addition, in these systems, declarative knowledge (factual knowledge) is typically encoded independently of procedural knowledge (knowledge about how to use the factual knowledge to solve problems). It is important to recognize, however, that attempting to elicit and encode knowledge in programs is nothing new.

> According to Cordingley (1989, p. 93) knowledge elicitation is a set of activities undertaken by a person, the knowledge elicitator, to:
>
> - obtain material from any relevant source
> - analyse and interpret that material,
> - put it in a pre-encoded form which, while useful to those who will encode the knowledge in the KBS [knowledge-based system] language, also allows it to be scrutinized by all parties interested in KBS development.

Auditors appear to make use of a variety of different categories of knowledge:

- *Organizational knowledge*. This is often embedded in manuals, established company practices, or even in the very way the company is structured (Lee, 1984). Much of this "knowledge" has never been fully codified, let alone verified. However, since such organizational knowledge is continually used to formulate auditing strategies over a long period of time, we may have some confidence in the validity of organizational knowledge.
- *Small group knowledge*. This category of knowledge is shared by a small group of individuals and relates to a specific domain or a specific client. Group knowledge may not have been codified in any formal manner.
- *Individual knowledge*. This knowledge may not be unique to the individual but it is significantly more "personal" than either of the two types of knowledge identified above. In a professional context, individual knowledge may vary significantly from the path of central

tendency represented by organizational and small group knowledge. Furthermore, such variation may not be viewed as deviant behaviour. It may be viewed not only as legitimate, but also, as an actual indicator of expertise.

One of our objectives in constructing CAPEX was to reduce the amount of what has been called "common sense" which had to be encoded in the system. As we proceeded with knowledge elicitation we realized that our ability to achieve this objective was limited. As we attempted to elicit more and more detailed knowledge of the domain we often encountered what might be called "business common sense". This type of knowledge related broadly to the domain of business organizations and operations. Failure to incorporate much of this knowledge can lead to lack of flexibility in the system's performance. As a result, audit plans generated by the system might not reflect the potential impact of full knowledge of the audit situation.

The next three sections consider each of the types of knowledge referred to above in more detail.

ORGANIZATIONAL KNOWLEDGE

Organizational knowledge may reside in a variety of different locations. The most obvious location is in company manuals and pre-defined procedures. Many firms have extensive manuals detailing expected performance in a variety of different situations. Burton and Shadbolt (quoted in Cordingley, 1989, p. 92) note that, " For many types of expert system, the whole set of domain knowledge may be found in documentation, books or in-house training manuals."

Use of these documentary sources as a basis for initial knowledge elicitation has a variety of problems even if such sources are structured in the form of rules. First, where they exist, the rule sets provided in manuals may be incomplete. They may be *syntactically incomplete*. That is, they may specify a set of rules to be applied in a variety of situations but they may not include sufficient rules to cover all the situations that may be encountered, or the rules may not allow for the precise identification of a particular course of action in a given situation. Thus, there may be a rule that specifies what should be done if the client's financial records are reliable. However, there may be no rule which specifies what should be done if the client's financial records are not reliable. This type of incompleteness can be established independently of the actual meaning of the terms which are used in the rules themselves. The set of all possible values for each of the variables which are valid is established at the outset. A rule must exist for every possible combination of values for each variable; otherwise, the rule set will be syntactically incomplete. Sometimes, this syntactic incompleteness is deliberate, as it allows for areas where judgment must be exercised. For instance, in the situation where a client's records are not reliable, the auditor may not want to state a rule to allow for more flexible behaviour. However, in other cases, syntactic incompleteness may simply be a result of our limited ability to draft complete sets of rules.

Second, the rule sets may be *semantically incomplete*. The terms used to specify the rules may be incompletely defined. For instance, in the example considered above, the term reliable may not be adequately defined. This type of incompleteness cannot be established by simply inspecting the rules. It will be discovered when an attempt is made to interpret the rules in a specific situation. As with syntactic incompleteness, this could be the result of oversight or be deliberate.

Third, textual encoded knowledge is often biased towards the encoding of factual, rather than procedural, knowledge. Even when procedural knowledge is textually encoded, it is often limited in a variety of ways. For instance, nested procedures or procedures with many conditions, or a large number of potential outcomes, are often difficult to represent in text.

It is worth noting that the way in which such procedural knowledge is presented will often vary, depending on the function of the textual material. If the material has been written expressly for the purpose of training individuals to perform certain tasks, then procedures will often be described in a relatively simple manner. If, however, the textual material is intended to represent a procedures "bible", a reference document on how procedures should be carried out, then the procedures are likely to be defined in greater detail.

It is interesting to note that the identification and elucidation of organizational knowledge may be a valuable activity in its own right, regardless as to whether it is subsequently encoded in some computable representation. Some organizations are not aware of the scope or richness of the organizational knowledge they possess. The public presentation of such organizational knowledge also provides opportunities for critiquing and validating this knowledge.

Many organizations develop procedural manuals which attempt to standardize the ways in which individuals make decisions, handle disputes, etc. These procedure manuals have similarities with regulatory texts which describe building regulations, regulations for the storage and handling of hazardous chemicals, etc. Moulin and Rousseau (1992) discuss a system for assisting in the acquisition of knowledge from regulatory texts. The regulatory texts they investigate contain three types of propositions: definitions, normative propositions and metatextual statements which provide cross-references of the type "subject to the provisions of article x" or "in spite of article y".

One interesting feature of regulatory texts is that the rules they contain are of the form "If A is true then B must be done". For example, a regulation concerning the storage of hazardous chemicals might state that "Chemical A must be stored in leak proof containers and at a temperature of not more than 60° C and not less that 10° C." They note that:

> *Reasoning in expert systems is usually based on the modus ponens inference rule: If A-> B, and if A is true, then B is true. But suppose that a ... knowledge-base contains the rule ""f situation X, then object A shall do action P," and that situation X is true in a given case. We cannot use the modus ponens inference rule to infer directly that A has done P. We can only check if A has done P; if it has not, we can conclude that the rule has been violated. p. 29*

Moulin and Rousseau's work highlights the fact that company manuals may encode knowledge in the form of *deontic* rules. Deontic rules differ from traditional expert systems rules in that they are associated with such notions as obligation, permission and interdiction. Thus, a deontic rule may state:

> *If an auditor detects any evidence of management fraud he is obliged to make such evidence public.*

This rule expresses an obligation that an auditor has to act in a certain way. The explanation for this action is that the auditor feels morally obliged to report evidence of management fraud. The detection of evidence of management fraud does not, of itself, cause the auditor to make such evidence public.

A further complication is that the type of deontic rules which are encoded in regulatory texts often use *modal* operators such as possible, necessary, probable etc. For example, a rule may state:

> *If it is probable that management fraud has been committed then the auditor is obliged to make public whatever evidence he may have.*

Moulin and Rousseau primarily focus on the evaluation of objects such as building plans to determine whether they comply with building regulations. If regulatory texts are used as the basis for *creating* building plans it may be appropriate to interpret deontic rules as production rules. In the context of the current research it is assumed that if an audit evidence-gathering procedure is planned for it will be carried out. However, if a particular audit plan is implemented it may be necessary to modify it during execution if some procedures cannot be carried out or do not provide the evidence which was expected.

Regulatory material relating to auditing in general, and audit planning in particular, may be found in standards promulgated by such bodies as the AICPA in the United States and the CICA in Canada. They may also be found in company manuals and auditing textbooks. In constructing CAPEX, use was made of all these sources of regulatory material.

The use of textbooks as a source of knowledge for constructing knowledge-bases is contentious. It can be argued that textbooks contain knowledge structured in such a way as to help novices develop audit planning skills. That is, textbooks do not contain encoded expert knowledge *per se*, but expert knowledge transformed in such a way as to be understandable to a novice. There are, however, well-established precedents for using textbook material as a basis for constructing prototype knowledge-bases. For instance, Meservy, Bailey and Johnson (1986) refer to the use of such textual material in developing prototype knowledge-bases:

> *We referred to textbooks in an attempt to provide a base of reference for the rules . . . Although these books did provide a reference point for basic internal control terminology and issues, only those rules elicited directly from the experts were used in model building . . . Subsequent discussions with the experts indicate that while the textbook rules were generally correct, they do not coincide with the auditor's decision processes. p. 57.*

The usefulness of the material provided by textbooks depends, to some extent, on the overall objectives which have been established for the knowledge-based system. Meservy, Bailey and Johnson (1986) were interested in building a computational model of the process followed by auditors when making internal control assessments. When textbook material is used for this purpose, it is not surprising that textbook rules may not necessarily map exactly to auditors' decision processes. However, in cases where the overall objective is to model the domain, textbook material may be more generally applicable with the following caveats:

1. Textbook knowledge may be little more than post-hoc rationalizations of the types of processes which *should* be followed. Although this type of knowledge may not provide an appropriate foundation for generating solutions, in a knowledge-based system it may be particularly useful when explanations and justifications of system behavior need to be constructed.

2. Even more so than manuals, textbooks are generally better at providing factual, as opposed to procedural, knowledge. Where they do provide procedural knowledge, it may be in a very general form. This may stem from the requirement that texts support learning rather than simply being compendia of facts about the domain and/or valid procedures for processing facts about the domain.

SMALL GROUP KNOWLEDGE

Organizations are comprised of many different, and often, overlapping, groups of individuals. There are groups which exist to complete certain tasks, groups which comprise individuals with similar skills and groups of individuals who have similar interests. In the following discussion we will focus on the first two types of groups. Although there has been extensive research into the nature of groups, relatively little attention has been directed towards the creation, modification and nature of the shared knowledge of different groups. This knowledge is often of considerable importance to industrial and social organizations.

Small group knowledge may be relatively well-structured, as in the case of the knowledge shared by a group of professionals, or, it may be relatively unstructured, as in the case of a work group which forms for a short period to solve a particular problem. Small group knowledge may be encoded in a number of different forms. It may be written down in manuals similar to the procedural manuals of organizations. Thus, professionals have codes of conduct and unions develop rules governing the behaviour of their members on the job. Sometimes the language used in these manuals is difficult to decode unless one is a member of the group. Knowledge may also be encoded in "stories" which group members share with each other. The sharing of these stories often leads to their enhancement and refinement. For example, doctors share stories about particular patients and Seeley Brown & Duguid (1991) refer to situations where engineers use stories as a way of representing knowledge and finding solutions to unique problems. Groups may also encode knowledge in the form of rituals and ceremonies. This type of knowledge encoding is discussed, in the context of memory, by Connerton (1989).

Recently, the popularity of such tools as electronic mail and new multimedia communications have created the possibility of creating new types of groups. With the emergence of these tools researchers have begun to investigate how some types of group knowledge can be captured as it is created in these electronic interactions.

Some of the most powerful tools for investigating the nature, creation, refinement and transmission of group knowledge have been provided by anthropologists and ethographers. In addition, sociologists of knowledge (e.g. Luckman, 1967) have provided useful insights.

Our overall objective in constructing CAPEX was to encode the knowledge of professional auditors. We expected that even though some professional auditors would not share some of the knowledge which is encoded in CAPEX they would at least find it acceptable. However, surprisingly, often we found that the knowledge we had encoded was shared by a relatively small group of auditors. In some cases, the group was comprised of auditors working for the same audit firm. In other cases the group was made up of auditors from the same firm and the same country. We initially became aware of these issues during knowledge elicitation for CAPEX. The existence of different types of knowledge also created difficulties during the validation of CAPEX. For example, some of the auditors who were asked to assess the solutions developed by CAPEX and other auditors rejected both solutions as being inappropriate. In addition, one auditor rejected the whole approach to constructing an audit program plan for banking audits.

It might be argued that the existence of different types of knowledge, which are often inconsistent, if not totally contradictory, is a demonstration of the lack of deep understanding of auditing as a field of knowledge. Some researchers have questioned whether it is appropriate to refer to auditors as experts given the limited learning opportunities they may have had compared to chess players, doctors and other acknowledged experts (see, for example, Bédard, 1989; Ashton 1991).

These varieties of different types of audit knowledge are worthy of considerable further research to investigate both their nature and examine ways in which they may be enhanced and combined. As a case in point, Johnson (1993) suggests that audit teams are likely to develop their own specialized knowledge of clients which they share between themselves and pass on to new team members. The nature of this specialized knowledge is not well understood nor do we know how it can be enhanced and potentially encoded so that it can become a resource for other members of a firm or, indeed, the audit profession.

Expert systems such as CAPEX can potentially be used as tools to investigate the nature of small group knowledge by providing a medium for encoding the knowledge and investigating its structure both statically and dynamically.

INDIVIDUAL KNOWLEDGE

The importance, nature and even, in specific areas, the very existence of some types of individual knowledge are contentious. There is considerable dispute as to the extent to which individuals have privileged access to their own mental processes. As one aspect of this controversy Gaines (1990) notes that:

> *Knowledge transfer is rarely a straightforward problem of obtaining knowledge in some form and encoding it for the computer. For example, experts may be able to* perform *complex tasks and yet have major problems in* understanding *and* communicating *how they do this. p. 53 (emphasis in original text)*

Thus, knowledge acquisition often requires the development of tools which can assist the expert in enunciating his/her individual knowledge. These tools may assist in the construction of what Johnson (1989) refers to as *mediating representations*. In the context of the research described in this book, we interpret this term in a somewhat different way from Johnson. In our work, the term "mediating representation" is used to refer to any representation of knowledge which is not in the form of a computer program. The mediating representations we focus on are often in the form of matrices. One example of a mediating representation is the relevance matrix presented in Appendix 3.1.

Mediating representations allow for the structuring and communication of knowledge. In addition, in some cases they may also be used to check on the integrity and accuracy of the knowledge which is elicited and to suggest refinements to the knowledge.

It has also been argued that much of the knowledge which governs our performance is "tacit" and essentially unexpressible. The term "tacit" knowledge was introduced by Polyani (1967) to refer to knowledge of a domain (in his case, the scientific domain) which to some extent is "wired in" and hence not open to conscious inspection.[1] A related concept was introduced by Anderson (1983) when he referred to "compiled" knowledge. In his view, once a set of mental activities become habitual, they will be compiled and, when invoked, will be processed without conscious awareness or intervention. This does not necessarily mean that individuals are unable to provide verbal "descriptions" of the processes and knowledge they use in problem solving, but that the descriptions offered may simply be *post hoc* rationalizations. This "covering up" of tacit knowledge may be a particular problem in what may be called "defensive" professions such as medicine or auditing. In these professions there is a need to defend oneself with verbal justifications, and a feeling of insecurity if a justification cannot be offered. Thus, some level of skepticism is appropriate when eliciting individual knowledge from practitioners in these areas.

Gaines (1990) has identified the following problems with respect to accessing experts' knowledge:

- Expertise may be fortuitous. Results may be dependent on features of the situation which the expert is not controlling.
- Expertise may not be available to awareness. An expert may not be able to transmit the expertise by critiquing the performance of others because he or she is not able to evaluate it.

---

[1] See, Schon (1983) and Dreyfus and Dreyfus (1986) for a discussion of the extent to which expertise can be made explicit and hence available for acquisition. Nisbett and Wilson (1977) also argue forcefully that many cognitive processes are not open to conscious inspection. Martin (1990) also provides an interesting discussion of the linkage between tacit knowledge and the nature of consciousness.

- Expertise may not be expressible in language. An expert may not be able to transmit the expertise explicitly because he or she is unable to express it.

- Expertise may not be understandable when it is expressed in language. An apprentice may not be able to convert verbal comprehension of the basis of a skill to skilled performance.

- Expertise expressed may be irrelevant. Much of what is learned, particularly under random reinforcement schedules, is superstitious behavior that neither contributes nor detracts from performance.

- Expertise expressed may be incomplete. There will usually be implicit situational dependencies that make explicit expertise inadequate for performance.

- Expertise expressed may be incorrect. Experts may make explicit statements which do not correspond to their actual behavior and lead to incorrect performance. (p. 55)

Expanding on the above, experts may find it difficult to explicate their knowledge because of the frameworks with which they are presented to encapsulate it. It may be necessary to investigate the development of alternative frameworks for representing an expert's knowledge. It is also possible that the frameworks which have traditionally been used are inappropriate. They may not have sufficient expressive power, they may be internally inconsistent, or they may be incomplete in unrecognized ways.

It is interesting how easily we fall into two traps if we focus on the elicitation of knowledge which is expressible by an expert or group of experts. The first trap is to consider that knowledge must be verbalizable by the knower. It is clear that a considerable amount of knowledge is implied by the way the expert structures the domain and acts within that structure. The expert him/herself may not be aware of such knowledge.

The second trap involves the myth that the "knowledge engineer" (a term which seems to carry echoes of Plato's philosopher kings) extracts or elicits knowledge from an expert. The use of the verbs "extracts" or "elicits" may be misleading. The knowledge engineer and the expert(s) may actually be engaged in a process of *knowledge construction*. The knowledge engineer contributes both to the structuring of knowledge and the construction of meaning.[2] Thus, the expert learns during his/her participation in the process of so-called knowledge acquisition and may come to have a markedly different understanding of the domain after participating in the process. This has implications for all stages of expert systems development. Of particular concern is that each method of knowledge acquisition may provide "knowledge" relating to a different view of the domain.

---

[2] See, Kjaergaard, 1987, and Langley and Carbonell, 1984, for further discussion of these issues.

SOME THOUGHTS ABOUT EPISTEMOLOGICAL STATUS

A variety of issues arise when we attempt to combine knowledge from a variety of different sources. First, we should be concerned with what we may term the "epistemological status" of individual items of knowledge. This may have an impact on all the subsequent stages of expert systems development. Second, we should investigate how items with different epistemological status should be combined (if at all).

Considering the epistemological status[3] of the "knowledge" that has been acquired by the researcher(s), some of the potential impacts are:

- The representation approach must be able to differentiate between different levels of certainty associated with the information that has been acquired. For example, some items of information may be known with certainty while others may only be probable. A production manager may be certain about yesterday's production but very uncertain about the production costs of a competitor.

- It is often important to identify and record the sources and foundations of knowledge claims. For example, a given client may be considered to be a credit risk. It is important to know the reasons for this judgment and the individual who made the judgment. Both of these items of information are relevant to assessing the trustworthiness, or otherwise, of the judgment.

- When attempts are made to "refine" the system, the action to be taken when information of different epistemological status conflicts is likely to be different than when information of the same status conflicts. For example, one statement in the knowledge-base is supported by a number of credible individuals who are unable to provide detailed justifications for their belief in the truth of the statement. Another statement in the knowledge-base, which conflicts with the first, is only supported by one credible individual. However, this individual is able to provide extensive justification for her belief in the truth of the statement. In "refining" the knowledge-base we may choose to discard the former statement in favor of the latter.

  In contrast to the above case let us consider the following situation. Two equally credible individuals have provided widely differing assessments concerning the probability of a particular event occurring. How are the different statements expressing their probability assessments to be "refined"? It all depends upon what explanation we accept for this divergence. If we genuinely believe that each individual is equally justified in their belief then we will probably choose either to combine their probability assessments in some way or seek to maintain their separate assessments in the knowledge-base.

  As a final example, consider again our two equally credible individuals. One firmly believes in the truth of statement, S, while the other staunchly maintains that P is true when P is, in fact, the negation of S. How do we reconcile this situation? One common approach would be to investigate whether the basis for their beliefs are the same. Put more technically, are they using the same information set as the basis for their beliefs. If the answer is no, we may choose to discard the statement supported by the individual whose information set, we consider to be inferior. If, on the other hand, they claim to share the same information set we are in a quandary and may well opt to collect more information before we make any decision as to how to refine the knowledge-base.

---

[3] In this context, the term "epistemological status" refers to whether the item of information in question is considered to be knowledge or belief. In addition, where appropriate, the strength of belief, the identity and credentials of the individual holding the belief, and the justification(s) for the belief should be recorded.

- Comprehensive explanation facilities require the identification of the epistemological status of different items. For example, users may ask "How has this conclusion been arrived at?" It is important to be able to provide the user with a chain of reasoning and indicate whether the links in the chain are logical, probable, or fuzzy.

- Subsequent implementation of the system can be improved. Since the epistemological basis of the system's contents is made explicit, revisions can be more easily "negotiated" with the users. For example, if a particular item was previously included purely on the basis of a particular individual's convictions, users may subsequently discard it once reliable evidence becomes available from a number of sources.

The methodology chosen to verify and validate the elicited knowledge will be contingent upon the epistemological status of the "knowledge" which has been elicited. For example, where the support for a particular knowledge item derives from the convictions of a particular individual, validation will involve confirming that the individual agrees that the particular knowledge item is, in fact, a knowledge item which he or she accepts. If, in contrast, a knowledge item is supported by a large body of evidence, its validity may be tested by investigating the body of evidence to determine whether it does support the knowledge item.

If distinctions between the epistemological status of different knowledge items are not made, users may well assume that all information contained in the knowledge-based system has the same status - namely, knowledge. In most cases this will lead to inappropriate conclusions, misleading explanations, severe difficulty with refinement, and many other problems.

Much has been said about the fact that in eliciting knowledge we are constructing models or theories of the domain. Chandrasekaran and Mittal (1983), Fu (1986) and others advocate building expert systems using "deep" knowledge rather than "surface" knowledge. One of the most powerful types of deep models are causal models (see, for example, Steels and Van de Velde, 1985 and Steels, 1990). However, in many fields this "surface" vs. "deep" dichotomy is very difficult to apply.

In the area of audit planning, the accounting model might seem to be a classic example of deep knowledge. This is not so. Although the accounting model defines an elegant logical structure which explains relationships among many accounting concepts, it is, at best, an intermediate level of knowledge. There are a number of reasons why the accounting model does not achieve the status of deep knowledge:

- Accounting concepts often map imperfectly to reality. For instance, the determination of revenue does not simply require observation, it also requires considerable judgement to be exercised.

- The accounting model may be imperfectly implemented by its user. Much as accountants may consider that the accounting model is a necessary description of reality, it is surely a contingent one in the hands of fallible and self-interested humans.

When presenting arguments for preferring deep to surface knowledge, it should be borne in mind that many areas where expert systems research is taking place are long on description and short on theory. Raufels (1981, p. 101) appropriately refers to these as areas of "diffuse" knowledge. Even the domain that was the original source of the terms, transformational grammar, has never been able to produce acceptable exemplars of items of deep knowledge or structure. In spite of the above caveats, the metaphor will remain very seductive. Deep knowledge will always sound far superior to surface knowledge.

Given our belief that the categorization of knowledge into surface and deep knowledge is generally not very enlightening or helpful for determining a knowledge acquisition strategy, are there other ways of categorizing knowledge? One approach which may be helpful is to distinguish between:

knowing that: factual knowledge. This has also been referred to as declarative knowledge.

knowing how: knowledge of how to bring something about. This has also been referred to as procedural knowledge.

Here we have come full circle to the distinction which has been noted earlier between declarative and procedural knowledge.

In the following section we will review the approach which was adopted to elicit the different types of knowledge which are represented in CAPEX.

KNOWLEDGE ACQUISITION FOR CAPEX

The sources which were used in knowledge acquisition for CAPEX and the corresponding elicitation methods are set out in Table 3.1.

Table 3.1 Sources of Knowledge and Acquisition Methods Used

Source	Knowledge Acquisition Method
Literature search	Text analysis
Initial experts	Interviews for initial knowledge acquisition
Initial experts	Additional knowledge acquisition using prototype computational model and knowledge-base. Interviews, observation of case solutions, review of plan assessment questionnaire.
Independent experts	Further knowledge acquisition using revised prototype computational model and knowledge-base. Observation of case solutions, interviews, review of plan assessment questionnaire.

LITERATURE SEARCH

The principal textual sources of domain knowledge used to generate a prototype knowledge-base were as follows:

- Relevant sections of the CICA and AICPA audit manuals.

- Various auditing texts, most particularly Anderson (1984), Mautz and Sharaf (1961) and Lemon, Arens and Loebbecke (1987). These texts were particularly useful for identifying procedures and clarifying the various important characteristics of evidence.

- Published research papers; for example, with respect to the evaluation of evidence, Mock and Wright (1982) and Mock (1976).
- A major accounting firm's audit planning manuals.
- A working paper by Boritz (1986) describing a spreadsheet-based decision aid.
- The personal knowledge of the researchers.
- A paper describing the Clarkson Gordon audit planning approach (Leslie *et al.*, 1986).

The above sources of domain knowledge provided the prototype knowledge-base structure as indicated in Figure 3.1.

Figure 3.1 Structure of the Initial Prototype CAPEX Knowledge-base

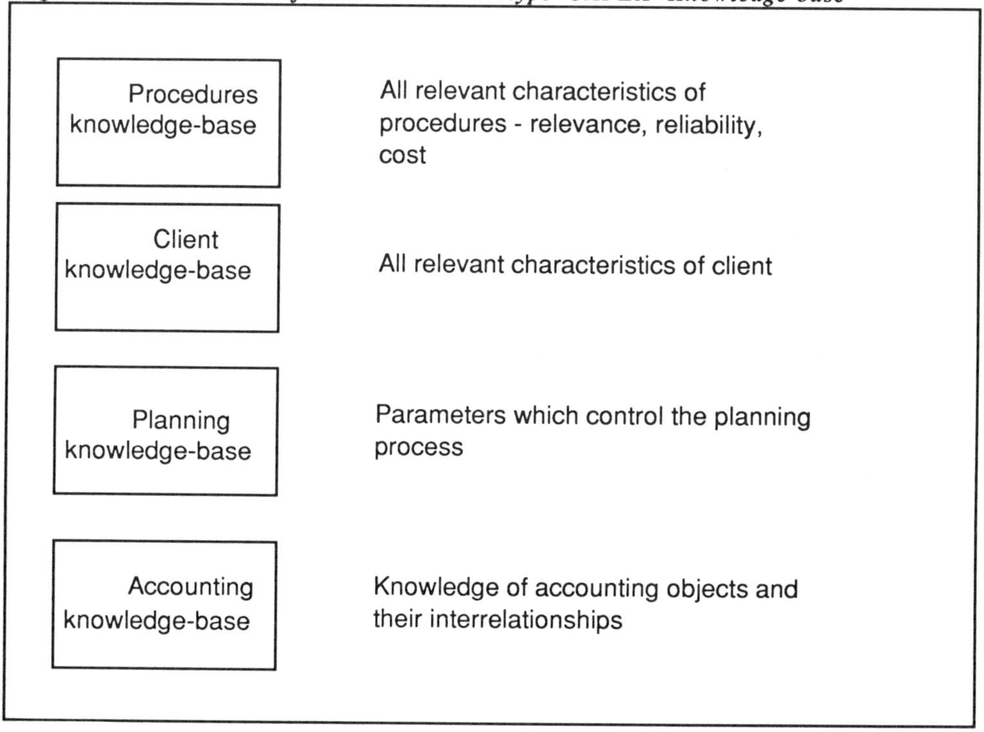

This initial prototype knowledge-base and computational model was used as the basis for interviews with audit managers and partners.

Knowledge which was obtained from external textual sources was used if the experts considered that such knowledge was entirely appropriate. Since the principal objective of this research was not to construct a computational model of the auditor's decision process, the restrictions which Meservy *et al.* (1986, p. 57) placed on their use of external textual sources of knowledge, referred to earlier, did not seem appropriate.

One of the principal problems which arise in situations where a knowledge-base is constructed from knowledge derived from a number of different sources is that of terminological consistency. A text or firm manual may use an accounting or auditing term in a significantly different way from the practicing auditor. Inconsistent or even contradictory information may therefore be included in the knowledge-base. It is impossible to control completely for this type of problem. To provide some protection, whenever external textual material was used, the experts were consulted and asked to comment and/or elaborate on the material.

Adding to the problems of the interpretation of the terminology was the fact that the accounting firm which provided the auditors who participated in the research was in process of revising its audit strategy extensively at the same time as this research was being carried out.

INTERVIEWS WITH EXPERTS

In addition to providing a critique of externally obtained textual data, four experts also provided a significant quantity of knowledge themselves in a series of interviews conducted over two years. The audit partners and managers who assisted in knowledge elicitation were broadly familiar and generally comfortable with assertion-based approaches to audit planning. The firm with which they were associated subscribed to a particular risk-based approach to assertion-based substantive audit planning. In the early stages of the interviewing process they were asked to identify financial statement items which should be addressed for different types of clients and their associated assertions. They were also asked to conduct a "walk-through" of a typical audit in order to identify critical financial statement item assertions, the order in which financial statement assertions are typically satisfied, and relevant client characteristics which might modify the audit planning process.

Assessing the Relevance of Evidence

Once a representative set of financial statement items and their associated assertions had been identified and agreed upon, a "relevance matrix" was constructed. Over a considerable period of time procedures were identified which provided relevant audit evidence for financial statement item assertions relevant to each of the three general types of client being investigated - manufacturing, merchandising and banking.

The principal instrument for eliciting relevance assessments was a relevance matrix that is presented in Appendix 3.2. This matrix has similarities with the type of matrices a number of accounting firms use to select appropriate audit procedures for audit engagements.

The matrix was used in the following way:

Step 1

Subjects were asked to identify the separate procedures that they would consider using in the substantive phase of an audit of the revenue/receipts/receivables cycle for manufacturing, retail, or banking clients.

Step 2

Subjects were asked to indicate the assertions for which support was provided by evidence generated by each procedure identified.

Step 3

The judgments of each subject were checked for consistency by taking each subject through a list of all the relevant financial statement item assertions. For each financial statement assertion, relevant procedures were identified from the relevance matrix. Each subject was asked to confirm that the procedures identified as providing relevant evidence in support of a particular financial statement item assertion were correctly recorded.

Step 3 represents an alternative way of framing questions concerning the relevance of evidence provided by a particular procedure. Thus, there are two approaches to framing a question concerning relevance:

Question 1: Procedure P_1 has been conducted and evidence E_1 obtained. For which financial statement item assertions does E_1 provide information relevant to determining the truth of the assertion?

Question 2: If you are planning to gather evidence to assist you in determining the truth of financial statement item assertion FSA_1 would you plan to conduct procedure P_1?

In the early stages of the development of the relevance matrix, relevance was expressed as being strong, strong limited, moderate, weak limited, and weak. As the interviews with auditors progressed, however, it was found that relevance terms other than strong often indicated the presence of other types of knowledge or inferences based on knowledge of the procedure in question, or of the client. For instance, initially a procedure, say, vouching entries in the sales ledger to supporting documentation, which provided evidence relevant to the assessment of the appropriateness of the *sales revenue occurrence overstatement* assertion, was considered to provide "weak" evidence relevant to the *accounts receivable existence overstatement* assertion. Subsequently, the latter type of evidential relationship was modeled explicitly in the form of an indirect supporting relationship. This indirect supporting relationship arises because of the basic accounting relationship:

Opening Accounts Receivable + Sales on Account - Cash Receipts on Account = Closing Accounts Receivable

It was also discovered that occasionally the term "weak" was used to indicate that a procedure might provide evidence with respect to a particular financial statement item assertion but that such evidence was by no means to be relied on. For example, positive confirmation of receivables, might provide evidence with respect to collectibility problems if a confirmation was returned indicating that the customer in question was in receivership. However, it was agreed that in these cases the possibility of obtaining such evidence would not generally be taken into account in planning an audit. Hence, weak relevance used in this sense was ignored for the purposes of generating an audit plan.

The use of the modifier "limited" also provided a further rich source of previously "hidden" knowledge. In some cases it was found that the term was used to indicate that a particular procedure provided evidence which was relevant to a sub-population of a particular financial statement item. Thus, for a banking client, a review of the previous period's outstanding loan balances provides evidence with respect to the sub-population of loan balances which have been outstanding for more than a year.

In other instances "limited" was found to mean that the evidence provided by a particular procedure was conditionally relevant. For example, recomputation of the allowance for doubtful accounts, using a percentage of aging categories approach, provides evidence which is relevant to the appropriateness of the allowance for doubtful accounts valuation assertion if the percentage of aging categories has proved to be an accurate method in the past and there have been no significant changes in the client's or the customer's financial circumstances in the meantime.

Assessing the Reliability of Evidence

In addition to eliciting information concerning the identity and relevance of procedures, subjects were asked to identify factors which they considered to be relevant in determining the reliability of the evidence provided by each procedure and the cost of performing each procedure. The factors which impacted on the reliability of the evidence provided by audit evidence-gathering procedures were identified from the literature by Ditner (1986) and confirmed with several experts. Ditner developed a scoring system for weighing the reliability of various evidence-gathering procedures, as discussed in Chapter 2 (see Table 3.2, Table 3.3 and Figure 3.2).

Table 3.2 Initial Scoring System for Reliability Factor Levels

Reliability Factor	Factor Level Reliability Score
Source of evidence:	
direct auditor knowledge,	7
external,	5
external/internal	3
internal	1
Complexity of client's records:	
high	1
medium	2
low	3
Type of evidence:	
positive	3
negative	1
Type of data:	
external,	5
external/internal	3
internal	1
Form of the evidence:	
oral	1
documentary	3
Non-sampling risk:	
high	0
moderate	2
low	3
Competence of the preparer:	
high	+2
medium	0
low	-2
Internal Control Environment:	
good	+1
moderate	0
poor	-1

Table 3.3 Relationship Between Reliability Scores and Assurance Levels

Reliability Score Derived from Table 3.2	Assurance Level Provided
18	0.95
.	.
14	.91
13	.90
.	.
6	0.55
5	0.50
.	.
1	.10
0	0.00

Figure 3.2 Graphical Representation of Relationship Between Verbal and Quantitative Expressions of Evidential Reliability

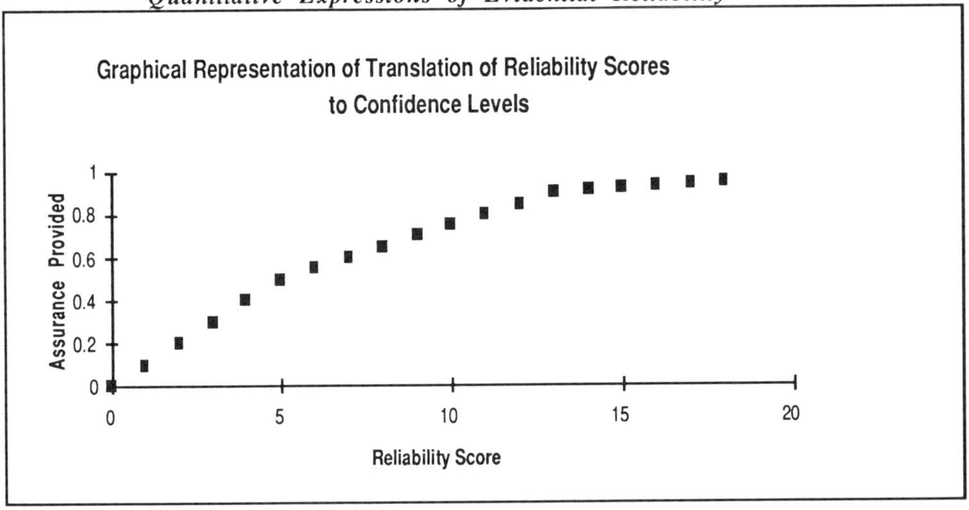

Subsequently, a number of experts were requested to provide assessments of the relative importance of each of these factors. The approach used to elicit these assessments was the Analytic Hierarchy Process (AHP).

Reliability Assessments Using the Analytic Hierarchy Process

Assessments of the relative importance of each reliability factor were elicited using a software package based on the Analytic Hierarchy Process called Expert Choice™. The Analytic Hierarchy Process was developed by Saaty (1977) and has been applied in a large number of different situations. It provides a methodology for eliciting judgments with respect to the importance of factors which may be related hierarchically to an overall objective.

Experts were asked to provide pairwise judgments concerning the relative importance of all possible combinations of reliability factors and reliability factor levels. For instance, they were asked to compare the reliability of audit evidence obtained from an external source with audit evidence obtained from an internal source, *ceteris paribus*. The importance or priority matrices that were constructed from these pairwise comparisons were transformed in a principled fashion to yield a ratio scale of the relative importance of each factor and each factor level.

In making pairwise comparisons the experts were asked to compare one factor or factor level to another with respect to their contribution to the reliability of the evidence provided by an audit evidence-gathering procedure. Concern has been expressed by researchers with respect to the way in which questions eliciting such assessments should be posed. Watson and Freeling (1982, 1983), as quoted by Wasil, Golden and Assad (1983), note that questions of the form:

> *Which attribute is more important when considering criterion X, characteristic Y or characteristic Z ?*

do not permit the assessment of *relative* significance or importance of each attribute at *different levels* of the attribute. They also suggest that, in providing an answer to such a question, a decision-maker typically imposes some underlying scale of measurement to address how much of one attribute is worth a particular amount of another attribute. Rarely are answers furnished without specification of the units of measurement. Watson and Freeling (1983, p.13) suggest that questions should refer to the relative importance of factor values over the options to be considered.

In their work using the Analytic Hierarchy Process to assess the importance of various attributes of audit procedures, Lin, Mock and Wright (1983, p.12) ask the following type of question:

Figure 3.3 Analytic Hierarchy Process Question Approach

> Criterion:
>
> *Cost*
>
> Under this criterion, which audit evidence-gathering procedure is superior:
>
> #1 Or #2?
>
> #N is better to what degree under this criterion (1-9)?
>
> (N represents the alternative selected by the subject.)

Lin et al. define the degree of importance in the following manner:

1 = Equally important

3 = Slightly more important

5 = Materially more important

7 = Significantly more important

9 = Absolutely more important

(2,4,6,8 are used for intermediate values)

They do not provide an indication of how they explained the meanings of such terms as "materially" and "significantly". It is likely that they used such terms because they would be familiar to practicing auditors. Saaty and Kerns (1985) use somewhat less context dependent interpretations of the numerical values:

1 = Two factors contribute equally to the objective.

3 = Experience and judgment slightly favour one factor over another.

5 = Experience and judgment strongly favour one factor over another.

7 = One factor is strongly favored and can be demonstrated in practice.

9 = One factor absolutely dominates the other factor.

In asking experts to make assessments it was found that most of the factors and factor levels were essentially self-explanatory. However, one particular factor whose meaning was not self-evident was the *complexity of audit issue*. One of the experts, referred to as Auditor 1, had suggested the factor and the associated factor levels himself. This subject was asked to provide an explanation of the meaning of the term and examples which would assist other auditors in making judgments with respect to each of the factor levels. He explained that the complexity of audit issue refers to the amount of judgment exercised by the auditor in assessing the evidence provided by a particular procedure. He offered the following explanatory examples of factor levels:

- Complexity of Audit Issue

  Medium - Positive confirmation of individual accounts.

  Low - Tracing or vouching transactions to supporting documents.

In the following sections the assessments of the various factors and factor levels made using Expert Choice™ by four different auditors are presented and analyzed.

Each of four different auditors was asked to make assessments of the relative importance of both reliability factors and then reliability factor levels using Expert Choice™. The results of these assessments are presented in Table 3.4.

Table 3.4 Reliability Factor Importance Assessments by Auditors

Level 1 - Reliability Factors	A 1	A 2	A3	A4
Complexity of the audit issue	0.439	0.297	0.355	0.652
Source of the audit evidence	0.248	0.399	0.125	0.173
Reliability of source	0.110	0.195	0.153	0.100
Type of audit evidence	0.128	0.106	0.312	0.036
Nature of audit evidence	0.075	0.053	0.055	0.034
Level 2 - Reliability Factor Levels				
Complexity of audit issue				
High complexity	0.079	0.105	0.078	0.067
Medium complexity	0.263	0.258	0.287	0.218
Low complexity	0.659	0.637	0.635	0.715
Source of audit evidence				
Direct	0.563	0.508	0.526	0.186 [4]
External	0.223	0.265	0.206	0.678
External/Internal	0.148	0.151	0.206	0.099
Internal	0.067	0.075	0.062	0.036
Reliability of Source				
Low	0.105	0.109 [5]		
Medium	0.258	0.309	0.246	0.344
High	0.637	0.582	0.754	0.656
Type of audit evidence				
Negative	0.300	0.300	0.172	0.338
Positive	0.700	0.700	0.828	0.662
Nature of audit evidence				
Oral	0.250	0.400	0.551	0.436
Written	0.750	0.600	0.449	0.564

[4] There was some discussion over this assessment with Auditor 4. However, he felt that this assessment reflected the relative reliabilities of evidence from the different sources.

[5] In the experiments conducted with Auditor 3 and Auditor 4 only two levels of source reliability were considered as was the case with the earlier assessments made by Auditor 1. At a later stage Auditor 1 felt that an additional level of source reliability should be added, namely low reliability. He felt that this level would correspond to situations where the source of the evidence was, for instance, a related party.

The relative importance values provided by the auditors were then converted into scores. To do this it was assumed that 100 reliability points were available for the most reliable procedure. Given the above assessments and rounding to the second decimal place, the number of reliability points available for each factor were determined for Auditor 1 as follows:

Table 3.5 Level 1 - Reliability Factor Points for Auditor 1

Complexity of audit issue	=	44 points
Source of audit evidence	=	25 points
Reliability of source	=	11 points
Type of evidence	=	13 points
Nature of evidence	=	7 points
		100 points

For example, since the relative importance of the factor, complexity of audit issue, is 0.439, it may be considered to provide a maximum potential contribution of 44% of the overall reliability of a procedure. Thus, if the total available "reliability points" are 100, the maximum number of reliability points which can be earned by the complexity of audit issue factor are 44.

The reliability points available for each factor were then allocated to factor levels in proportion to the assessed importance of the factor level in question . For example, for the factor "Complexity of audit issue" for the factor levels "high", "medium", and "low", the following calculation was used:

low:	.659/.659	*	44	=	44
medium:	.263/.659	*	44	=	18
high:	.08/.659	*	44	=	5

Table 3.6 contains the reliability scores for each reliability factor by factor level.

Table 3.6 Level 2 - Reliability Factor Level Points for Auditor 1

Complexity of audit issue	
High complexity	= 5 points
Medium complexity	= 18 points
Low complexity	= 44 points
Source of audit evidence	
Direct auditor knowledge	= 25 points
External source	= 10 points
External/Internal	= 7 points
Internal	= 3 points
Reliability of source	
Low	= 2 points
Medium	= 5 points
High	= 11 points
Type of audit evidence	
Negative	= 6 points
Positive	= 13 points
Nature of audit evidence	
Oral	= 2 points
Written	= 7 points
	100 points

These points were used to assign an overall reliability score to each procedure. The overall reliability score for a given procedure was determined by adding together the scores for the individual factor levels assessed for the procedure by auditor. For example, the audit procedure "positive confirmation of accounts receivable and alternate procedures" was considered to have the following characteristics by Auditor 1:

Source = External, Complexity = Medium, Reliability of source = High, Nature = Positive, Type = Written

In this case, the total number of reliability points, out of 100, that would be awarded to vouching of accounts receivable is determined as follows:

Internal source = 3, Low = 44, Moderate reliability of source = 5,
Positive evidence = 13, Written evidence = 7

Total reliability points = 72

The methodology described above provided a way of developing a reliability scoring function from an auditor's assessments of the relative importance of each audit evidence-gathering procedure from the stand-point of the reliability of the evidence provided by the procedure. There is no unique way to translate this reliability score into a probability value. We used the following approach to generating probabilities from overall reliability scores:

Step 1

Auditor 1 was asked to provide his assessment of the reliability of the most reliable procedure available for the revenue cycle and also assess the reliability of the least reliable procedure. He was asked to use a scale from 0.5 to 1 where 0.5 indicates a procedure which provides the correct signal 50% of the time and 1 indicates a procedure which provides a correct signal 100% of the time.[6] He indicated that the most reliable procedure in this cycle would have a reliability of 0.98, or 98% while the least reliable procedure would have a reliability of 0.80 or 80%.

Step 2

The procedures with the highest and lowest overall reliability scores were identified. In the case of manufacturing the most reliable procedure was considered to be the vouching of accounts receivable whereas the least reliable procedure was identified as "discussing the collectibility of accounts receivable with management". This procedure has the following characteristics and reliability points associated with it:

Internal source = 3, Medium complexity = 18, Moderate reliability of source = 5,
Positive evidence = 13, Oral evidence = 2

Total number of reliability points = 41

The reliability scores of these procedures were then scaled using an appropriate scaling factor to correspond to the maximum and minimum reliability values. Therefore the difference in reliability points between the most reliable and least reliable procedure (72 - 41 = 31) corresponds to a change in reliability of (0.98-0.80) or 0.18. The change in the reliability for each change of a reliability point equals 0.18/31 or 0.006. The scaling factor obtained in this manner allows all overall reliability scores to be mapped to probability values.

Taking a specific example, consider vouching of accounts receivable to underlying documentation. This procedure has the following characteristics:

External source = 10, Medium complexity = 18, High reliability of source = 11,
Positive evidence = 13, Written evidence = 7

Total number of reliability points = 59

The reliability of this procedure will be 0.80 + (59-41)x 0.006 = 0.80 + 0.11
= 0.91

---

[6] The identity of the procedures was not of concern at this stage only the maximum and minimum reliability values.

Reliability Factor Levels for Test of Detail Procedures

Auditor 1 and Auditor 2 were asked to determine the appropriate reliability factor levels for every procedure contained in the procedural knowledge base. This information was elicited using a matrix of the type presented in Appendix 3.2. These factor levels were then used to generate numerical reliabilities for each procedure using the reliability scoring function described above.

Questions Concerning Reliability Determination

The principal problem with the approach described above is that it does not provide for the direct assessments of the reliability of evidence provided by audit evidence-gathering procedures in probabilistic terms. However, the approach that we adopted can be justified in a number of ways. First, it provides a ranking of procedures consistent with the experts' assessments of the relative importances of the various factor levels in determining the reliability of a particular procedure. Second, when experts were asked to make direct reliability assessments of procedures which differed by only one factor level these assessments were generally found to be inconsistent. Thus, two procedures which had the same factor levels except that one provided oral evidence and the other written might well be assessed in a way that resulted in the former being more reliable than the latter when the assessor readily accepts that written evidence is more reliable than oral evidence. The approach adopted here avoids such inconsistencies and illustrates the difference between our *paramorphic* approach of modeling the audit process and an *isomorphic* approach of modeling the auditor.

As can be seen in Table 3.4, there was considerable variation between auditors with respect to their assessments of the relative importance of each of the factors. There was also considerable variation in the assessments of the importance of the different factor levels for each factor. As a partial explanation for these variations it is appropriate to note that Auditor 2 worked for the same firm as Auditor 1 but specialized in auditing financial institutions. Auditors 3 and 4 were from the Research Center of the same firm which was located in the United States. They had not previously been involved with the research and had not had access to any CAPEX literature concerning reliability and reliability determination.

Generally speaking, the relative importances of the various factor and factor level assessments were consistent with the relative importances previously identified from reviews of the literature and in discussions with practicing auditors. However, for Auditor 1 part of the reason for this consistency may result from the fact that he had been involved with the project for a considerable time and had been made aware of the literature on reliability. This may have resulted in his assessments being biased or adjusted by him to "fit" the literature. However, the assessments obtained from three other managers, detailed below, provides some evidence against the existence of such a bias.

It is interesting to note that there was a considerable variation in the assessments of the importances of the factors but considerable consistency in the assessments in the relative importances of the factor levels between Auditor 1 and Auditor 2.

It is worth noting that Auditor 1 and Auditor 3 are in fairly close agreement both with respect to the importance of the factors and also in terms of the importance of the factor levels. Auditor 4 deviates considerably in his assessments. Also, apart from the notable pessimism Auditor 4 has concerning the reliability of evidence provided by direct auditor knowledge, all three experts are in broad agreement with the previously established evidential reliability relationships. One demonstration of the degree of congruity between the judgments made by different auditors is provided by determining the mean distance between the importance vectors for the factors and factor levels. The mean distance between two vectors is defined in this instance as:

$$\sum(X_{1,n} - X_{2,n})^2/n$$

Where:
$X_{1,n}$ is the nth element of importance vector 1 and
$X_{2,n}$ is the nth element of importance vector 2.

The mean distances between the different experts' assessments of the importance of reliability factors are as follows:

Table 3.7 Differences Between Experts' Reliability Ratings

Auditor 1-Auditor 2	0.00711
Auditor 1-Auditor 3	0.01137
Auditor 1-Auditor 4	0.000544

Thus, relatively speaking, the judgments of Auditor 1 are more congruent with the judgments of Auditor 4 than with those of Auditor 2 or Auditor 3. Interestingly, this relationship is reversed when assessments of the importance of reliability factor levels are compared.

Table 3.8 Differences Between Experts' Reliability Factor Ratings

Auditor 1-Auditor 2	0.004049
Auditor 1-Auditor 3	0.008963
Auditor 1-Auditor 4	0.036754

The above distance statistics provide an indication that the three managers diverge from each other but the extent of the divergence is relatively low.

Reliability Assessments for Analytical Procedures

Following a procedure similar to that used for test of detail procedures, Auditor 1 provided the following assessments regarding the relative importance of factors and factor levels in determining the reliability of evidence obtained from analytic review procedures. (The factors and factor levels were identified through literature review and discussions with practicing auditors).

Table 3.9 Reliability Ratings for Analytical Procedures

Level 1 - Type of Analytic Procedures	
Ratio analysis	0.054
Trend analysis - non statistical	0.111
Trend analysis - statistical	0.162
Regression analysis - univariate	0.376
Analytic recomputation	0.296
Level 2 - Reliability Factors	
Variability of data	0.113
Reliability of data	0.130
Frequency of data	0.563
Homogeneity of population	0.195
Level 3 - Reliability Factor Levels	
Variability of data	
High	0.079
Medium	0.263
Low	0.659
Reliability of data	
High	0.735
Medium	0.207
Low	0.058
Frequency of data	
Annual	0.040
Monthly	0.087
Weekly	0.251
Daily	0.622
Homogeneity of population	
Very high	0.573
High	0.286
Medium	0.102
Low	0.039

A reliability score was developed for each analytic review procedure from the priority scores presented above. For example, the most reliable analytic review procedure, univariate regression analysis, was given a possible total score of 100 points. The possible total reliability points for ratio analysis can then be calculated as: (100/0.376)x 0.054, or 14 points.

Table 3.10 Reliability Scores for Level 1 - Type of Analytic Review Procedures

Ratio analysis	14 points
Trend analysis - non statistical	29 points
Trend analysis - statistical	43 points
Regression analysis - univariate	100 points
Analytic recomputation	79 points

The method for calculating the overall reliability score was as follows:

Step 1

Identify the procedure as one of the five analytic review procedures. This indicates the MAXIMUM number of reliability points which could be awarded to the procedure.

Step 2

For each level 2 factor multiply the score for Level 1 by the relative importance weight for the Level 2 factor. This calculates the MAXIMUM number of points which are available from that Level 2 factor for the particular analytic review procedure identified.

Step 3

Multiply the MAXIMUM number of Level 2 points available by the weight assigned to the relevant Level 3 factor by the normalized importance vector at this level.

Step 4

The points available from the Level 3 factor levels are summed to give the overall reliability points for the procedure.

To demonstrate this method consider the following situation:

Auditor 1 identified the following procedure as the analytic procedure which he considered to be the least reliable procedure:

Ratio analysis with moderately variable, annual, moderately reliable, moderately homogeneous data.

This procedure has a maximum available number of reliability points equal to 14. These 14 points may be distributed over the four level 2 factors according to the assessed priorities of each of the factors. Thus, the variability of data factor will potentially contribute (0.113) x 14, or 1.582 points. The reliability factor points available are detailed below:

Table 3.11 Reliability Scores for Level 2 - Factor Reliability Scores

Variability	1.582
Reliability	1.820
Frequency	7.882
Homogeneity	2.716

The above level 2 factor reliability points may be interpreted as follows: if an analytic review procedure is directed towards a population with low variability, this fact will contribute 1.582 reliability points to the overall total reliability points for the procedure. If the variability of the population is medium or high, the procedure will receive less than 1.582 reliability points. The difference in the reliability points earned with respect to the variability factor can be determined from the normalized priority values for Level 3 factors presented below:

Table3.12 Reliability Scores for Level 3 - Normalized Factor Level Scores

Variability of data	
High	0.120
Medium	0.400
Low	1.000
Reliability of data	
High	1.000
Medium	0.282
Low	0.079
Frequency of data	
Annual	0.064
Monthly	0.139
Weekly	0.404
Daily	1.000
Homogeneity of population	
Very high	1.000
High	0.499
Medium	0.178
Low	0.068

The same procedure can be followed for each of the level 3 factors. Thus, for the analytic review procedure: ratio analysis with moderately variable, annual, moderately reliable, moderately homogeneous data the total reliability points are:

Table 3.13 Reliability Score Calculations for Analytical Procedures

Points for medium variability	= (1.582x0.4) = 0.6328 points
Points for annual frequency	= (7.882x0.064) = 0.50445 points
Points for medium reliability	= (1.82x0.282) = 0.51324 points
Points for medium homogeneity	= (2.716x0.178) = 0.48345 points

Hence, the total number of points available is 2.13. These are the reliability points which correspond to the least reliable analytic review procedure. The most reliable analytic review procedure would be awarded 100 points. As in the case of developing a reliability mapping for test of detail procedures, Auditor 1 provided the following maximum and minimum reliability assessments for analytic review procedures:

Maximum reliability = 0.96
Minimum reliability = 0.55

To determine the increase in reliability for each reliability it is necessary to perform the following calculation:

Reliability value of 1 reliability point = (0.96-0.55)/(100-2.10)
= 0.0042

These steps were used to generate numerical values for the reliabilities of analytic review procedures for each type of account. This is necessary because a number of the reliability factors would tend to vary between clients. For example, the degree of homogeneity in the population would be much greater if loan balances are being considered than sales of many different items of approximately the same value.

Limitations of Reliability Assessments

Although there was general agreement with respect to factors which influenced the reliability of the audit evidence provided by audit evidence-gathering procedures, there was considerable variation in the assessments of the importance of the various factors. One explanation for the differences is that the different experts who were questioned made different implicit assumptions in order to make their assessments. Another possible explanation is that each subject was exhibiting his or her own preferences with respect to risk. Different experts may also have made assessments based on different interpretations of the terms. Also, experts may have been biased in their assessments of the reliabilities of the most reliable and least reliable procedures. There is both general anecdotal evidence and specific objective evidence (Hubbard and Ballington, 1972) that auditors tend to overstate the reliability of audit procedures. This has the general effect of potentially overstating the reliability of individual procedures and understating the impact of individual reliability factors. In addition, the judgment task may not have been consistently complex for all experts. The relative complexity of a judgment task for a particular individual depends, among other factors, on:

1. The experience of the subject.

2. The manner in which the problem is presented.

3. The nature of the problem itself.

It might be argued that reducing a problem of global assessment to assessments concerning a number of relatively simple factors should inevitably reduce the complexity of the task. However, Burns and Pearl (1981, p.391), referring to analytic methods which decompose complex global judgments into a series of simpler judgments, caution that:

> *one should approach the "divide and conquer""ritual with caution; not every division leads to conquest . . . [inappropriate forms of decomposition] may lead to inferences of lower quality than direct, "holistic" judgments.*

Since, in this case, the decomposition used (in terms of reliability factors) has both a pragmatic basis (the factors were obtained from a consideration of the professional literature and agreed to by expert auditors) and a logical basis, it is to be hoped that the decomposition does actually reduce the cognitive load associated with the task of reliability assessment.

Another potential limitation stems from the fact that there is no unique way of mapping overall importance scores obtained through the use of AHP to probability values. The approach adopted in this research generally preserves order relationships between reliabilities, but there is no guarantee that the absolute numerical reliability values are valid. Nor is it clear exactly how one could go about obtaining more precise reliability values. At the very least it would be necessary to conduct extensive empirical studies to investigate appropriate mapping functions and where possible compare the results to "objective" values or values obtained from realistic simulations. This may be possible for some procedures and would be useful as a source of data with which to calibrate auditors' reliability judgments.

The use of an additive weighting function may not be appropriate. However, there is a considerable body of evidence that an additive combination of factor values often outperforms expert assessments. A weak test of the additive weighting approach to reliability determination is provided by the extensive validation tests described in Chapter 4.

Finally, there may not be general agreement with respect to the factors which should be considered in procedural reliability assessments. For the present research the factors were identified from extensive literature search (Ditner, 1986) and were agreed to by several experienced auditors who participated in providing the AHP assessments.

Cost Assessments

Auditors 1,2 and 4 were asked to consider a set of cost factors (Auditor 2 was not available at the time). These factors were developed following a literature search, conducted by Ditner (1986), and extensive discussion with experts. Once the relevant factors had been identified, three experts were asked to provide assessments of the relative importance of each factor. Once again, the Analytic Hierarchy Process was used.

Considerably greater congruence was found between the assessed importance of cost factors provided by different experts than between their assessments of the importance of reliability factors. This may partially be explained by the greater ease with which the cost factors could be defined compared to reliability factors and the significantly more objective nature of cost.

Cost Assessments for Tests of Detail Procedures

The Analytic Hierarchy Process was also used to assist the auditors to assess the relative importances of the three cost factors and their associated factor levels. The results that were obtained are presented in Table 3.3.

Table 3.14 Cost Factor Importance Assessments by Auditors

Level 1 - Cost Factors	Auditor 1	Auditor 3	Auditor 4
Seniority	0.618	0.644	0.633
Time taken	0.297	0.271	0.304
Behavioral cost	0.085	0.085	0.063
Level 2 - Cost Factor Levels			
Seniority			
High	0.628	0.637	0.669
Medium	0.230	0.258	0.243
Low	0.122	0.105	0.008
Time taken			
High	0.571	0.637	0.584
Medium	0.286	0.258	0.281
Low	0.143	0.105	0.135
Behavioral cost			
High	0.571[7]		
Medium	0.286		
Low	0.143		

[7] Although Auditor 1 felt that behavioral costs were important, he rated them as of very low importance at the procedural level. As a result they were not included in the scoring function.

The cost scoring function for auditors was developed in a similar fashion to the reliability scoring function:

Table 3.15 Level 1 - Cost Factor Points

Seniority	= 62 points
Time taken	= 30 points
Behavioral Cost	n/a

The relative importance of the cost factor levels was assessed as follows:

Table 3.16 Level 2 - Cost Factor Level Points

Seniority	
High	= 62 points
Medium	= 23 points
Low	= 12 points
Time taken	
High	= 30 points
Medium	= 15 points
Low	= 8 points
Behavioral Cost	n/a

In contrast to the overall reliability scores, the overall cost score was determined by multiplying the scores for each of the two factor levels. Thus, a procedure requiring audit partners and high time would be assigned a score of 62x30 or 1860 points. A procedure which could be conducted by staff in low time would be assigned 12x8 or 96 points. The use of a multiplicative rule is broadly consistent with the interpretation of the factors and factor levels.

Auditor 1 was also asked to provide examples to assist other auditors in interpreting the factor levels for the time taken and the behavioral cost of audit evidence-gathering procedures. He provided the following guidelines:

- Time taken to perform procedure:
    - High - loan review
    - Medium - selecting and sending out accounts receivable confirmations
    - Low - tracing or vouching
- Behavioral cost
    - High - a complex and tedious task
    - Medium - a complex and somewhat challenging task
    - Low - a simple and quick task

The preceding cost factor level assessments exhibit less variability than the reliability assessments. The degree of congruency, as measured by the mean distance criterion, is also greater:

Table 3.17 Differences Between Auditors' Cost Assessments

Auditor 1 - Auditor 3	0.001649
Auditor 1 - Auditor 4	0.00201

There are a number of possible reasons why the cost factor level assessments were more congruent than the reliability factor or factor level assessments. First, the overall criterion in the case of cost is more easily assessed by the managers than reliability. Second, the relationships between the cost factors and the overall cost are more transparent and easier to grasp than the relationships between the reliability factors and the overall reliability.

In previous AHP studies using a number of assessors, individual assessments have sometimes been combined. Saaty (1975) suggests that a geometric mean combination rule may be appropriate. Although four different assessments were available for each reliability level and three for each cost level, these were not combined to obtain a composite assessment. Auditor 1's assessments were used in the prototype of CAPEX.

Cost Factor Level Assessment for Test of Detail Procedures

As in the case of the reliability factor assessments, Auditor 1 was presented with a cost factor matrix and asked to identify cost factor levels for each procedure (refer to Appendix 3.2).

Cost Assessment for Analytic Procedures

One auditor was asked to provide an assessment of the cost of performing each type of analytic review procedure. In order to ensure that the costs of analytic review procedures were comparable to those assessed for test of details procedures, he was asked to assess the cost of substantive analysis procedures in terms of a reference cost - in this case, the cost of performing a single accounts receivable confirmation by a moderately competent auditor when the client has a moderately complex and a moderately reliable set of records. It was assumed that the cost of a positive confirmation of a single item was 100 units. The cost scores for each different type of analytic procedure are listed below.

Table 3.18 Cost Factor Scores

Ratio analysis	1000
Random walk forecasting	2000
Moving average forecasting	2000
Regression analysis	2000
Analytic recomputation	2000

Since analytic procedures are non-sampling procedures, the above cost figures represent the total costs of applying the procedures.

KNOWLEDGE ELICITATION USING A PROTOTYPE VERSION OF THE KNOWLEDGE-BASE

Once a prototype knowledge-base and computational model had been developed, they were used to further refine the knowledge-base. This knowledge refinement took place in two stages:

Stage I

During the initial knowledge elicitation stage, a prototype of the computational model and the knowledge-base was run using simplified client data to detect, with the help of the experts, major omissions in terms of procedures or necessary and sufficient conditions for invoking particular procedures.

Stage II

Once a set of comprehensive cases had been developed, these were used to provide for more detailed investigation of the contents and behavior of the prototype computational model and knowledge-base. Two senior managers, who had not been involved in the earlier stages of the research were asked to work through the manufacturing and retail cases. They were also requested to "think aloud" during this task and what they said was tape recorded.

Both the debriefing of the managers and a review of the tapes provided examples of information which was missing from the prototype. Since the banking cases were developed at a late stage it was not possible to perform such extensive testing of the part of the knowledge-base which applied specifically to banking audits. This would partially explain some of the problems which were experienced in validating audit plans which were generated for the banking cases.

SUMMARY

This chapter describes the acquisition of knowledge which was subsequently encoded in CAPEX's various knowledge-bases. There are a variety of different types of knowledge: organizational, small-group, and individual. Each of these three types of knowledge have different characteristics, are available from different sources and, as we note, may well have different epistemological status. We introduce this technical term to refer to whether an item of information is to be considered to really have the status of knowledge or if it is rather a belief. In addition, in considering epistemological status we suggest that it is appropriate to be concerned with the strengths of beliefs, the identity and credentials of the individual(s) holding the beliefs, and the justification(s) for the beliefs. It is important to establish the epistemological status of knowledge claims before they are encoded in knowledge-bases because it will have an impact on how we are likely to revise the knowledge-base on the receipt of new information, how we generate explanations, and how we handle conflicts between knowledge which encoded in the knowledge-bases.

In constructing CAPEX we have a logical basis for some of the knowledge which needs to be encoded - the accounting model. However, although the accounting model is a logical model in the abstract, when it is implemented, the model is no longer necessarily logical.

Knowledge elicitation was directed towards identifying audit evidence-gathering procedures and establishing their relevance, reliability and cost. Elicitation primarily made use of interviewing, supplemented by the use of paper and computer-based tools. In assessing the relevance of audit evidence we made use of relevance matrices which were patterned on the types of matrices used by accounting firms.

As we discussed in Chapter 2, audit evidence-gathering procedures may be divided into tests of detail and analytic procedures. In this chapter we indicate how reliability assessments were made for the two different types of procedures. Reliability assessments were made in two distinct ways. One way involved the determination of reliability factor weights directly. The other way made use of the Analytic Hierarchy Process (AHP). The AHP assessments were made using a computer program to capture and process the assessments made by the experts who were interviewed.

Assessments of the costs of applying audit procedures were made using the AHP and two different sets of cost factors; one set for tests of detail procedures and one set for analytic procedures.

Chapter 4

EVALUATING CAPEX

INTRODUCTION

Knowledge-based systems (or expert systems) designed to produce outputs of the complexity of audit plans, which consist of numerous components, many interdependencies among those components, and many alternative solutions, raise important questions about the type of evaluation approach needed to evaluate them.

The development of effective approaches to the evaluation of such systems is important for a number of reasons:

- From both a pragmatic and a research standpoint such a methodology can be a useful tool for validating processes which generate multivariate outputs such as audit program plans regardless of how they may be generated; i.e., whether by knowledge-based systems, conventional programs, or even manual systems based on forms and tables.
- Knowledge-based systems (KBSs) can be powerful research tools in their own right provided that they have been adequately verified and validated. For example, once validated, an audit planning KBS can be used to explore the impact of alternative heuristics for determining the reliability of audit evidence-gathering procedures. Another potential research application for such a system is to use it to investigate the impact of using different approaches for combining the uncertainties associated with audit planning objectives.
- With respect to accounting and auditing knowledge-based systems, many accounting firms are looking to use knowledge-based systems for supporting audit decision making. Clearly, an investment in validation of such systems will be required to warrant their use in practice. Indeed the use of such systems could affect the risks associated with external audits (e.g., refer to Richmond *et al.* 1987).

As Phillips, Brown and Nielsen (1991) point out, many expert systems are proprietary and few opportunities exist for independent evaluations of their performance and comparisons with other similar systems. Also, methods for evaluating expert systems with complex outputs are not well developed in the literature and few opportunities exist for critically considering the effectiveness of such methods. This chapter describes the approach used to evaluate CAPEX and reports on the evaluation results. We believe that our approach and experience, including the limitations reported here, will contribute to the development of appropriate evaluation methodologies for knowledge-based systems and expert systems.

Knowledge-based systems can be evaluated according to a number of different criteria. For example correctness, robustness, usability, reliability, etc. Our tests were primarily directed to evaluating the correctness of outputs generated by CAPEX. In the past, tests designed to evaluate the correctness of the outputs of knowledge-based systems or expert systems in the field of auditing have concentrated mainly on a single judgment variable or decision. As O'Leary (1987, p. 475) points out, the number of correct responses obtained in a decision situation, often used to measure the quality of human decisions, has also been the criterion used to evaluate the performance of expert systems. For example, Dungan (1983) focused on the appropriateness of his expert system's bad debt provisions and Steinbart (1985) focused on the appropriateness of the materiality values provided by his system.

Unlike the systems described above, a system that produces an entire audit plan results in a multivariate array of outputs. For example, CAPEX was designed to produce an audit plan consisting of a listing of suggested audit procedures, their timing and their extent. To adequately test the performance of CAPEX, it was necessary to identify appropriate performance variables and design instruments to elicit judgments from experts concerning these variables. To adequately evaluate the performance of CAPEX it was necessary to design appropriate evaluation cases and instruments. These cases and instruments were designed with the active involvement of domain experts. Independent auditors evaluated the performance of CAPEX using these cases and instruments. To avoid biasing the evaluators' judgments, we carried out a single-blinded study whereby independent experts evaluated the system-produced audit plans as well as human-expert-produced plans without knowing which were which, nor even that some of the plans were produced by a system.

In the following sections, we first discuss the broad objectives established for evaluating CAPEX. This is followed by a discussion of the criteria chosen to measure the extent to which these objectives had been achieved. The next section discusses the methodology used to evaluate the system, including a description of the cases used in the evaluation process and the questionnaires used to elicit expert auditors' assessments. (A number of appendices at the end of the book reproduce the materials used in the evaluation). Next, we report the results of experts' assessments of the acceptability, effectiveness and efficiency of both human-produced and system-produced plans. We conclude with a discussion of the limitations of the evaluation process and suggestions for enhancing evaluation procedures.

EVALUATION, VALIDATION AND VERIFICATION - A BRIEF REVIEW

Evaluating knowledge-based systems or expert systems involves, among other activities, verification and validation. Other aspects of evaluation may involve investigating the usability, robustness, cost effectiveness, efficiency etc. of the system being investigated. We will focus on verification and validation issues in this chapter.

There is a considerable research literature which addresses validity and verification issues in the social sciences (Brinberg and McGrath, 1982, 1985), simulation (Shannon, 1975), and software engineering (Martin and McClure, 1985; Geissman and Schultz, 1988). However, until relatively recently (see, for example, O'Leary, 1986, 1987, 1988; Klein and Mathlie, 1990) little of this work has been examined for its relevance to expert systems research.

O'Leary (1987) uses the social sciences research tradition as a foundation on which to develop an analysis of a variety of different types of validity and construct a validation "framework" which he subsequently uses to examine the extent to which previously developed expert systems in accounting and auditing have been validated. While O'Leary discusses a number of previous approaches to validating expert systems in accounting and auditing, he does not explicitly consider the need to develop multi-dimensional approaches to validation, particularly in the domains of accounting and auditing. One reason for this omission may be that the validation work he reviews related to expert systems whose performance could be measured using univariate approaches. When expert systems generate "rich" outputs whose essential nature can only be characterized multi-dimensionally, the validation process must itself become significantly more complex. In these cases, it becomes necessary to address the following questions:

1. What are the variables which appropriately characterize the outputs being generated by the system?

2. What instruments can be used to provide measurements of these variables?

3. How reliable are these instruments?

4. If it is not possible to measure the relevant variables directly, are the variables which can be measured reliable and valid?

5. How competent are the assessors in making the types of judgments that they are required to make in order to provide the necessary assessments of the variables?

Hollnagel (1989) investigates a variety of different validation techniques and considers the appropriateness of each technique and ways in which the reliability and validity of the technique may be increased. In particular, he suggests that experts should be called upon to compare the performance of expert systems to that of other experts and that explicit criteria should be established for performance assessment. For example, in a medical context, Yu et al. (1979) found that a group of expert evaluators who agreed with the diagnosis of an expert system 75% of the time were themselves rated at a 70-80% level by other experts. On the strength of these results, the investigators concluded that the expert system matched the performance of the "best" experts in the field.

We have taken account of the issues raised by Bonnet et al. (1988), most particularly those relating to the creation of the information sets which are used as the basis for any validation tests. They caution that any validation methodology must ensure that such information sets provide a sufficiently rich basis for eliciting expert behavior. In addition, they propose methods which can be used to ensure that both the system and the experts are provided with the identical information.

The next section reviews the concepts of verification and validation from a general perspective.

THE PROCESSES OF VERIFICATION AND VALIDATION

The model of audit knowledge on which CAPEX is based is in the form of a computer program. Thus, it would seem appropriate to initially investigate the concepts of verification and validation from the standpoint of software engineering. Although O'Leary (1987) concluded that traditional software validation techniques were inappropriate for expert systems and proposed an alternative approach based on social sciences research design principles, we believe that it is necessary to revisit these techniques, particularly those derived from software engineering, for a number of reasons:

1. Software engineering provides a basis for making a clear distinction between verification and validation. We believe that this distinction, often glossed over in expert systems research, is an important one to recognize if robust validation and verification methodologies are to be developed for expert systems.

2. Software engineering stresses the need for clear and precise specifications to be established for any computer program. There are good reasons for it being difficult to provide such specifications for expert systems (see below). However, since the strength of any validation tests depends on the precision of the performance specification there is a need to develop specifications which are as precise as possible.

3. As expert systems are increasingly based on "deep" knowledge of a domain it becomes both possible and increasingly necessary to develop formal specifications for these systems.

Formal methods developed by software engineers distinguish between verification and validation:[1]

- *Verification:* the correctness and completeness of the processes whereby software specifications are converted into software.
- *Validation*: the processes which determine whether the initial requirements correctly and completely specify the behaviors which the user(s) wanted the system to have.

One way of clarifying the differences between the two concepts is provided by Figure 4.1. This figure demonstrates that computer systems are constructed to satisfy some set of user requirements. In order to construct the system, in the first place, it is necessary to translate the user's requirements into a set of system specifications. Once these specifications have been established, the system can be developed. Generally speaking, the greater the confidence we have in the processes which are used to map from system specifications to the completed code (labeled SYSTEM in Figure 4.1), the less we need to be concerned with verification tests which check whether the system meets the specifications established for it. Similarly, the greater the confidence we have in the processes which are used to map from user requirements to system specifications, the less we need to be concerned with validation tests which seek to determine the extent to which the system satisfies user requirements.

Figure 4.1 Distinction Between Verification and Validation

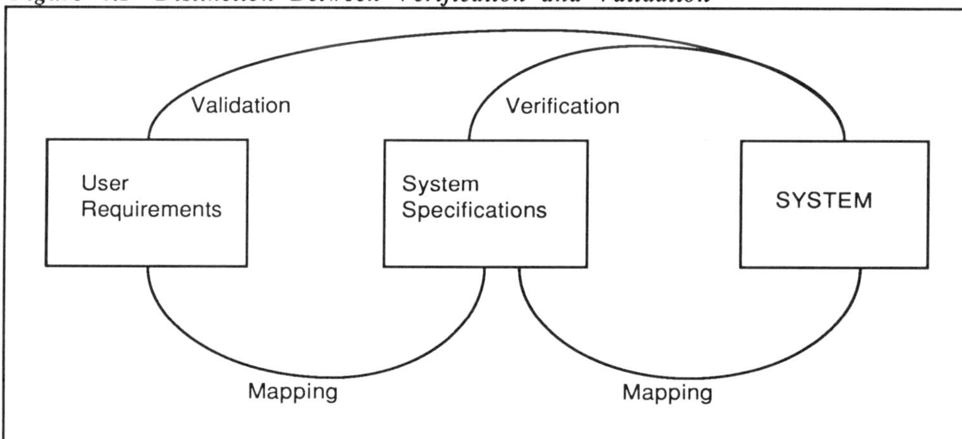

Computer systems and programs have a particular internal structure. Some verification tests may involve investigating this structure **statically**; i.e, simple inspection or comparison with system specifications. However, it is often necessary to investigate the actual behavior of the system or program. That is, the internal structure can also be investigated **dynamically** by investigating the types of behavior, in terms of intermediate results, processes invoked, and outputs which result from providing the system or program with a variety of different sets of input

---

[1] For instance, O'Leary [1986, p. 8] states: "Verification is defined as an attempt to find errors by executing a program in a simulated environment. Validation is defined as an attempt to find errors by executing a program in a real environment. Testing [assessment] is the process of executing a program to find errors."

information. Verification of computer systems and programs generally requires both static and dynamic testing.

Developing extensive and reliable verification tests for expert systems may not be possible for a number of reasons:

1. A particular set of users may not be explicitly identified for an expert system; hence, little, or no attempt is made to identify user requirements. Thus, it is very difficult to demonstrate that the mapping between user requirements and system specifications is accurate.

2. Even if a set of users has been identified, system specifications are often very vaguely defined. This causes problems with respect to verifying that higher level requirements are accurately translated into lower level requirements. It also creates significant problems with any attempts to determine whether an expert system is meeting its specifications and thus reduces the strength of any validation tests which can be applied to the system.

3. Development methodologies for expert systems are relatively undeveloped and untested. Thus little confidence can be placed in their reliability.

Therefore, it is almost always necessary to also perform some form of validation tests on a computer program. In some situations it may only be necessary to perform very limited validation tests. For instance, if it is possible to elicit, and refine, user requirements in a form which can be translated into system specifications in a straightforward manner, then it may be sufficient to show that the system which has been developed meets these specifications. Thus, the overall confidence that user requirements are satisfied will be high if:

1. The confidence level that user requirements have been accurately mapped to system specifications is high, and

2. The confidence level that the system actually developed meets system specifications is high.

Each of these confidence levels is a combination of the confidence levels associated with the relevant mapping process and the confidence level associated with the verification or validation tests which have been performed.

Validation tests are particularly important for expert systems because, even when some attempt is made to refine user requirements they are usually at a different logical level to system specifications. Usually, system specifications relate to the *content* of the expert systems knowledge-base rather than the *behavior* which is expected of the system. It is tacitly assumed that behavior which will satisfy user requirements will be generated using a system which contains some representation of domain knowledge, either constructed in concert with experts or obtained from other sources. In this type of situation the terms verification and validation may be defined in the following way:

1. Verification = Determining that the knowledge which is encoded in the knowledge-base corresponds to the knowledge which has been specified in the system specifications.

2. Validation = Determining whether the knowledge possessed by the knowledge sources corresponds to the knowledge specified in the system specifications.

However, user requirements may specify a system which exhibits certain behaviors which are typical of individuals possessing a particular level of expertise. In this case, it becomes critical to establish a robust validation methodology for investigating the actual behavior of the system. Since, in our opinion, this type of validation is critical to the overall confidence that we are able to invest in a particular expert system, we have required that both the structure and behavior of CAPEX be evaluated.

There are a variety of other problems which arise with respect to developing validation tests for expert systems. Usually, validation involves comparing the behavior of a system to the behavior of the actual system being modeled. However, in the case of many expert systems, this comparison cannot be made directly. Addressing this issue, O'Leary (1987) advocates that the performance of expert systems should be compared to the performance of other models wherever possible. While this suggestion may be appropriate in some limited circumstances, it fails to recognize that expert systems are most likely to be developed when there are no other practical alternatives. Therefore, in most domains in which it is sensible to develop an expert system in the first place, the ultimate arbiter of the quality of the solution provided by such a system is an expert or set of experts. It is unlikely that there would be other models of similar complexity to that embedded in the expert system in question.

CAPEX encodes a variety of different types of knowledge about audit planning. Thus, in a broad sense, it encodes a theory of audit planning and specific data which can be used, along with the theory, to generate behavior. In this case, the behavior of the system involves the construction of an audit program plan. At the present time we possess insufficient knowledge to be able to assess the validity and other properties of an audit program plan objectively. Therefore, it is necessary to rely on experienced audit planners to provide these assessments.

Using experts to evaluate the performance of expert systems raises a number of important methodological questions which have rarely been addressed in the verification and validation literature.[2] For instance:

- What types of information do experts require to be able to assess the performance of either other experts or an expert system?
- How skilled are the experts selected at judging the behavior of others?
- How reliable and/or valid are the assessments provided by experts?

Expert systems create additional difficulties for designing and conducting validation tests. For example, if an expert system is built to satisfy user requirements of the following form:

> *Expert system **A** should exhibit behavior consistent with that exhibited by individuals with an expertise level **X** given a variety of different information sets.*

One important aspect of behavior relates to the **output** provided by the expert or the system. Thus, in the context of audit planning it is to be expected that the system will generate certain types of audit program plans given certain types of input. However, this seems hardly sufficient to characterize the richness of the term behavior. There are also **process** dimensions. That is, experts do not generate audit program plans at random. They follow some generally accepted procedure for generating plans. Both of these types of behavior need to be explicated in much more detail.

Another aspect of the preceding type of specification is that the notion of expertise level needs considerable exploration. To what extent is it possible to identify a variety of different expertise levels? Do they overlap? Is it possible to identify, with any degree of accuracy, what expertise level

---

[2] Finlay, *et al.* [1988] and Hollnagel [1989] make some references to problems discussed in this section.

a particular individual has achieved? At the very least some attempt must be made to specify expected expertise levels and develop ways of measuring the expertise level of the resulting system.

The expertise level exhibited by any expert system is likely to depend on several factors, most importantly: (1) the content of the knowledge-base and (2) the heuristics used in processing the knowledge in the knowledge base. Thus, to generate a system to exhibit a certain level of expertise it is necessary to construct a knowledge-base and set of heuristics which have been provided by individuals whose expertise level is equal to, or greater than, the expertise level which has been specified in the initial specifications.

An additional problem arises if the solution itself does not indicate the level of expertise, but requires an explanation to, in some sense, validate the solution. In other words, the line of reasoning used in developing a given solution may be more important than the actual solution itself. Similarly, in some circumstances, expertise may be evidenced not so much by the solution itself, but by the response of the individual to slight perturbations of the initial conditions which were used to develop the initial solution.

In the following section we move from the general to the specific and focus our attention on CAPEX.

EVALUATION OBJECTIVES

Our primary evaluation objective was to determine whether the system could produce correct substantive audit programs for the revenue/receivables/receipts cycle for three different types of client namely: manufacturing, retailing and banking. A subsidiary objective was to identify shortcomings in outputs and trace them to system features such as the knowledge-base, the plan generating process, or other features (e.g., user interface, explanation facility, etc.). Since correctness is not easily established when the output is an entire audit plan, we focused on several criteria by which correctness could be established, as discussed in the following section.

EVALUATION CRITERIA

CAPEX was not designed to model the process by which human experts actually combine knowledge in order to generate audit program plans. As a result the system's behavior was evaluated with reference to the following two related criteria:

Criterion 1

System "behavior" should correspond to the behavior exhibited by an individual with expertise level X by processing a variety of information inputs in a way which generates acceptable behavior although that behavior would not necessarily be identical to the behavior of any particular expert.

Criterion 2

System "behavior" should correspond to the behavior exhibited by an individual with expertise level X by processing a variety of information inputs in a way which generates acceptable outcomes, decisions, etc.

The first criterion is akin to the "reasonable person" test used in legal reasoning. Under this criterion, an assessment of system behavior is not based on whether it is an isomorph of an expert; but rather, whether the behavior would be acceptable to other experts (because it is reasonable) even though they themselves might not necessarily behave in the identical way. For example, the use of Bayesian revision by a system might be considered acceptable by an expert because it is a reasonable computational approach to evidence aggregation, although an expert might not actually use this type of computation to revise his or her own evidential assessments.

The second criterion involves the indirect evaluation of the process by considering the outputs of the process and inferring that, if the output is correct, the process that produced it must have been appropriate.

OUTPUT RELATED CRITERIA

Tests of system outputs have relied on experts' ratings of those outputs. However, merely considering experts' assessments of system outputs alone may not be appropriate, since many factors can bias experts' ratings of system-produced outputs. For example, experts may systematically rate system-produced outputs as better or worse than human-produced outputs. Reliance on blind evaluations alone may not eliminate all sources of bias. For example, evaluators may systematically rate others more or less harshly than they would rate themselves.

Partly in response to concerns such as those raised above, Hollnagel (1989) suggests that experts should compare the performance of expert systems to the performance of other experts. Therefore, our evaluation approach involved comparing experts' blind assessments of the acceptability, efficiency, and effectiveness of system-produced outputs with their assessments of plans prepared by other experts. The experts that we relied upon were "blind" as to the source of the plans they were assessing and were not told that any system-produced plans were being assessed. We reasoned that if both the human experts and the system could produce acceptable, effective and efficient outputs in response to the information contained in the case material, it would be reasonable to conclude that the system's behavior in response to the input was appropriate/correct. The information provided should, of course, be appropriate and, moreover, should not exceed the information required by an experienced auditor to complete the planning task. If we wished to test the robustness of the system, we would also need to test the system's ability to handle irrelevant and conflicting information. This type of test is important for a "delivery" version of a system; however, the criterion of robustness was outside the scope of the tests reported here.

Judgments of "acceptability" were intended to encompass both the consideration of the appropriateness of the plan in a technical sense, as well as indicating the degree of tolerance or acceptance of the approach implicitly used to produce the plan. For example, a plan could satisfy target levels of assurance, but use procedures that the auditor's firm or the auditor did not like to employ. We also asked the auditors to rate the plan's effectiveness and efficiency for the same reason that Type I and Type II error are both considered in auditing. An audit plan could be made effective by requiring dozens of extensive procedures, although its degree of inefficiency would cast doubt on the degree of expertise being applied.

Although our central concern in evaluating CAPEX was the correctness of its outputs, we recognized that a correct result could be achieved in ways that would not be considered generally acceptable. For instance, the system could generate acceptable audit program plans using a combination of inaccurate or incorrect knowledge and/or inappropriate approaches to processing knowledge. One way to reduce the possibility of spurious or chance agreement between the system's outputs and experts is to use a large volume of testing under a variety of conditions. Limited resources and, especially, scarcity of expert time, limits such testing to final stages of development of "delivery" versions of systems (e.g., refer to Ribar *et al.* 1991). However, we took several steps to reduce the possibility of obtaining favorable results due to chance. These involved careful construction of several cases, checks of the knowledge-base and tests of system processing.

INPUT CASES

As will be discussed more fully below, the cases were carefully screened to ensure that they contained appropriate information and furthermore, that it was the minimum information needed to enable an experienced auditor to generate a competent audit program plan. The two case writers and four of the five auditors acting as evaluators, who had no previous exposure to the system or the case material, were able to use the information provided to generate audit program plans consisting of lists of audit procedures and their extents. CAPEX was also able to generate audit program plans based on the same information.

KNOWLEDGE-BASE CONTENT

Knowledge encoded in CAPEX's knowledge-base was structured primarily according to accounting theory, convention, and current literature (discussed in Boritz and Wensley, 1990). Some of the planning and evidential assessment heuristics used to generate audit program plans were obtained from research literature or firm manuals, while others were provided by experienced auditors. Four different auditors from the same auditing firm provided the bulk of the knowledge encoded in CAPEX's knowledge-base.

The knowledge-base was subjected to intensive informal evaluation, throughout the system development process, involving extensive interaction with practicing auditors whose knowledge was being encoded. In addition, we tested various algorithms and we developed a set of programs to check the consistency and completeness of some of the key information encoded in the knowledge-base. However, due to resource limitations, no additional independent comprehensive verification of the accuracy of coding was carried out, on the assumption that the output evaluation process would identify any significant coding errors. In practice, such verification is a critical part of the expert system development and maintenance process as described by Graham *et al.* (1990).

PROCESS

To check on program processing, we developed and studied program trace information to determine that the order of program execution was in accordance with the model. We also discussed the process with the participating experts who agreed that the process should result in the construction of acceptable audit program plans.

PARTICIPANTS IN EVALUATION PROCESS

The total number of auditors involved across all aspects of the evaluation is comparable to other evaluation studies. As indicated in Figure 4.2, two senior audit managers were involved throughout all phases of system development and evaluation. There were four auditors involved in pre-testing the questionnaire and case materials and five senior audit managers were involved in the formal output evaluation, four from the U.S. practice of one "Big Six" accounting firm and one from the Canadian practice of a different "Big Six" accounting firm. None of the managers had any prior involvement with CAPEX, and they were all selected by the participating firms, not by us. We simply requested that they should have the appropriate levels of experience; two of the managers were required to have had experience managing audits of manufacturing clients, two were required to have had experience managing audits of financial institutions (only one of them provided usable responses) and the last auditor was required to have had experience with audits of retail clients. The average industry-specific audit experience of the managers was 6.75 years with a range from 4 to 9 years. The average number of years experience in managing audits was 2.5 years, with a range from 1 to 4 years. In addition, several senior practitioners and technical specialists periodically reviewed the underlying structure and approach, as well as the detailed source code.

Figure 4.2 Summary of Participants in Evaluation

Stage	Participant
case preparation	2 senior audit managers (1 mfg & retail; 1 banking)
initial evaluation of cases and questionnaires	same two audit managers as above, plus 4 additional audit managers from same firm, different office
independent evaluations of solution plans	5 audit managers (2 manufacturing; 2 banking; 1 retail); manufacturing and banking from same firm, different office; retail from different firm

EVALUATION INSTRUMENTS

To assess the performance of CAPEX with respect to the established criteria it was necessary to develop two instruments: a set of cases which would provide input information to CAPEX and a questionnaire which would be used to elicit experts' assessments of the plans generated by CAPEX. The cases are presented in full in Appendices 4.1 through 4.6 and the different versions of the questionnaire, one for each case, in Appendices 4.7 through 4.12.

CASE PREPARATION AND TESTING

Six cases were developed – two cases for each of three industries: manufacturing, retail and banking. Each case consisted of numerical information together with judgmental and qualitative information. The case material was patterned, as much as possible, on the type and structure of information that would be available to an experienced auditor in the firm.[3] These cases were developed principally by two senior managers from a large accounting firm over a period of nine months. One of the managers had considerable experience with managing audits of merchandising and manufacturing clients, while the other had managed audits of a variety of financial institutions. The cases were designed to be challenging to audit managers with specific industry experience and included only the minimum information that the case writer and pre-testing indicated was necessary to enable the construction of revenue cycle substantive audit program plans by an experienced auditor.

To ensure that the cases provided sufficient information to engage the subjects' expertise, the cases were subjected to a number of pre-testing stages. Except for the case developers, the auditors who participated in the pre-testing phases had neither any prior exposure to any aspect of the research nor any subsequent role in the evaluation. The tests consisted of requiring each auditor to provide "solutions" to two cases in terms of suggested substantive audit program plans for the revenue/receivables/receipts cycle. The participants were also asked to "think aloud" as they worked through the cases, and a debriefing was conducted at the end of each session. Participants were particularly directed to identify information they thought was lacking and the assumptions they made to compensate for the missing information.

---

[3] The case material provided to the assessors contained summary inherent risk and control risk assessments and summary information concerning the client being audited. Specific areas in which information was missing were: Previous period's working papers, details supporting the inherent risk assessment, details supporting the control risk assessment, and detailed information concerning the environment in which the client operates.

THE OUTPUT EVALUATION INSTRUMENT

Each of the independent experts was asked to assess the proposed solutions to four cases -- two of which were produced by the case writers and two produced by CAPEX. The order of case presentation was varied to counteract potential order effects. The experts rated the solutions at the financial statement level, at the financial statement item (i.e., account) level, and at the financial statement item assertion level. Rating scales such as the one in Figure 4.3 were used to assist the experts in making these assessments.

Figure 4.3 Sample Acceptability Rating Scale

1 =	The plan is **fundamentally unacceptable** and even **major** revisions cannot change this conclusion.
2 =	The plan is **unacceptable** and can only be made acceptable through **major** revisions.
3 =	The plan is **generally acceptable** but **some** significant revisions are necessary.
4 =	The plan is **generally acceptable** but some **minor** revisions are necessary.
5 =	The plan is **acceptable** without any revisions being required.

A score of 5 with respect to a particular plan indicates that it is not only appropriate in a technical sense, but acceptable to the evaluator. In contrast, a score of 1 would indicate that, even if it could be shown to be, in some sense, technically appropriate, the plan was not acceptable to the evaluator. For example, a plan could satisfy target levels of assurance, but use procedures that the auditor's firm or the auditor did not like to employ.

As mentioned earlier, we also asked the auditors to rate the plan's effectiveness and efficiency by account and assertion using rating scales similar to Figure 4.3. In addition, we asked the auditors to identify procedures which should have been included in the plan but were not, and any procedures included in the plan which should not have been. This information could be particularly useful for indicating refinements which might improve the performance of the system.

The output evaluation questionnaire was pre-tested by presenting it, together with the case materials (but not solutions), to the case developers and four additional auditors from the same firm as the case preparers, but from a different office. These auditors were involved only in the pre-testing phase of the evaluation, not the evaluation itself. The objective of this step was to determine whether the questionnaire and scales seemed usable in making evaluations of solutions to the case materials. The pre-testers were asked to informally evaluate the questionnaire for understandability and appropriateness. They all stated that they found the questionnaire generally understandable, though one auditor suggested a number of wording changes. In some cases they felt that the required evaluations were rather detailed; but, on the whole, they considered them to be appropriate. Apart from these assessments, we did not carry out any additional formal validity and reliability tests on these scales.

OUTPUT EVALUATION METHODOLOGY

The output produced by CAPEX was an audit plan in the form of a list of procedures and their extents. The principal test performed to assess the appropriateness of the system output required the two case writers and five other experienced audit planners to assess the performance of CAPEX using a number of cases, as described earlier. Except for the case writers, the auditors involved in this part of the evaluation had not been previously involved in the development of the system and its knowledge-base, or the cases, or in pre-testing of the cases and questionnaires.

Each participant was presented with two cases pertaining to the type of client with which he/she had had most experience. Each case was presented in two different forms: one specifying target assurances for all the relevant financial statement item assertions and the other which left all target assurances unspecified. The version of the case with target assurances unspecified was always presented first. Auditors were requested to provide detailed audit program plans using the types of worksheets they would use in normal practice. The auditors were first asked to construct a substantive audit program plan to achieve target assurances set by themselves for the first case. They were then requested to consider the second version of the case, the version with target assurances provided, and asked whether the additional information would lead them to revise their initial plan. The purpose of this stage was to help the auditors focus attention on the case material before actually assessing the acceptability of the plans which were the subject of the evaluation effort. In addition, we hoped to control any anchoring effects which might arise by having subjects anchor on their own plans rather than any of the solutions presented to them. Thus, any potential bias due to anchoring would be "against" the evaluation of the system.

After completing the planning task themselves, the evaluators were presented with two "solutions" to the case. One solution had been generated by CAPEX, while the other was provided by the case writer.[4] Evaluators were asked to fill out the same planning assessment questionnaire as the case writers had used. They were not told which plans they were assessing (auditor-produced or CAPEX-produced), or even that they were assessing any system-produced plans at all.

Having completed the assessments of all the solution plans, evaluators were asked to re-inspect their own solution and decide whether they wanted to change it in any way. If they felt that any changes were necessary they were asked to indicate the precise nature of these changes. This process was repeated, in its entirety, for the second case.

Throughout all the activities described above, auditors were asked to "think-aloud" into a tape recorder. They were directed to explain why they selected certain procedures over others, what assumptions they found they had to make if they felt that they had insufficient information, and any other comments that they had on the difficulties of solving the case or inconsistencies they perceived in the case material.

---

[4] The participating auditors were not made aware that they were participating in the evaluation of an expert system. They were told that each of the case solutions was the work of a human auditor. This type of blinding is somewhat loosely referred to as a Turing test (O'Leary, 1988). A true Turing test would allow for the interrogation of both the system and experts by the evaluators.

RESULTS OF EVALUATIONS

In the following sections, the results of the evaluations are presented and discussed. These results are presented in tables summarizing the detailed assessments of efficiency and effectiveness of the various solution plans. The detailed responses themselves are not reported here, but are available from the authors upon request. The numerical values presented in each table refer to the effectiveness and efficiency ratings using the 5-point scales similar to Figure 4.3 described earlier.

OVERALL PLAN ACCEPTABILITY RATINGS

The assessments of the overall acceptability of both human-generated and CAPEX-generated plans made using the rating scale illustrated in Figure 4.3 are presented in Table 4.1.

Table 4.1 Overall Plan Acceptability Ratings by Independent Experts

Case	Evaluator	Human-generated	CAPEX-generated
Case 1	Case writer 1	n/a	4
Manufacturing	Auditor 1	4	4
	Auditor 2	3	3
Case 2	Case writer 1	n/a	3
Manufacturing	Auditor 1	4	2
	Auditor 2	3	1
Case 3	Case writer 1	n/a	4
Retail	Auditor 3	3	2
Case 4	Case writer 1	n/a	4
Retail	Auditor 3	3	3
Case 5	Case writer 2	n/a	4
Bank	Auditor 4	n/r	n/r
Case 6	Case writer 2	n/a	2
Bank	Auditor 4	3	3

As Table 4.1 indicates, all of the human-generated plans were deemed to be generally acceptable (ratings > 2) and nine of the thirteen CAPEX-generated plans for which assessments were made were judged to be generally acceptable. No plans were accepted by the assessors without reservation (i.e., there were no ratings of 5); thus, most of the human-generated and CAPEX-generated plans were judged to require some significant revisions in order to be acceptable. Some of the assessors indicated that it was difficult to assess the solution plans because they deviated from 'firm practice'.

Our results seem to be consistent with those reported by Yu *et al.* (1979) who found, in a medical context, that a group of expert evaluators who agreed with the diagnosis of an expert system 75% of the time were themselves rated at a 70-80% level by other experts. On the strength of these results, the investigators concluded that the expert system matched the performance of the "best" experts in the field, although we make no such claims about CAPEX.

EFFECTIVENESS AND EFFICIENCY RATINGS BY THE CASE WRITERS

The case writers' detailed assessments of the effectiveness and efficiency of CAPEX's proposed audit program plans for the six test cases are summarized in Table 4.2. Cases 1, 2, 3 and 4 were evaluated by Case Writer 1, while cases 5 and 6 were evaluated by Case Writer 2. For each case, the case writer was asked to assess the efficiency and effectiveness of the proposed audit program plan at achieving target risks with respect to each financial statement item assertion. In the table, a score above 2 indicates that portion of the plan is at least as efficient or effective as any other alternative of which the assessor was aware. In contrast, a score of 1 or 2 represents the evaluator's judgment that the plan is less effective or less efficient than any alternative plan. For example, Case 1 involved a total of 13 individual planning decisions. Each of these decisions was evaluated by case writer 1 using a 5-point effectiveness scale and a 5-point efficiency scale similar to that in Figure 4.3. The entries in Table 4.2 report the number of ratings given for each scale value; i.e., 5 of the 13 decisions earned an effectiveness rating of 3, 4 of them earned a rating of 4, and 4 of them earned a rating of 5.

Table 4.2 Frequency Distributions of Effectiveness and Efficiency Ratings by Case Writers

		Effectiveness Ratings					Efficiency Ratings				
	Total Number of Judgments	1	2	3	4	5	1	2	3	4	5
Case 1	13			5	4	4		2	11		
Case 2	8		7	1					8		
Case 3	15				2	13			15		
Case 4	15				3	12			15		
Case 5	37				2	35				23	14
Case 6	37					37			9	3	25
Totals	125		7	6	11	101		2	58	26	39
	100%		6	5	9	80		2	46	21	31

It can be observed that, with the exception of the plan developed for Case 2, the case writers judged that CAPEX-generated audit program plans to be at least as effective as those they themselves could develop. From the stand-point of efficiency, the case writers provided a slightly less skewed set of judgments. This may be attributed, at least partially, to their concern that some of the audit plans would result in some of the financial statement items being over-audited.

EFFECTIVENESS AND EFFICIENCY RATINGS BY INDEPENDENT EXPERTS

The detailed results obtained in this part of the evaluation are summarized in Table 4.3. In each cell the first figure relates to judgments made by one of the four auditors, identified in column 2, with respect to the human-generated plan while the second figure relates to judgments concerning the CAPEX-generated plan. For example, Case 1 involved 13 planning judgments. Each of these judgments reported in the solution was evaluated by auditor 1 using the 5-point effectiveness scale and the 5-point efficiency scale. Table 4.3 reports the number of judgments for each scale value; i.e., for all 13 of the variables an effectiveness rating of 4 was given to both the human-generated judgments and the CAPEX-generated judgments. In contrast, for the 13 efficiency ratings, a rating of 3 was given to all of the human-generated judgements and 10 of the CAPEX-generated judgments, while 1 of the CAPEX-generated judgments was given a rating of 2 and 2 of them were given a rating of 4. The totals simply summarize the frequency distributions of the ratings given over all 146 judgments on the effectiveness and efficiency rating scales. Statistical analysis was precluded by the limited number of subjects and cases used. It should also be noted that, although a large number of assessments were made by each assessor with respect to each "solution" plan, these assessments are unlikely to be independent of each other.

Table 4.3 Frequency Distributions of Effectiveness and Efficiency Ratings by Independent Experts

			Effectiveness Ratings					Efficiency Ratings				
Case	A	Total Number of Judgments	1	2	3	4	5	1	2	3	4	5
1	1	13				13,13			0,1	13,10	0,2	
	2	13	0,2	8,3	5,8					13,13		
2	1	08				8,6	0,2		4,7	4,1		
	2	08		1,5	3,2	0,1	4,0	0,8		8,0		
3	3	15	1,6	9,3	3,4		2,2	.		.		
4	3	15	1,0	4,6	7,7	1,0	2,2	.		.		
5	4	37		17,0	19,15	1,20	0,2		2,3	23,32	12,2	
6	4	37		11,20	15,14	11,3			18,23	14,14	5,0	
Totals		146	2,8	50,37	52,50	34,43	8,8	0,8	24,34	75,70	17,4	

Note: A = Auditor ID number; Table entries represent rating frequencies for (Human, CAPEX)

There was considerable disagreement among assessors' views with respect to the same audit program plan. In Table 4.3 it can be observed that there is considerable variation between the judgments made by the two auditors who assessed the human-generated and CAPEX-generated "solutions" for cases 1 and 2. Although the differences between the judgments are considerable, both auditors seemed to make relatively little distinction between the human-generated plan and the CAPEX-generated plan. With respect to the auditor assessing human and CAPEX-generated plans for cases 3 and 4, both types of plan were considered to be relatively ineffective. Indeed, the auditor in question was not prepared to make any assessments concerning the efficiency of the plans since she considered them to be ineffective.

It is important to note that assessors were asked to make a large number of judgments; for example, each banking case required 37 judgments to be made. An inspection of the overall totals at the bottom of Table 4.3 indicates a fairly close match between the judgments concerning the efficiency and effectiveness of both human and CAPEX-generated plans. Most of the independent assessors rated the solution plans of both CAPEX and the case writers as being relatively inefficient. One explanation for this may be that, in assessing the cases, they were implicitly considering the types of evidence they would typically obtain from other procedures directed towards financial statement items in other cycles. Another reason that CAPEX's audit program plans may have been perceived as being somewhat inefficient could stem from the fact that even procedures with very small sample sizes were included in the solution plan.

LIMITATIONS OF THE APPROACH USED TO EVALUATE CAPEX

While we attempted to implement a comprehensive evaluation approach, in retrospect we can identify a number of limitations of the approach. Auditors rarely develop a substantive audit program plan "cold". An audit program plan is constructed sequentially and is subject to fairly extensive revisions throughout the duration of the audit. The distinctive expertise of the auditor may not be evidenced in the initial audit program plan, but rather, may be exercised through creative revisions of a relatively generic default plan as more information becomes available (Ribar *et al.* 1991). This may suggest that, while there may be relatively little difference between the initial plans produced by individuals with significantly different levels of competence, the final plans may be significantly different.

The evaluation approach described here is a "laboratory approach". Ribar *et al.* (1991) assert that evaluation requires that the task be performed by its ultimate user rather than the expert and that the evaluation must be carried out in the "real world" in the ultimate context for which it is destined. In this regard, we are mindful of the R1/XCON experience of having a system with a 90% accuracy in the laboratory drop to a 60% accuracy in the real world, because users were unfamiliar with the system, incorrect input data was used, the problem mix was different, and so on (Feigenbaum and McCorduck 1984, p. 92). Therefore, the evaluations made of expert systems in a research environment can only be rough approximations of the results to be obtained when the systems are placed before users.

However, it is important to recognize that while performing an evaluation in the "real" environment may be necessary, it is not sufficient to guarantee that the tests performed will be adequate to completely evaluate a system. Software testing literature is filled with reports of systems in which "old" undetected errors are discovered after user acceptance testing and implementation (e.g., see Jensen and Tonies, p. 402-405). Thus, extensive field experience may be needed to assess the long term impact and acceptability of an expert system; for example, in a financial planning context, Sviokla (1986, cited in Benbasat and Nault 1988) reports that even after an evaluation the principals of the firm that developed the PlanPower expert system felt that it would take them 1-2 years to clearly assess the implications of using this expert system.

If an expert system cannot be completely evaluated in a laboratory, what is the value of laboratory evaluation activity? One way of addressing this question is to separate the issue of "prototype" evaluation from the issue of "delivery system" evaluation (Geissman and Schultz 1988). Using this distinction, the laboratory setting can be appropriate, perhaps even ideal, for prototype evaluation, with "real world" evaluation reserved for delivery systems. Ribar *et al.* (1991) describe a variety of evaluation activities, many of which are similar to conventional software testing, that were deemed to be required to evaluate a delivery system.

In the context of our laboratory evaluation, a number of potential limitations stem from the design of the cases and questionnaires used to elicit evaluation responses. A potential limitation of the input is that, while the information provided in the cases was not artificial, it was somewhat structured in its presentation and limited in its scope. Although we went to great pains to ensure that the cases would represent engaging tasks for the exercise of audit planning judgments, it is nevertheless true that, no matter how realistic it is, a case is merely a simulation of the environment, not the environment itself. Since different subjects may make significantly different assumptions to make up for missing information, cross-sectional comparisons of assessments may reflect the effects of such different assumptions.

Also, as mentioned earlier, the information provided was the minimum necessary to produce acceptable audit plans. The provision of limited information and the absence of conflicting or extraneous information could lead to attenuation of responses and more consensus than might otherwise be observable.

The writers of the cases, the generators of the case solutions, and all except one of the assessors of the case solutions were employees of the same accounting firm and were able to use firm guidance materials in making their plans and assessments. Nevertheless, we noted the absence of consensus in the audit plan assessments. This could stem from the fact that the case writers worked in Canada, while most of the solution assessors worked in the United States. Although there is considerable uniformity in the audit approaches adopted by the firm's offices in both countries, it is to be expected that there are significant differences in the interpretation and application of the standard audit approach. Although the firm's audit approach exhibits considerable structure, it still allows considerable latitude for judgment. This, in turn, could lead to considerable variations in the procedures selected and the extents specified for each procedure.

In a slightly different vein, since the cases were developed to conform to the firm's audit planning worksheet, the results might be more favorable than would be the case with a completely generic approach. Some evidence for this is provided by the ratings reported in Table 3 for Auditor 3 who was from a different firm than the other evaluators.

To the extent that both CAPEX and the cases were developed to investigate structured approaches to constructing substantive audit program plans, subjects may exhibit bias either for or against them according to their attitudes to structuring audit planning in the first place. There is some indication of this type of bias with respect to the assessment of the proposed solutions to the banking cases. One assessor objected to the structured approach to generating an audit program plan for banking clients and refused to make any assessments.

As for the questionnaire, the interpretation of scale values and the related judgments may require a level of analysis that experienced auditors are unable to provide. Most of the auditors felt relatively uneasy with the numerical scale used to assess the efficiency of a particular plan. Some of the assessors indicated that they had interpreted the efficiency assessments as efficiency with respect to achieving the target risks. In this case, a plan which resulted in an achieved risk level significantly lower than the target risk level would inevitably be considered to be relatively inefficient at achieving target risks. Thus, a plan which was considered to be ineffective would automatically be considered to be inefficient too.

Our evaluation considered a large number of individual judgments which comprise a substantive audit program for a revenue/receivables/receipts cycle. An alternative approach might be to subdivide the audit program into even smaller parts which could be investigated separately. More detailed information could then be elicited about the appropriateness of the system's handling of each part, or weaknesses in a sub-part which might otherwise be submerged in the evaluation of the whole.

A limitation of the output used in our evaluation test is that no explanations were provided for the system-produced outputs; i.e., the system's line of reasoning was not available to the auditors. Audit plans produced in practice typically contain a good deal of supporting documentation, including responses to questionnaires, checklists, and forms, and free form narratives. Also, plan preparers are available to answer questions and defend their rationale. Because of our decision to use single-blind testing, it was impossible to provide users with access to the system itself.

Clearly, while this approach to evaluation may have a higher internal validity, it carries with it some limitations with respect to external validity.

SUMMARY

The construction of CAPEX's knowledge-bases represents a significant part of the research enterprise described in this book. An equally important part of this enterprise is described in this chapter - the evaluation of CAPEX. We have noted that the overall objectives which we established for our research was to build a prototype knowledge-based system which was capable of constructing audit program plans which were acceptable to practicing auditors. This chapter presents and discusses the approach we adopted to assess whether we achieved our objective.

We consider some of the reasons why knowledge-based systems, and in particular expert systems, may present significant difficulties to any researcher who tries to rely extensively on verification tests. We argue that the specifications which are established for expert systems are often vague. Thus, establishing that an expert system is built in accordance with pre-established objectives may not constitute a very strong test of the system. As in the case of CAPEX, considerable effort needs to be expended developing validation tests.

Since CAPEX accepts various input data and processes this data against previously encoded data, we propose evaluation criteria for input data, output data and the manner in which CAPEX processes these data. Having established a set of criteria for evaluating the different aspects of CAPEX, we describe the development of our evaluation instruments. To provide CAPEX with appropriate input data we worked with a number of practicing auditors to develop six comprehensive cases. These cases were designed to provide human auditors with sufficient information to be able to construct audit programs plans since it was our intention to compare the performance of CAPEX with practicing auditors using the same "input" data.

The next task we undertook was to develop a comprehensive instrument to evaluate assertion-based audit plan. This instrument, in the form of a detailed questionnaire, was also developed in close association with practicing auditors since it was vitally important that it be comprehensible and relatively easy to complete.

Once the instruments were developed, it was necessary to decide on a suitable experimental protocol. The protocol we describe in this chapter involves the presentation of human-generated and CAPEX-generated solutions to independent auditors in a single-blinded experimental design - the auditors did not know which of the solutions was human-generated and which was CAPEX-generated.

Having discussed the evaluation instruments and the experimental methodology in some detail, we present the results of the evaluation experiments. One particular strength of our approach is that it provides for the principled evaluation of an expert system with a very large number of outputs. Unlike much previous evaluation research involving expert systems, it is not possible to establish a single criterion of correctness. It is also worth noting that we made some attempts to assess the appropriateness of the process by which CAPEX generated audit plans. However, this area needs considerable more investigation since there is some question as to whether human experts can actually assess the process by which CAPEX processes audit evidence.

There are several limitations to the evaluation approach we adopted. We attempt to highlight the principal limitations in the concluding section of the chapter. Many of our concerns relate to the complexity of the evaluation process, the quality of the case material, and the lack of "real world" testing.

Chapter 5

SUMMARY AND FUTURE RESEARCH DIRECTIONS

INTRODUCTION

The purpose of this chapter is to review the material which has been presented in the preceding chapters and discuss future research directions for the CAPEX project in particular and knowledge-based audit planning research in general.

Interest in automated audit support tools was very strong in the middle to late 1980s but has waned somewhat in recent years. In part this can be attributed to the fact that these tools proved to be very difficult and time consuming to construct. Another reason for reduced interest in automated tools is that they were oversold as systems which would replace auditors rather than as primarily research or decision support tools. Finally, significant pressures on margins in the accounting profession have led many accounting firms to shy away from the investment of money and, especially, experts' time that is required in expert systems research and development.

While the amount of investment in computer-based decision support/expert systems has been reduced, it nonetheless continues, with major development projects being pursued by all the international accounting firms. Slowly, but surely, all of the major firms are putting in place important computer-based support tools. Initially, these tools are limited in the amount of expertise embedded within them. We expect, however, that future versions will embed increasing amounts of knowledge, to the point that the systems will evolve into full-fledged knowledge-based or expert systems.

REVIEW

CAPEX was designed to construct audit program plans for firms in three different industries: banking, retailing and manufacturing. Academic auditors have utilized expert systems methodology to investigate a number of different areas of auditing. These areas include materiality determination, internal control assessment and going concern determination. To our knowledge there have only been two academic attempts to apply expert systems methodology to audit planning - CAPEX and a system which is under development by Vinze et al. (1991). The latter system does not provide for the generation of a substantive audit program plan as does CAPEX.

In addition to academic applications of expert systems methodology to auditing most of the major accounting firms have developed expert systems over the last ten years. As with the academic systems, these systems address a range of audit issues, including audit program planning (e.g., Grant Thornton's ADAPT system (Gillett, 1993), which can trace its parentage and many aspects of its structure and function to CAPEX).

CAPEX requires three different types of inputs: specifications of audit objectives, data concerning the client being audited, and parameter values for a number of variables which influence the manner in which an audit program plan is constructed. During the course of constructing an audit program plan for a particular client, CAPEX generates a trace which details every stage of the planning process. In addition, having constructed a complete plan or, at least, a plan which comes closest to achieving pre-specified audit objectives, CAPEX provides an output which details how close it has come to achieving each objective.

The audit planning methodology which lies at the heart of CAPEX is referred to as an assertion-based risk oriented approach. This approach allows for the decomposition of an overall audit objective into a number of sub-objectives, or assertions. CAPEX constructs audit program plans by constructing sub-plans for each sub-objective sequentially. This type of decomposition is a very powerful method for generating complex plans. One of the characteristics of audit planning is that actions which lead to the satisfying of one audit objective may also partially satisfy one or more other objectives. Further, there are likely to be a number of ways of satisfying each sub-objective. Thus, provision has to be made to reflect these complexities in any expert system which purports to address audit planning.

Auditing involves the collection of evidence concerning the veracity of statements made in an organization's financial statements. It is generally not possible to collect sufficient evidence to achieve absolute certainty about the completeness and accuracy of a set of financial statements. As a result, audit standards require an auditor to collect sufficient appropriate evidence to support an opinion on the financial statements in question. The notion of sufficiency relates to the fact that there will always be some finite chance that the opinion expressed by the auditor based on the evidence collected is, in fact, wrong. Uncertainty is thus an integral aspect of audit program planning and must therefore be represented in some appropriate way in any audit planning expert system.

A key component of any expert system is its knowledge-base. In an audit planning context, the knowledge-base contains knowledge which can be processed to generate audit program plans. CAPEX has a particularly rich knowledge-base which contains knowledge gleaned from a number of different sources. Another key component is the user-interface which for CAPEX supports the user in a windowing environment.

The richness of the knowledge which is represented in CAPEX can be demonstrated in a number of different ways. In the first place, the knowledge was obtained from a variety of different types of sources. Some knowledge took the form of assessments which were made by practicing auditors. Other knowledge was extracted from audit planning manuals and auditing textbooks. Although these sources initially seemed to provide a convenient way of obtaining knowledge, it was found that much of the knowledge which was available from these sources was incomplete and sometimes even inaccurate.

Another way of demonstrating the richness of the knowledge encoded in CAPEX is to detail the different types of knowledge which have to be encoded to enable CAPEX to generate audit program plans. CAPEX has to "know" about audit evidence gathering procedures, the evidence they typically provide, the reliability of that evidence, the audit objectives which are supported by the evidence, and the cost of obtaining it.

CAPEX must also be able to handle uncertain knowledge and be able to manage uncertainties. In addition, CAPEX needs to know how to construct audit program plans.

The range of different types of knowledge which have to be represented in CAPEX creates challenges both for actually representing the knowledge in such a way that different types of knowledge can be combined together and for eliciting the specific knowledge needed.

Knowledge elicitation may involve reference to auditing texts and the extraction of the factual or procedural knowledge they contain. Although this type of task would seem to be straightforward, it can often be made significantly more complex if the knowledge is incomplete or badly expressed. It is also difficult to establish a consistent terminology so that knowledge from two different sources can be effectively combined.

Although textual sources of audit knowledge provided a number of useful approaches to developing and evaluating audit program plans it was also necessary to rely on knowledgeable individuals. The need at some stage to obtain knowledge from a human being with specialist credentials is itself often problematic. Techniques which assist the providers of knowledge in determining what they know - the structure of their knowledge - are vital in such areas as audit planning.

In attempting to reduce the "bottle-neck" wherever possible, familiar structuring tools were used during the knowledge elicitation phase. This approach allowed the provider of the knowledge to concentrate on the knowledge being provided.

Although planning, as a generic task, has been investigated over many decades, there has been relatively little research into how audit planning should be carried out. CAPEX constructs audit programs in a sequential fashion taking into account the fact that many of the sub-objectives cannot be satisfied independently of other sub-objectives.

The development of effective approaches to evaluating systems of the complexity of CAPEX is important both for practice and research. For the standpoint of practice, the development of robust evaluation methodologies becomes more and more critical as knowledge-based tools are used in the construction of audit program plans. On the other hand, research into evaluation methodologies for such systems is still in its infancy.

Generally speaking, knowledge-based systems are best evaluated according to a number of different criteria. Examples of suitable evaluation criteria are correctness, robustness, usability, and reliability. Some of these criteria relate to the performance of the system, some to the structure of the system, and some to the characteristics of the interface for the individual who interacts with the system. The tests which were performed on CAPEX were primarily directed towards establishing the correctness of the outputs generated - specific audit plans for particular clients.

One of the problems which arises with respect to any system is that it may fail to generate correct outputs for a number of reasons. It may have been constructed incorrectly leading it to transform correct inputs into incorrect outputs. Such construction failures may arise from correct specifications being translated incorrectly or specifications which are incorrect in the first place. Broadly speaking, verification methodologies address questions relating to the correct translation of specifications into systems while validation methodologies focus on whether the specifications themselves are correct.

In constructing tools for evaluating CAPEX it was decided that both the outputs generated by CAPEX and the process by which CAPEX actually generated its outputs would be scrutinized. Tests were carried out to ensure the completeness of the input data, the correctness of the knowledge-base, and to ensure that the pre-specified process for generating audit program plans had been correctly implemented. Both outputs and behaviour were evaluated in terms of their "acceptability" to practicing auditors. The former tests relate to the verification of CAPEX while the latter relate to its validation.

An additional feature of the evaluation methodology was the comparison of the performance of CAPEX as evaluated directly by practicing auditors with the performance of other auditors performing the planning task with the same inputs as those provided to CAPEX. Our desire to enrich the tests in this way made it necessary for us to develop cases which provided sufficient information for the human audit planner. This approach had a number of side benefits. It ensured that there was no inherent bias in the case material favoring CAPEX over human auditors. Indeed, if anything, there was a bias in favor of the human auditors since information was included which we knew CAPEX could not process. Second this approach ensured that the information contained in the case material was correct and coherent. The cases related to three distinct industries: banking, retailing and manufacturing.

CAPEX's outputs were evaluated using an elaborate questionnaire which required the assessors make a significant number of detailed assessments of each audit program plan generated by CAPEX and a human auditors based on identical input data.

The results of the evaluation phase indicate that although in some areas CAPEX performed less well than practicing auditor in many other areas its performance was comparable.

THE FUTURE

We hope that the existence of a variety of reasonably mature research-oriented expert systems in auditing and audit planning will stimulate further research in the following areas:

- How can the existing systems be refined in the light of extensive validation testing?
- In systems which require the assessment by the user of a variety of different factors, how sensitive is the system to these assessments.
- What structural effects are there in terms of the order in which the user is asked to provide assessments?

Often such questions have been asked in experimental psychology or cognitive psychology. The potential contribution of such investigations will probably be in terms of the degree of control that an expert system environment provides to the experimental setting.

A second contribution of such research is to an understanding of how to design decision supporting tools. These tools typically support the user through the provision of knowledge-structuring tools and/or additional information. To the extent that expert systems research provides a deeper understanding of how assessments can be structured, it is likely to lead to the development of more effective decision-supporting tools.

Another general set of research questions relates to the potential impact of knowledge-based systems on the individual (s) or groups using the tool. The types of questions which would be of interest are:

- To what extent does the use of a knowledge-based system alter the user's perception of the planning problem?
- To what extent does the use of an expert system alter the process by which a user reaches a conclusion?
- How do conclusions reached using the expert system differ from conclusions reached without the use of the expert system?
- How does the use of a knowledge-based system by an individual (individuals) belonging to a group change the allocation of tasks within the group, the dynamic interaction of group members, or the quality of the solution.

Finally, it is appropriate to investigate the impact of any expert systems at the organizational level. For instance, does the extensive use of expert systems reduce the variety of approaches adopted to solving specific problems or does it stimulate such variety? The extensive use of expert systems by an organization is also likely to have an impact on the allocation of responsibility, power and rewards. Other areas which may be impacted relate to what might be termed organizational adaptability and, more generally, an organization's learning style.

It should be emphasized that CAPEX is primarily a research tool. In its present incarnation it provides a flexible platform to conduct research into audit planning. It is not restricted to only one approach to structuring audit evidence or one approach to aggregating evidential support.

STRUCTURING AUDIT EVIDENCE

Considerable research has been conducted into appropriate approaches to structuring audit evidence. The dominant approach advocated by professional regulatory bodies and by many accounting firms may be referred to as the *assertion-based* approach. This approach structures the audit problem as one which requires establishing the credibility of a number of assertions which can be made with respect to a client's financial statements. Computer-based knowledge processing tools such as CAPEX allow for the principled investigation of these types of approaches to structuring the external audit.

One way in which CAPEX has proved useful in this area is in investigating the full complexity of the assertion-based approach. Indeed, it may be argued that CAPEX potentially demonstrates that no individual is capable of fully implementing an assertion-based approach to audit planning because the demands, in terms of information availability and processing, are simply too onerous. However, the concept of assertion-based audit planning can be realized through computerized knowledge-based systems. To the extent that assertion-based auditing is a valuable approach, the development of such systems can move the entire field of auditing forward.

It is interesting to note that the problem of identifying appropriate audit assertions became particularly acute when banking audits were investigated. In these cases it became necessary to subdivide outstanding balances in a very detailed way in order to appropriately reflect the impact of the evidence provided by audit evidence-gathering procedures.

CAPEX provides a flexible platform for investigating alternative approaches to constructing an assertion hierarchy. This issue is also relevant when it comes to considering the most appropriate approach to modeling uncertainty and assessing the impact of different items of audit evidence.

INVESTIGATING ALTERNATIVE AUDIT POLICIES

As initially conceived, CAPEX is capable of developing audit program plans using two basic policies: a transaction-oriented approach and a balance-sheet approach.

The transaction-oriented approach assumes that transaction stream financial statement item assertions will be selected first and audit evidence-gathering procedures will be directed towards gathering sufficient assurance with respect to appropriate transaction stream assertions prior to any attempt being made to plan for balance sheet financial statement items.

The balance-sheet approach, involves selecting audit evidence-gathering procedures to provide sufficient assurance with respect to balance-sheet financial statement items, and taking credit for the evidential spin-offs pertaining to transaction stream assertions.

Until the advent of such automated tools as CAPEX it has not been possible to investigate the relative merits of these different policies. Different firms have firmly-held beliefs as to which policy is most appropriate, efficient, effective, etc. However, conclusions have been based on limited argument and conviction rather than extensive analysis.

CAPEX provides sufficient flexibility to allow for the adoption of a combination of the above policies. At the extreme, a policy which details the precise order in which financial statement item assertions are to be planned for can be developed. In this case, the higher level policy issue - what order are financial statement items to be planned for - is being mixed with the next level of policy making, namely: what order should assertions be planned in.

Other policy issues relate to the automatic exclusion of some audit evidence-gathering procedures. For instance, some accounting firms consider that *negative confirmations* should not be used under some or all circumstances.

ALTERNATIVE APPROACHES TO MODELLING UNCERTAINTY

One of the most complex and interesting areas of research which has been pursued in the construction of CAPEX concerns the issues relating to uncertainty or assurance modelling. There are many unanswered questions concerning these issues. In the following discussion we will start by considering the modelling of uncertainty generally and then proceed to consider more specific questions relating to auditing in general and CAPEX in particular.

Historically, a number of different approaches have been adopted to modeling uncertainty in an auditing context. Many firms and a number of researchers have adopted what is essentially a *classical* approach to uncertainty modelling. This type of approach assumes that the uncertainties which have to be modeled in auditing can be represented as classical probabilities and combined accordingly.

Many researchers and practitioners have indicated serious problems with applying the classical interpretation of the uncertainties which face an external auditor.[1] One of the most serious criticisms concerns the fact that it is difficult to interpret the meaning of classical probabilities in the auditing domain. The two dominant interpretations of classical probabilities are the frequency approach and the exhaustive equiprobable state of affairs approach. The frequency approach interprets probabilities as expressing the long term frequency of occurrence. It is extremely unlikely that all of the events with which the auditor is concerned occur often enough to establish credible frequencies. With respect to the second approach to interpreting probabilities in the classical framework, it seems unlikely that a set of exhaustive possible events can be established in order to allow the determinations of this interpretation.

In order to address some of these criticisms, researchers advocated the use of Bayesian or quasi-Bayesian approaches to modelling uncertainty. These approaches have found support in the research literature but have not been widely accepted by practitioners. Bayesian approaches face some similar problems to the classical approach. In addition, various researchers have argued that neither the classical approach nor the Bayesian approach allow for the representation of ignorance.

More recently a number of researchers have advocated using belief functions.[2] These are uncertainly modelling functions which address some of the criticisms which can be laid both at the door of classical probability and the door of Bayesian probability interpretations.

---

[1] See, for example, Boritz and Wensley (1992) who discuss these issues at considerable length. Also of interest is the work of Srivastava and Shafer (1992).

[2] See, for example, Shafer (1975), Srivastava and Shafer (1992).

CAPEX can be used to investigate the impact of such alternative approaches to representing uncertainty.

AUDIT EVIDENCE-GATHERING PROCEDURE SELECTION HEURISTICS

In addition to the higher level policy issues with respect to generating audit program plans discussed earlier, it is important to consider how audit evidence-gathering procedures are selected for possible inclusion in an audit program plan. Some of these heuristics are essentially top-down while others are bottom-up. This distinction is important to keep in mind. The advantage of systems such as CAPEX is that they can be used to investigate the impact of both types of heuristics.

The principal selection heuristic utilized by CAPEX is a bottom-up heuristic and is based on the notion of **evidential power**. Essentially, evidential power is a measure of the total quantity of evidential support provided per unit cost. Suggestions have been made for alternative heuristics (e.g., Gillett 1992a).

Gillett (1992b) has suggested that it might be interesting to investigate the performance of various genetic algorithms in this area. It also might be worth considering a revised planning approach where audit evidence-gathering procedures *compete* to be used in completing a particular audit program plan.

THE RELIABILITIES AND RELEVANCES OF THE EVIDENCE PROVIDED BY AUDIT EVIDENCE-GATHERING PROCEDURES

CAPEX provides for the determination of the reliability and relevance of procedures in a principled way. Gillett (1992a) adopted a similar approach. Gillett (1992a) also implemented an interesting approach to the determining the reliability of audit evidence by providing a measure of the diversity of audit evidence based on work done by Spires (1989) which suggests that evidence concerning the same assertion derived from different types of procedures is more persuasive than evidence of similar individual strength derived from the same type of procedure. This is an interesting approach and one which could be encoded in CAPEX by adding a heuristic called Diversity paralleling the existing heuristic which measures Evidential Power.

THE COSTS OF AUDIT EVIDENCE-GATHERING PROCEDURES

In developing CAPEX we developed a detailed approach to accounting for the costs of various audit evidence-gathering procedures. These costs were derived by taking into account a variety of factors elicited from practicing professionals and gleaned from reviews of the professional literature. Other researchers have used a different approach to developing costs associated with audit evidence-gathering procedures. Gillett (1992a) and Lynch (1988) use estimates of the time taken to complete procedures. As in the case of other characteristics of audit evidence-gathering procedures, the costs associated with all procedures are generated in a separate module within CAPEX. This allows for the flexible calculation of costs.

Clearly, it is important to calculate the costs of applying procedures in a consistent and meaningful manner. There is considerable scope for further research both into developing costs measures for substantive and analytic audit evidence-gathering procedures.

Since CAPEX is a heuristic system, it is not guaranteed to produce an optimal audit plan. It could be that a cheaper plan could meet the target levels of assurance just as well as the plan that is generated. In the absence of a linear programming or other optimizing solution to the audit planning problem it will be impossible to guarantee that the most efficient audit program was produced to meet the target levels of assurance. Nevertheless, it is possible to implement heuristics which perturb the plan in various ways and lead to improvements in terms of cost reductions without loss of the required levels of assurance. For example, one heuristic may require the system to remove the most costly procedure from a plan, adjust the levels of assurance to new levels resulting from the deletion of the particular procedure, identify the assertions falling below target levels, and attempt to satisfy the assurance targets for those assertions by either increasing the extents of procedures already in the plan or by choosing new procedures that are less expensive than the cost of adding the removed procedure back in to the plan.

USER INTERACTIONS

In as much as there has been relatively little research into the development of automated audit support tools there has also been little research into the impact of such tools on the users. One of the most exciting future areas of research involving CAPEX has to do with extensive studies of the interaction between users and CAPEX.

SUMMARY

In this final chapter of the book we review the issues which have been presented in the preceding chapters. We then pose a number of research questions, some of which relate to issues of knowledge representation and others to the impact on users of using CAPEX. Following this general identification of interesting research questions, we focus on a number of promising areas for the future development of CAPEX. We first discuss the structuring of audit evidence and note that CAPEX provides a rich environment within which to explore different approaches to structuring audit evidence. CAPEX also provides a rich and fruitful tool for investigating the impact of adopting different audit planning policies. In the past audit firms have developed and followed such policies more on faith than as a result of detailed analysis. We propose that tools like CAPEX provide an opportunity for investigating the nature of such policies in detail.

In Chapter 2 we discussed some aspects of the approach to uncertainty modeling which we have adopted in CAPEX. As we note in this chapter there are a number of different approaches which can be adopted to modeling the uncertainties associated with audit planning. Although CAPEX, as originally conceived, generally uses a Bayesian or quasi-Bayesian approach to representing uncertainty it can be adapted to reflect other approaches to modeling uncertainty, including Dempster-Shafer belief functions.

Another interesting area which is worth exploring relates to the heuristics which are used to select procedures during the construction of audit plans. CAPEX provides the researcher with an unique opportunity of investigating the efficiency and effectiveness of audit procedure selection heuristics other than the *evidential power* heuristic which lies at the heart of the audit plan construction methodology we have presented in this book.

In earlier chapters of the book we have discussed the key characteristics of audit evidence gathering procedures. We identified these characteristics as the relevance and reliability of the evidence which is provided by the procedure and the cost of applying the procedure. Although these characteristics have been discussed and analyzed by researchers in the past we propose that the building of tools like CAPEX can and should stimulate further investigation of the nature of audit evidence-gathering procedures.

Appendix 2.1

PROLOG ENCODING OF THE ACCOUNTING MODEL

ITEM

```
item(balance_sheet, asset).
item(asset, cash_Balances).
item(asset, accounts_Receivable).
item(asset, inventory).
item(asset, non_demand_Dp__and_Mkt__Sec_).
item(asset, plant).
item(asset, equipment).
item(asset, land).
item(balance_sheet, contra_asset_allocation).
item(contra_asset_allocation, allowance_for_Doubtful_Account).
item(balance_sheet, contra_asset_non_allocation).
item(contra_asset_non_allocation, write_offs).
item(contra_asset_non_allocation, plant___Accumulated_Depreciati).
item(contra_asset_non_allocation, equipment___Accumulated_Deprec).
item(balance_sheet, liability).
item(liability, accounts_Payable).
item(liability, payroll_Taxes_Payable).
item(liability, loans_Payable).
item(liability, dividends_Payable).
item(liability, income_Taxes_Payable).
item(liability, payable_Payable).
item(balance_sheet, contra_liability_allocation).
item(balance_sheet, contra_liability_non_allocation).
item(balance_sheet, owners_equity).
item(owners_equity, capital_Stock).
item(owners_equity, paid_in_Capital_in_Excess_of_P).
item(owners_equity, retained_Earnings).
item(transaction_stream, cash_disbursements).
item(cash_disbursements, cash_Disbursements).
item(transaction_stream, cash_receipts).
item(cash_receipts, cash_Receipts).
```

```
item(transaction_stream, revenue).
item(revenue, sales_Revenues).
item(revenue, interest_Revenue_from_AR).
item(transaction_stream, contra_revenue_allocation).
item(transaction_stream, contra_revenue_non_allocation).
item(contra_revenue_non_allocation, sales_Returns).
item(transaction_stream, expense).
item(expense, purchases).
item(expense, expenses).
item(expense, production_Costing).
item(expense, customer_Discounts_Taken).
item(expense, salaries_Expense).
item(expense, fringe_Benefits).
item(expense, payroll_Tax_Expense).
item(expense, bad_Debt_Expense).
item(expense, rent_Expense).
item(expense, depreciation_Expense).
item(expense, utilities_Expense).
item(expense, advertising_Expense).
item(expense, professional_Fees).
item(expense, insurance_Expense).
item(expense, supplies_Expense).
item(expense, postage_Expense).
item(expense, miscellaneous_Expense).
item(expense, interest_Expense).
item(expense, purchase_Discounts_Lost).
item(transaction_stream, contra_expense_allocation).
item(transaction_stream, contra_expense_non_allocation).
item(cash_Balances, cash_Balances_on_hand).
item(allowance_for_Doubtful_Account, allowance_for_Doubt_Acct___1).
item(sales_Revenues, sales_on_Account___2ns).
item(sales_Revenues, sales_on_Account___1s).
item(sales_Revenues, sales_on_Account___1ns).
item(accounts_Receivable, accounts_Receivable___1ns).
item(accounts_Receivable, accounts_Receivable___1s).
item(accounts_Receivable, accounts_Receivable___2ns).
item(accounts_Receivable, accounts_Receivable___2s).
```

item(allowance_for_Doubtful_Account, allowance_for_Doubt_Acct___2).
item(cash_Receipts, cash_Receipts_on_acct___2ns).
item(cash_Receipts, cash_Receipts_on_acct___2s).
item(sales_Revenues, cash_Sales___1ns).
item(cash_Balances, cash_Balances_on_deposit___ns).
item(cash_Balances, cash_Balances_on_deposit___s).
item(cash_Receipts, cash_Receipts_on_Account___1ns).
item(cash_Receipts, cash_Receipts_on_Account___1s).
item(cash_Receipts, cash_Receipts_cash_sales_1).
item(cash_Receipts, cash_Receipts___1ns).

PRIORITY

priority(cash_Balances_on_hand, existence, over, 1).
priority(cash_Balances_on_hand, completeness, under, 2).
priority(cash_Balances_on_hand, valuation_hard, over, 3).
priority(cash_Balances_on_hand, valuation_hard, under, 4).
priority(allowance_for_Doubt_Acct___1, valuation_soft, over, 1).
priority(allowance_for_Doubt_Acct___1, valuation_soft, under, 2).
priority(sales_on_Account___2ns, completeness, under, 1).
priority(sales_on_Account___2ns, occurence, over, 2).
priority(sales_on_Account___2ns, measurement_hard, over, 3).
priority(sales_on_Account___2ns, measurement_hard, under, 4).
priority(sales_on_Account___1s, completeness, under, 1).
priority(sales_on_Account___1s, occurence, over, 2).
priority(sales_on_Account___1s, measurement_hard, over, 3).
priority(sales_on_Account___1s, measurement_hard, under, 4).
priority(sales_on_Account___1ns, completeness, under, 1).
priority(sales_on_Account___1ns, occurence, over, 2).
priority(sales_on_Account___1ns, measurement_hard, over, 3).
priority(sales_on_Account___1ns, measurement_hard, under, 4).
priority(accounts_Receivable___1ns, existence, over, 1).
priority(accounts_Receivable___1ns, completeness, under, 2).
priority(accounts_Receivable___1ns, valuation_hard, over, 3).
priority(accounts_Receivable___1ns, valuation_hard, under, 4).
priority(accounts_Receivable___1s, existence, over, 1).
priority(accounts_Receivable___1s, completeness, under, 2).
priority(accounts_Receivable___1s, valuation_hard, over, 3).

```
priority(accounts_Receivable___1s, valuation_hard, under, 4).
priority(accounts_Receivable___2ns, existence, over, 1).
priority(accounts_Receivable___2ns, completeness, under, 2).
priority(accounts_Receivable___2ns, valuation_hard, over, 3).
priority(accounts_Receivable___2ns, valuation_hard, under, 4).
priority(accounts_Receivable___2s, existence, over, 1).
priority(accounts_Receivable___2s, completeness, under, 2).
priority(accounts_Receivable___2s, valuation_hard, over, 3).
priority(accounts_Receivable___2s, valuation_hard, under, 4).
priority(allowance_for_Doubt_Acct___2, valuation_soft, over, 1).
priority(allowance_for_Doubt_Acct___2, valuation_soft, under, 2).
priority(cash_Receipts_on_acct___2ns, completeness, under, 1).
priority(cash_Receipts_on_acct___2ns, occurence, over, 2).
priority(cash_Receipts_on_acct___2ns, measurement_hard, over, 3).
priority(cash_Receipts_on_acct___2ns, measurement_hard, under, 4).
priority(cash_Receipts_on_acct___2s, completeness, under, 1).
priority(cash_Receipts_on_acct___2s, occurence, over, 2).
priority(cash_Receipts_on_acct___2s, measurement_hard, over, 3).
priority(cash_Receipts_on_acct___2s, measurement_hard, under, 4).
priority(cash_Sales___1ns, completeness, under, 1).
priority(cash_Sales___1ns, occurence, over, 2).
priority(cash_Sales___1ns, measurement_hard, over, 3).
priority(cash_Sales___1ns, measurement_hard, under, 4).
priority(cash_Disbursements_type_nf, completeness, under, 1).
priority(cash_Disbursements_type_nf, occurence, over, 2).
priority(cash_Disbursements_type_nf, measurement_hard, over, 3).
priority(cash_Disbursements_type_nf, measurement_hard, under, 4).
priority(cash_Balances_on_deposit___ns, existence, over, 1).
priority(cash_Balances_on_deposit___ns, completeness, under, 2).
priority(cash_Balances_on_deposit___ns, valuation_hard, over, 3).
priority(cash_Balances_on_deposit___ns, valuation_hard, under, 4).
priority(cash_Balances_on_deposit___s, existence, over, 1).
priority(cash_Balances_on_deposit___s, completeness, under, 2).
priority(cash_Balances_on_deposit___s, valuation_hard, over, 3).
priority(cash_Balances_on_deposit___s, valuation_hard, under, 4).
priority(cash_Receipts_on_Account___1ns, completeness, under, 1).
priority(cash_Receipts_on_Account___1ns, occurence, over, 2).
```

priority(cash_Receipts_on_Account___1ns, measurement_hard, over, 3).

priority(cash_Receipts_on_Account___1ns, measurement_hard, under, 4).

priority(cash_Receipts_on_Account___1s, completeness, under, 1).

priority(cash_Receipts_on_Account___1s, occurence, over, 2).

priority(cash_Receipts_on_Account___1s, measurement_hard, over, 3).

priority(cash_Receipts_on_Account___1s, measurement_hard, under, 4).

priority(cash_Receipts_cash_sales_1, completeness, under, 1).

priority(cash_Receipts_cash_sales_1, occurence, over, 2).

priority(cash_Receipts_cash_sales_1, measurement_hard, over, 3).

priority(cash_Receipts_cash_sales_1, measurement_hard, under, 4).

priority(sales_Returns_type_nf, completeness, under, 1).

priority(sales_Returns_type_nf, occurence, over, 2).

priority(sales_Returns_type_nf, measurement_hard, over, 3).

priority(sales_Returns_type_nf, measurement_hard, under, 4).

priority(allowance_for_Doubtful_Acc_t, valuation_soft, over, 1).

priority(allowance_for_Doubtful_Acc_t, valuation_soft, under, 2).

priority(cash_Receipts_type_nf, completeness, under, 1).

priority(cash_Receipts_type_nf, occurence, over, 2).

priority(cash_Receipts_type_nf, measurement_hard, over, 3).

priority(cash_Receipts_type_nf, measurement_hard, under, 4).

priority(sales_Revenues___1ns, completeness, under, 1).

priority(sales_Revenues___1ns, occurence, over, 2).

priority(sales_Revenues___1ns, measurement_hard, over, 3).

priority(sales_Revenues___1ns, measurement_hard, under, 4).

priority(cash_Receipts___1ns, completeness, under, 1).

priority(cash_Receipts___1ns, occurence, over, 2).

priority(cash_Receipts___1ns, measurement_hard, over, 3).

priority(cash_Receipts___1ns, measurement_hard, under, 4).

INDIRECT SUPPORTING RELATIONSHIP

indirect_supporting_relationship(cash_Receipts_type_nf, occurence, over, cash_Balances_on_hand, existence, over, strong, weak).

indirect_supporting_relationship(cash_Receipts_type_nf, completeness, under, cash_Balances_on_hand, completeness, under, strong, weak).

indirect_supporting_relationship(cash_Receipts_type_nf, measurement_hard, over, cash_Balances_on_hand, valuation_hard, over, strong, weak).

indirect_supporting_relationship(cash_Receipts_type_nf, measurement_hard, under, cash_Balances_on_hand, valuation_hard, under, strong, weak).

indirect_supporting_relationship(cash_Disbursements_type_nf, completeness, under, cash_Balances_on_hand, existence, over, strong, weak).

indirect_supporting_relationship(cash_Disbursements_type_nf, occurence, over, cash_Balances_on_hand, completeness, under, strong, weak).

indirect_supporting_relationship(cash_Disbursements_type_nf, measurement_hard, over, cash_Balances_on_hand, valuation_hard, over, strong, weak).

indirect_supporting_relationship(cash_Disbursements_type_nf, measurement_hard, under, cash_Balances_on_hand, valuation_hard, under, strong, weak).

indirect_supporting_relationship(sales_Revenues___1ns, occurence, over, accounts_Receivable___1ns, existence, over, strong, weak).

indirect_supporting_relationship(sales_Revenues___1ns, completeness, under, accounts_Receivable___1ns, completeness, under, strong, weak).

indirect_supporting_relationship(sales_Revenues___1ns, measurement_hard, over, accounts_Receivable___1ns, valuation_hard, over, strong, weak).

indirect_supporting_relationship(sales_Revenues___1ns, measurement_hard, under, accounts_Receivable___1ns, valuation_hard, under, strong, weak).

indirect_supporting_relationship(cash_Receipts___1ns, completeness, under, accounts_Receivable___1ns, existence, over, strong, weak).

indirect_supporting_relationship(cash_Receipts___1ns, occurence, over, accounts_Receivable___1ns, completeness, under, strong, weak).

indirect_supporting_relationship(cash_Receipts___1ns, measurement_hard, over, accounts_Receivable___1ns, valuation_hard, over, strong, weak).

indirect_supporting_relationship(cash_Receipts___1ns, measurement_hard, under, accounts_Receivable___1ns, valuation_hard, under, strong, weak).

indirect_supporting_relationship(sales_Revenues___1ns, occurence, over, accounts_Receivable___1s, existence, over, strong, weak).

indirect_supporting_relationship(sales_Revenues___1ns, completeness, under, accounts_Receivable___1s, completeness, under, strong, weak).

indirect_supporting_relationship(sales_Revenues___1ns, measurement_hard, over, accounts_Receivable___1s, valuation_hard, over, strong, weak).

indirect_supporting_relationship(sales_Revenues___1ns, measurement_hard, under, accounts_Receivable___1s, valuation_hard, under, strong, weak).

indirect_supporting_relationship(cash_Receipts_type_nf, completeness, under, accounts_Receivable___1s, existence, over, strong, weak).

indirect_supporting_relationship(cash_Receipts_type_nf, occurence, over, accounts_Receivable___1s, completeness, under, strong, weak).

indirect_supporting_relationship(cash_Receipts_type_nf, measurement_hard, over, accounts_Receivable___1s, valuation_hard, over, strong, weak).

indirect_supporting_relationship(cash_Receipts_type_nf, measurement_hard, under, accounts_Receivable___1s, valuation_hard, under, strong, weak).

indirect_supporting_relationship(sales_Revenues___1ns, occurence, over, accounts_Receivable___2ns, existence, over, strong, weak).

indirect_supporting_relationship(sales_Revenues___1ns, completeness, under, accounts_Receivable___2ns, completeness, under, strong, weak).

indirect_supporting_relationship(sales_Revenues___1ns, measurement_hard, over, accounts_Receivable___2ns, valuation_hard, over, strong, weak).

indirect_supporting_relationship(sales_Revenues___1ns, measurement_hard, under, accounts_Receivable___2ns, valuation_hard, under, strong, weak).

indirect_supporting_relationship(cash_Receipts_type_nf, completeness, under, accounts_Receivable___2ns, existence, over, strong, weak).

indirect_supporting_relationship(cash_Receipts_type_nf, occurence, over, accounts_Receivable___2ns, completeness, under, strong, weak).

indirect_supporting_relationship(cash_Receipts_type_nf, measurement_hard, over, accounts_Receivable___2ns, valuation_hard, over, strong, weak).

indirect_supporting_relationship(cash_Receipts_type_nf, measurement_hard, under, accounts_Receivable___2ns, valuation_hard, under, strong, weak).

indirect_supporting_relationship(sales_Revenues___1ns, occurence, over, accounts_Receivable___2s, existence, over, strong, weak).

indirect_supporting_relationship(sales_Revenues___1ns, completeness, under, accounts_Receivable___2s, completeness, under, strong, weak).

indirect_supporting_relationship(sales_Revenues___1ns, measurement_hard, over, accounts_Receivable___2s, valuation_hard, over, strong, weak).

indirect_supporting_relationship(sales_Revenues___1ns, measurement_hard, under, accounts_Receivable___2s, valuation_hard, under, strong, weak).

indirect_supporting_relationship(cash_Receipts_type_nf, completeness, under, accounts_Receivable___2s, existence, over, strong, weak).

indirect_supporting_relationship(cash_Receipts_type_nf, occurence, over, accounts_Receivable___2s, completeness, under, strong, weak).

indirect_supporting_relationship(cash_Receipts_type_nf, measurement_hard, over, accounts_Receivable___2s, valuation_hard, over, strong, weak).

indirect_supporting_relationship(cash_Receipts_type_nf, measurement_hard, under, accounts_Receivable___2s, valuation_hard, under, strong, weak).

indirect_supporting_relationship(cash_Receipts_type_nf, occurence, over, cash_Balances_on_deposit___ns, existence, over, strong, weak).

indirect_supporting_relationship(cash_Receipts_type_nf, completeness, under, cash_Balances_on_deposit___ns, completeness, under, strong, weak).

indirect_supporting_relationship(cash_Receipts_type_nf, measurement_hard, over, cash_Balances_on_deposit___ns, valuation_hard, over, strong, weak).

indirect_supporting_relationship(cash_Receipts_type_nf, measurement_hard, under, cash_Balances_on_deposit___ns, valuation_hard, under, strong, weak).

indirect_supporting_relationship(cash_Disbursements_type_nf, completeness, under, cash_Balances_on_deposit___ns, existence, over, strong, weak).

indirect_supporting_relationship(cash_Disbursements_type_nf, occurence, over, cash_Balances_on_deposit___ns, completeness, under, strong, weak).

indirect_supporting_relationship(cash_Disbursements_type_nf, measurement_hard, over, cash_Balances_on_deposit___ns, valuation_hard, over, strong, weak).

indirect_supporting_relationship(cash_Disbursements_type_nf, measurement_hard, under, cash_Balances_on_deposit___ns, valuation_hard, under, strong, weak).

indirect_supporting_relationship(cash_Receipts_type_nf, occurence, over, cash_Balances_on_deposit___s, existence, over, strong, weak).

indirect_supporting_relationship(cash_Receipts_type_nf, completeness, under, cash_Balances_on_deposit___s, completeness, under, strong, weak).

indirect_supporting_relationship(cash_Receipts_type_nf, measurement_hard, over, cash_Balances_on_deposit___s, valuation_hard, over, strong, weak).

indirect_supporting_relationship(cash_Receipts_type_nf, measurement_hard, under, cash_Balances_on_deposit___s, valuation_hard, under, strong, weak).

indirect_supporting_relationship(cash_Disbursements_type_nf, completeness, under, cash_Balances_on_deposit___s, existence, over, strong, weak).

indirect_supporting_relationship(cash_Disbursements_type_nf, occurence, over, cash_Balances_on_deposit___s, completeness, under, strong, weak).

indirect_supporting_relationship(cash_Disbursements_type_nf, measurement_hard, over, cash_Balances_on_deposit___s, valuation_hard, over, strong, weak).

indirect_supporting_relationship(cash_Disbursements_type_nf, measurement_hard, under, cash_Balances_on_deposit___s, valuation_hard, under, strong, weak).

Appendix 2.2

PROLOG ENCODING OF THE PROCEDURES

DICTIONARY ENTRY

dictionary_entry(1, 'Perform cash count of cash balances - ns')

dictionary_entry(2, 'Vouch from sales items to supporting documents Type 2 - ns')

dictionary_entry(3, 'Trace from shipping documents to sales ledger Type 2 - ns')

dictionary_entry(4, 'Year end positive confirmation of sales balances and alt. proc. Type 2 - ns')

dictionary_entry(5, 'Year end negative confirmation of sales balances and alt. procs. Type 2 - ns')

dictionary_entry(6, 'Vouch from sales items to supporting documents Type 2 - sig')

dictionary_entry(7, 'Trace from shipping documents to sales ledger Type 2 - sig')

dictionary_entry(8, 'Year end positive confirmation of sales balances and alt. proc. Type 2 - sig')

dictionary_entry(9, 'Year end negative confirmation of sales balances and alt. procs. Type 2 - sig')

dictionary_entry(10, 'Vouch from sales items to supporting documents Type 1 - ns')

dictionary_entry(11, 'Trace from shipping documents to sales ledger Type 1 - ns')

dictionary_entry(12, 'Year end positive confirmation of sales balances and alt. proc. Type 1 - ns')

dictionary_entry(13, 'Year end negative confirmation of sales balances and alt. procs. Type 1 - ns')

dictionary_entry(14, 'Review subsequent receipts relating to open accounts in A/R sub-ledger at Y/E Type 1 - ns')

dictionary_entry(15, 'Vouch from items in aged Trial Balance to supporting documents Type 1 - ns')

dictionary_entry(16, ' Type 1 - ns')

dictionary_entry(17, 'Review subsequent payments against items in aged Trial Balance at Y/E. Type 1 - ns')

dictionary_entry(18, 'Review subsequent receipts relating to open accounts in A/R sub-ledger at Y/E Type 1 - sig')

dictionary_entry(19, 'Vouch from items in aged Trial Balance to supporting documents Type 1 -sig')

dictionary_entry(20, ' Type 1 - sig')

dictionary_entry(21, 'Review subsequent payments against items in aged Trial Balance at Y/E. Type 1 - sig')

dictionary_entry(22, 'Review subsequent receipts relating to open accounts in A/R sub-ledger at Y/E Type 2 - ns')

dictionary_entry(23, 'Vouch from items in aged Trial Balance to supporting documents Type 2 - ns')

dictionary_entry(24, ' Type 2 - ns')

dictionary_entry(25, 'Review subsequent payments against items in aged Trial Balance at Y/E. Type 2 - ns')

dictionary_entry(26, 'Review subsequent receipts relating to open accounts in A/R sub-ledger at Y/E Type 2 - sig')

dictionary_entry(27, 'Vouch from items in aged Trial Balance to supporting documents
Type 2 - sig')

dictionary_entry(28, ' Type 2 - sig')

dictionary_entry(29, 'Review subsequent payments against items in aged Trial Balance at Y/E. Type 2 - sig')

dictionary_entry(30, 'Year end negative confirmation of cash receipts Type 2 - ns')

dictionary_entry(31, 'Year end positive confirmation of cash receipts Type 2 - ns')

dictionary_entry(32, 'Year end negative confirmation of cash receipts Type 2 - sig')

dictionary_entry(33, 'Year end positive confirmation of cash receipts Type 2 - sig')

dictionary_entry(34, 'Vouch from sales items to supporting documents Type 1 - ns')

dictionary_entry(35, 'Trace from shipping documents to sales ledger Type 1 - ns')

dictionary_entry(36, 'Year end positive confirmation of sales balances and alt. proc.
Type 1 - ns')

dictionary_entry(37, 'Year end negative confirmation of sales balances and alt. procs.
Type 1 - ns')

dictionary_entry(38, 'Perform cash count of cash balances - ns')

dictionary_entry(39, 'Perform cash count of cash balances - sig')

dictionary_entry(40, 'Year end negative confirmation of cash receipts Type 1 - ns')

dictionary_entry(41, 'Year end positive confirmation of cash receipts Type 1 - ns')

dictionary_entry(42, 'Year end negative confirmation of cash receipts Type 1 - sig')

dictionary_entry(43, 'Year end positive confirmation of cash receipts Type 1 - sig')

dictionary_entry(44, 'Year end negative confirmation of cash receipts - ns')

dictionary_entry(45, 'Year end positive confirmation of cash receipts - ns')

dictionary_entry(46, 'Year end negative confirmation of cash receipts - ns')

dictionary_entry(47, 'Year end positive confirmation of cash receipts - ns')

dictionary_entry(48, 'Vouch from sales items to supporting documents Type 1 - ns')

dictionary_entry(49, 'Trace from shipping documents to sales ledger Type 1 - ns')

dictionary_entry(50, 'Year end positive confirmation of sales balances and alt. proc. Type 1 - ns')

dictionary_entry(51, 'Year end negative confirmation of sales balances and alt. procs. Type 1 - ns')

dictionary_entry(52, 'Year end negative confirmation of cash receipts Type 1 - ns')

dictionary_entry(53, 'Year end positive confirmation of cash receipts Type 1 - ns')

PROCTYPE

procType(1, detail).

procType(2, detail).

procType(3, detail).

procType(4, detail).

procType(5, detail).

```
procType(6, detail).
procType(7, detail).
procType(8, detail).
procType(9, detail).
procType(10, detail).
procType(11, detail).
procType(12, detail).
procType(13, detail).
procType(14, detail).
procType(15, detail).
procType(16, detail).
procType(17, detail).
procType(18, detail).
procType(19, detail).
procType(20, detail).
procType(21, detail).
procType(22, detail).
procType(23, detail).
procType(24, detail).
procType(25, detail).
procType(26, detail).
procType(27, detail).
procType(28, detail).
procType(29, detail).
procType(30, detail).
procType(31, detail).
procType(32, detail).
procType(33, detail).
procType(34, detail).
procType(35, detail).
procType(36, detail).
procType(37, detail).
procType(38, detail).
procType(39, detail).
procType(40, detail).
procType(41, detail).
procType(42, detail).
```

procType(43, detail).
procType(44, detail).
procType(45, detail).
procType(46, detail).
procType(47, detail).
procType(48, detail).
procType(49, detail).
procType(50, detail).
procType(51, detail).
procType(52, detail).

UNSAMPLED PROCEDURE

unsampled_procedure(1).
unsampled_procedure(14).
unsampled_procedure(16).
unsampled_procedure(17).
unsampled_procedure(18).
unsampled_procedure(20).
unsampled_procedure(21).
unsampled_procedure(22).
unsampled_procedure(24).
unsampled_procedure(25).
unsampled_procedure(26).
unsampled_procedure(28).
unsampled_procedure(29).
unsampled_procedure(38).
unsampled_procedure(39).

CONFLICTING PROCEDURE

conflicting_procedures(300, 301).
conflicting_procedures(302, 303).
conflicting_procedures(304, 305).
conflicting_procedures(306, 307).

FIXED EXTENT PROCEDURE

fixed_extent_procedure(none, none).

Appendix 2.3

PROLOG ENCODING OF THE PROCEDURE-ASSERTION SUPPORT MATRIX

PROC SUPPORT

proc_support(1, cash_Balances_on_hand, existence, over, strong).
proc_support(1, cash_Balances_on_hand, valuation_hard, over, strong).
proc_support(1, cash_Balances_on_hand, valuation_hard, under, strong).
proc_support(2, sales_on_Account___2ns, completeness, under, strong).
proc_support(2, sales_on_Account___2ns, occurence, over, strong).
proc_support(2, sales_on_Account___2ns, measurement_hard, over, strong).
proc_support(3, sales_on_Account___2ns, occurence, over, strong).
proc_support(3, sales_on_Account___2ns, measurement_hard, over, strong).
proc_support(4, sales_on_Account___2ns, completeness, under, strong).
proc_support(4, sales_on_Account___2ns, occurence, over, strong).
proc_support(4, sales_on_Account___2ns, measurement_hard, over, strong).
proc_support(5, sales_on_Account___2ns, completeness, under, strong).
proc_support(5, sales_on_Account___2ns, occurence, over, strong).
proc_support(5, sales_on_Account___2ns, measurement_hard, over, strong).
proc_support(6, sales_on_Account___1s, completeness, under, strong).
proc_support(6, sales_on_Account___1s, occurence, over, strong).
proc_support(6, sales_on_Account___1s, measurement_hard, over, strong).
proc_support(7, sales_on_Account___1s, occurence, over, strong).
proc_support(7, sales_on_Account___1s, measurement_hard, over, strong).
proc_support(8, sales_on_Account___1s, completeness, under, strong).
proc_support(8, sales_on_Account___1s, occurence, over, strong).
proc_support(8, sales_on_Account___1s, measurement_hard, over, strong).
proc_support(9, sales_on_Account___1s, completeness, under, strong).
proc_support(9, sales_on_Account___1s, occurence, over, strong).
proc_support(9, sales_on_Account___1s, measurement_hard, over, strong).
proc_support(10, sales_on_Account___1ns, completeness, under, strong).
proc_support(10, sales_on_Account___1ns, occurence, over, strong).
proc_support(10, sales_on_Account___1ns, measurement_hard, over, strong).
proc_support(11, sales_on_Account___1ns, occurence, over, strong).
proc_support(11, sales_on_Account___1ns, measurement_hard, over, strong).
proc_support(12, sales_on_Account___1ns, completeness, under, strong).

proc_support(12, sales_on_Account___1ns, occurence, over, strong).
proc_support(12, sales_on_Account___1ns, measurement_hard, over, strong).
proc_support(13, sales_on_Account___1ns, completeness, under, strong).
proc_support(13, sales_on_Account___1ns, occurence, over, strong).
proc_support(13, sales_on_Account___1ns, measurement_hard, over, strong).
proc_support(14, accounts_Receivable___1ns, valuation_hard, under, strong).
proc_support(15, accounts_Receivable___1ns, existence, over, strong).
proc_support(15, accounts_Receivable___1ns, valuation_hard, over, strong).
proc_support(15, accounts_Receivable___1ns, valuation_hard, under, strong).
proc_support(16, accounts_Receivable___1ns, completeness, under, strong).
proc_support(16, accounts_Receivable___1ns, valuation_hard, over, strong).
proc_support(16, accounts_Receivable___1ns, valuation_hard, under, strong).
proc_support(17, accounts_Receivable___1ns, valuation_hard, under, strong).
proc_support(18, accounts_Receivable___1s, valuation_hard, under, strong).
proc_support(19, accounts_Receivable___1s, existence, over, strong).
proc_support(19, accounts_Receivable___1s, valuation_hard, over, strong).
proc_support(19, accounts_Receivable___1s, valuation_hard, under, strong).
proc_support(20, accounts_Receivable___1s, completeness, under, strong).
proc_support(20, accounts_Receivable___1s, valuation_hard, over, strong).
proc_support(20, accounts_Receivable___1s, valuation_hard, under, strong).
proc_support(21, accounts_Receivable___1s, valuation_hard, under, strong).
proc_support(22, accounts_Receivable___2ns, valuation_hard, under, strong).
proc_support(23, accounts_Receivable___2ns, existence, over, strong).
proc_support(23, accounts_Receivable___2ns, valuation_hard, over, strong).
proc_support(23, accounts_Receivable___2ns, valuation_hard, under, strong).
proc_support(24, accounts_Receivable___2ns, completeness, under, strong).
proc_support(24, accounts_Receivable___2ns, valuation_hard, over, strong).
proc_support(24, accounts_Receivable___2ns, valuation_hard, under, strong).
proc_support(25, accounts_Receivable___2ns, valuation_hard, under, strong).
proc_support(26, accounts_Receivable___2s, valuation_hard, under, strong).
proc_support(27, accounts_Receivable___2s, existence, over, strong).
proc_support(27, accounts_Receivable___2s, valuation_hard, over, strong).
proc_support(27, accounts_Receivable___2s, valuation_hard, under, strong).
proc_support(28, accounts_Receivable___2s, completeness, under, strong).
proc_support(28, accounts_Receivable___2s, valuation_hard, over, strong).
proc_support(28, accounts_Receivable___2s, valuation_hard, under, strong).
proc_support(29, accounts_Receivable___2s, valuation_hard, under, strong).

```
proc_support(30, cash_Receipts_on_acct___2ns, completeness, under, strong).
proc_support(30, cash_Receipts_on_acct___2ns, occurence, over, strong).
proc_support(30, cash_Receipts_on_acct___2ns, measurement_hard, over, strong).
proc_support(31, cash_Receipts_on_acct___2ns, completeness, under, strong).
proc_support(31, cash_Receipts_on_acct___2ns, occurence, over, strong).
proc_support(31, cash_Receipts_on_acct___2ns, measurement_hard, over, strong).
proc_support(32, cash_Receipts_on_acct___2s, completeness, under, strong).
proc_support(32, cash_Receipts_on_acct___2s, occurence, over, strong).
proc_support(32, cash_Receipts_on_acct___2s, measurement_hard, over, strong).
proc_support(33, cash_Receipts_on_acct___2s, completeness, under, strong).
proc_support(33, cash_Receipts_on_acct___2s, occurence, over, strong).
proc_support(33, cash_Receipts_on_acct___2s, measurement_hard, over, strong).
proc_support(34, cash_Sales___1ns, completeness, under, strong).
proc_support(34, cash_Sales___1ns, occurence, over, strong).
proc_support(34, cash_Sales___1ns, measurement_hard, over, strong).
proc_support(35, cash_Sales___1ns, occurence, over, strong).
proc_support(35, cash_Sales___1ns, measurement_hard, over, strong).
proc_support(36, cash_Sales___1ns, completeness, under, strong).
proc_support(36, cash_Sales___1ns, occurence, over, strong).
proc_support(36, cash_Sales___1ns, measurement_hard, over, strong).
proc_support(37, cash_Sales___1ns, completeness, under, strong).
proc_support(37, cash_Sales___1ns, occurence, over, strong).
proc_support(37, cash_Sales___1ns, measurement_hard, over, strong).
proc_support(38, cash_Balances_on_deposit___ns, existence, over, strong).
proc_support(38, cash_Balances_on_deposit___ns, valuation_hard, over, strong).
proc_support(38, cash_Balances_on_deposit___ns, valuation_hard, under, strong).
proc_support(39, cash_Balances_on_deposit___s, existence, over, strong).
proc_support(39, cash_Balances_on_deposit___s, valuation_hard, over, strong).
proc_support(39, cash_Balances_on_deposit___s, valuation_hard, under, strong).
proc_support(40, cash_Receipts_on_Account___1ns, completeness, under, strong).
proc_support(40, cash_Receipts_on_Account___1ns, occurence, over, strong).
proc_support(40, cash_Receipts_on_Account___1ns, measurement_hard, over, strong).
proc_support(41, cash_Receipts_on_Account___1ns, completeness, under, strong).
proc_support(41, cash_Receipts_on_Account___1ns, occurence, over, strong).
proc_support(41, cash_Receipts_on_Account___1ns, measurement_hard, over, strong).
proc_support(42, cash_Receipts_on_Account___1s, completeness, under, strong).
proc_support(42, cash_Receipts_on_Account___1s, occurence, over, strong).
```

```
proc_support(42, cash_Receipts_on_Account___1s, measurement_hard, over, strong).
proc_support(43, cash_Receipts_on_Account___1s, completeness, under, strong).
proc_support(43, cash_Receipts_on_Account___1s, occurence, over, strong).
proc_support(43, cash_Receipts_on_Account___1s, measurement_hard, over, strong).
proc_support(44, cash_Receipts_cash_sales_1, completeness, under, strong).
proc_support(44, cash_Receipts_cash_sales_1, occurence, over, strong).
proc_support(44, cash_Receipts_cash_sales_1, measurement_hard, over, strong).
proc_support(45, cash_Receipts_cash_sales_1, completeness, under, strong).
proc_support(45, cash_Receipts_cash_sales_1, occurence, over, strong).
proc_support(45, cash_Receipts_cash_sales_1, measurement_hard, over, strong).
proc_support(46, cash_Receipts_type_nf, completeness, under, strong).
proc_support(46, cash_Receipts_type_nf, occurence, over, strong).
proc_support(46, cash_Receipts_type_nf, measurement_hard, over, strong).
proc_support(47, cash_Receipts_type_nf, completeness, under, strong).
proc_support(47, cash_Receipts_type_nf, occurence, over, strong).
proc_support(47, cash_Receipts_type_nf, measurement_hard, over, strong).
proc_support(48, sales_Revenues___1ns, completeness, under, strong).
proc_support(48, sales_Revenues___1ns, occurence, over, strong).
proc_support(48, sales_Revenues___1ns, measurement_hard, over, strong).
proc_support(49, sales_Revenues___1ns, occurence, over, strong).
proc_support(49, sales_Revenues___1ns, measurement_hard, over, strong).
proc_support(50, sales_Revenues___1ns, completeness, under, strong).
proc_support(50, sales_Revenues___1ns, occurence, over, strong).
proc_support(50, sales_Revenues___1ns, measurement_hard, over, strong).
proc_support(51, sales_Revenues___1ns, completeness, under, strong).
proc_support(51, sales_Revenues___1ns, occurence, over, strong).
proc_support(51, sales_Revenues___1ns, measurement_hard, over, strong).
proc_support(52, cash_Receipts___1ns, completeness, under, strong).
proc_support(52, cash_Receipts___1ns, occurence, over, strong).
proc_support(52, cash_Receipts___1ns, measurement_hard, over, strong).
proc_support(53, cash_Receipts___1ns, completeness, under, strong).
proc_support(53, cash_Receipts___1ns, occurence, over, strong).
proc_support(53, cash_Receipts___1ns, measurement_hard, over, strong).
```

Appendix 2.4

PROLOG ENCODING OF PROCEDURE RELIABILITIES

PROCEDURE RELIABILITY

```
procedure_reliability(1, 0.863636).
procedure_reliability(2, 0.863636).
procedure_reliability(3, 0.863636).
procedure_reliability(4, 0.863636).
procedure_reliability(5, 0.043182).
procedure_reliability(6, 0.863636).
procedure_reliability(7, 0.863636).
procedure_reliability(8, 0.863636).
procedure_reliability(9, 0.043182).
procedure_reliability(10, 0.863636).
procedure_reliability(11, 0.863636).
procedure_reliability(12, 0.863636).
procedure_reliability(13, 0.043182).
procedure_reliability(14, 0.950000).
procedure_reliability(15, 0.863636).
procedure_reliability(16, 0.863636).
procedure_reliability(17, 0.906818).
procedure_reliability(18, 0.950000).
procedure_reliability(19, 0.863636).
procedure_reliability(20, 0.863636).
procedure_reliability(21, 0.906818).
procedure_reliability(22, 0.950000).
procedure_reliability(23, 0.863636).
procedure_reliability(24, 0.863636).
procedure_reliability(25, 0.906818).
procedure_reliability(26, 0.950000).
procedure_reliability(27, 0.863636).
procedure_reliability(28, 0.863636).
procedure_reliability(29, 0.906818).
procedure_reliability(30, 0.043182).
procedure_reliability(31, 0.863636).
procedure_reliability(32, 0.043182).
```

```
procedure_reliability(33, 0.863636).
procedure_reliability(34, 0.863636).
procedure_reliability(35, 0.863636).
procedure_reliability(36, 0.863636).
procedure_reliability(37, 0.043182).
procedure_reliability(38, 0.863636).
procedure_reliability(39, 0.863636).
procedure_reliability(40, 0.043182).
procedure_reliability(41, 0.863636).
procedure_reliability(42, 0.043182).
procedure_reliability(43, 0.863636).
procedure_reliability(44, 0.043182).
procedure_reliability(45, 0.863636).
procedure_reliability(46, 0.043182).
procedure_reliability(47, 0.863636).
procedure_reliability(48, 0.863636).
procedure_reliability(49, 0.863636).
procedure_reliability(50, 0.863636).
procedure_reliability(51, 0.043182).
procedure_reliability(52, 0.043182).
procedure_reliability(53, 0.863636).
```

Appendix 2.5

PROLOG ENCODING OF PROCEDURE COSTS

PROCEDURE SET UP COST

```
procedure_set_up_cost(1, 0.0).
procedure_set_up_cost(10, 0.0).
procedure_set_up_cost(11, 0.0).
procedure_set_up_cost(12, 0.0).
procedure_set_up_cost(13, 0.0).
procedure_set_up_cost(14, 0.0).
procedure_set_up_cost(15, 0.0).
procedure_set_up_cost(16, 0.0).
procedure_set_up_cost(17, 0.0).
procedure_set_up_cost(18, 0.0).
procedure_set_up_cost(19, 0.0).
procedure_set_up_cost(2, 0.0).
procedure_set_up_cost(20, 0.0).
procedure_set_up_cost(21, 0.0).
procedure_set_up_cost(22, 0.0).
procedure_set_up_cost(23, 0.0).
procedure_set_up_cost(24, 0.0).
procedure_set_up_cost(25, 0.0).
procedure_set_up_cost(26, 0.0).
procedure_set_up_cost(27, 0.0).
procedure_set_up_cost(28, 0.0).
procedure_set_up_cost(29, 0.0).
procedure_set_up_cost(3, 0.0).
procedure_set_up_cost(30, 0.0).
procedure_set_up_cost(31, 0.0).
procedure_set_up_cost(32, 0.0).
procedure_set_up_cost(33, 0.0).
procedure_set_up_cost(34, 0.0).
procedure_set_up_cost(35, 0.0).
procedure_set_up_cost(36, 0.0).
procedure_set_up_cost(37, 0.0).
procedure_set_up_cost(38, 0.0).
```

```
procedure_set_up_cost(39, 0.0).
procedure_set_up_cost(4, 0.0).
procedure_set_up_cost(40, 0.0).
procedure_set_up_cost(41, 0.0).
procedure_set_up_cost(42, 0.0).
procedure_set_up_cost(43, 0.0).
procedure_set_up_cost(44, 0.0).
procedure_set_up_cost(45, 0.0).
procedure_set_up_cost(46, 0.0).
procedure_set_up_cost(47, 0.0).
procedure_set_up_cost(48, 0.0).
procedure_set_up_cost(49, 0.0).
procedure_set_up_cost(5, 0.0).
procedure_set_up_cost(50, 0.0).
procedure_set_up_cost(51, 0.0).
procedure_set_up_cost(52, 0.0).
procedure_set_up_cost(53, 0.0).
procedure_set_up_cost(6, 0.0).
procedure_set_up_cost(7, 0.0).
procedure_set_up_cost(8, 0.0).
procedure_set_up_cost(9, 0.0).
```

PROCEDURE VARIABLE COST

```
procedure_variable_cost(1, 12.0).
procedure_variable_cost(10, 10.0).
procedure_variable_cost(11, 10.0).
procedure_variable_cost(12, 1.0).
procedure_variable_cost(13, 1.0).
procedure_variable_cost(14, 12.0).
procedure_variable_cost(15, 10.0).
procedure_variable_cost(16, 10.0).
procedure_variable_cost(17, 12.0).
procedure_variable_cost(18, 12.0).
procedure_variable_cost(19, 10.0).
procedure_variable_cost(2, 10.0).
procedure_variable_cost(20, 10.0).
procedure_variable_cost(21, 12.0).
```

```
procedure_variable_cost(22, 12.0).
procedure_variable_cost(23, 10.0).
procedure_variable_cost(24, 10.0).
procedure_variable_cost(25, 12.0).
procedure_variable_cost(26, 12.0).
procedure_variable_cost(27, 10.0).
procedure_variable_cost(28, 10.0).
procedure_variable_cost(29, 12.0).
procedure_variable_cost(3, 10.0).
procedure_variable_cost(30, 1.0).
procedure_variable_cost(31, 10.0).
procedure_variable_cost(32, 1.0).
procedure_variable_cost(33, 10.0).
procedure_variable_cost(34, 10.0).
procedure_variable_cost(35, 10.0).
procedure_variable_cost(36, 1.0).
procedure_variable_cost(37, 1.0).
procedure_variable_cost(38, 12.0).
procedure_variable_cost(39, 12.0).
procedure_variable_cost(4, 1.0).
procedure_variable_cost(40, 1.0).
procedure_variable_cost(41, 10.0).
procedure_variable_cost(42, 1.0).
procedure_variable_cost(43, 10.0).
procedure_variable_cost(44, 1.0).
procedure_variable_cost(45, 10.0).
procedure_variable_cost(46, 1.0).
procedure_variable_cost(47, 10.0).
procedure_variable_cost(48, 10.0).
procedure_variable_cost(49, 10.0).
procedure_variable_cost(5, 1.0).
procedure_variable_cost(50, 1.0).
procedure_variable_cost(51, 1.0).
procedure_variable_cost(52, 1.0).
procedure_variable_cost(53, 10.0).
procedure_variable_cost(6, 10.0).
procedure_variable_cost(7, 10.0).
procedure_variable_cost(8, 1.0).
```

Appendix 2.6

PROLOG ENCODING OF CLIENT SPECIFIC KNOWLEDGE

PARAMETERS

```
assurance_revision_method(bayesian).

minimum_mandatory_sampling_confidence_factor(0.65).
maximum_sampling_confidence_factor(0.980000).
minimum_sampling_confidence_factor(0.0).

maximum_indirect_assurance_for_derived_item(0.950000).
maximum_indirect_assurance_for_generating_item(0.750000).
maximum_singular_indirect_assurance(0.95).
maximum_total_indirect_assurance(0.95).

recurse_depth(2).
materiality(0).
maximumTolerableError(0.000000).
```

NUMBER OF ITEMS

```
number_of_items(cash_Balances_on_hand, 2).
number_of_items(allowance_for_Doubt_Acct___1, 3).
number_of_items(sales_on_Account___2ns, 171).
number_of_items(sales_on_Account___1s, 88).
number_of_items(sales_on_Account___1ns, 187).
number_of_items(accounts_Receivable___1ns, 26).
number_of_items(accounts_Receivable___1s, 14).
number_of_items(accounts_Receivable___2ns, 22).
number_of_items(accounts_Receivable___2s, 14).
number_of_items(allowance_for_Doubt_Acct___2, 2).
number_of_items(cash_Receipts_on_acct___2ns, 114).
number_of_items(cash_Receipts_on_acct___2s, 36).
number_of_items(cash_Sales___1ns, 10).
number_of_items(cash_Disbursements_type_nf, 10).
number_of_items(cash_Balances_on_deposit___ns, 2).
number_of_items(cash_Balances_on_deposit___s, 1).
```

number_of_items(cash_Receipts_on_Account___1ns, 135).
number_of_items(cash_Receipts_on_Account___1s, 45).
number_of_items(cash_Receipts_cash_sales_1, 10).
number_of_items(sales_Returns_type_nf, 10).
number_of_items(allowance_for_Doubtful_Acc_t, 0).
number_of_items(cash_Receipts_type_nf, 0).
number_of_items(sales_Revenues___1ns, 0).
number_of_items(cash_Receipts___1ns, 0).

TARGET ASSURANCE

target_assurance(cash_Balances_on_hand, existence, over, 0.980000).
target_assurance(cash_Balances_on_hand, completeness, under, 0.980000).
target_assurance(cash_Balances_on_hand, valuation_hard, over, 0.980000).
target_assurance(cash_Balances_on_hand, valuation_hard, under, 0.980000).
target_assurance(allowance_for_Doubt_Acct___1, valuation_soft, over, 0.960000).
target_assurance(allowance_for_Doubt_Acct___1, valuation_soft, under, 0.960000).
target_assurance(sales_on_Account___2ns, completeness, under, 0.870000).
target_assurance(sales_on_Account___2ns, occurence, over, 0.870000).
target_assurance(sales_on_Account___2ns, measurement_hard, over, 0.870000).
target_assurance(sales_on_Account___2ns, measurement_hard, under, 0.870000).
target_assurance(sales_on_Account___1s, completeness, under, 0.870000).
target_assurance(sales_on_Account___1s, occurence, over, 0.870000).
target_assurance(sales_on_Account___1s, measurement_hard, over, 0.870000).
target_assurance(sales_on_Account___1s, measurement_hard, under, 0.870000).
target_assurance(sales_on_Account___1ns, completeness, under, 0.870000).
target_assurance(sales_on_Account___1ns, occurence, over, 0.870000).
target_assurance(sales_on_Account___1ns, measurement_hard, over, 0.870000).
target_assurance(sales_on_Account___1ns, measurement_hard, under, 0.870000).
target_assurance(accounts_Receivable___1ns, existence, over, 0.990000).
target_assurance(accounts_Receivable___1ns, completeness, under, 0.990000).
target_assurance(accounts_Receivable___1ns, valuation_hard, over, 0.990000).
target_assurance(accounts_Receivable___1ns, valuation_hard, under, 0.990000).
target_assurance(accounts_Receivable___1s, existence, over, 0.990000).
target_assurance(accounts_Receivable___1s, completeness, under, 0.990000).
target_assurance(accounts_Receivable___1s, valuation_hard, over, 0.990000).
target_assurance(accounts_Receivable___1s, valuation_hard, under, 0.990000).
target_assurance(accounts_Receivable___2ns, existence, over, 0.990000).

target_assurance(accounts_Receivable___2ns, completeness, under, 0.990000).

target_assurance(accounts_Receivable___2ns, valuation_hard, over, 0.990000).

target_assurance(accounts_Receivable___2ns, valuation_hard, under, 0.990000).

target_assurance(accounts_Receivable___2s, existence, over, 0.990000).

target_assurance(accounts_Receivable___2s, completeness, under, 0.990000).

target_assurance(accounts_Receivable___2s, valuation_hard, over, 0.990000).

target_assurance(accounts_Receivable___2s, valuation_hard, under, 0.990000).

target_assurance(allowance_for_Doubt_Acct___2, valuation_soft, over, 0.980000).

target_assurance(allowance_for_Doubt_Acct___2, valuation_soft, under, 0.980000).

target_assurance(cash_Receipts_on_acct___2ns, completeness, under, 0.870000).

target_assurance(cash_Receipts_on_acct___2ns, occurence, over, 0.870000).

target_assurance(cash_Receipts_on_acct___2ns, measurement_hard, over, 0.870000).

target_assurance(cash_Receipts_on_acct___2ns, measurement_hard, under, 0.870000).

target_assurance(cash_Receipts_on_acct___2s, completeness, under, 0.870000).

target_assurance(cash_Receipts_on_acct___2s, occurence, over, 0.870000).

target_assurance(cash_Receipts_on_acct___2s, measurement_hard, over, 0.870000).

target_assurance(cash_Receipts_on_acct___2s, measurement_hard, under, 0.870000).

target_assurance(cash_Sales___1ns, completeness, under, 0.750000).

target_assurance(cash_Sales___1ns, occurence, over, 0.750000).

target_assurance(cash_Sales___1ns, measurement_hard, over, 0.750000).

target_assurance(cash_Sales___1ns, measurement_hard, under, 0.750000).

target_assurance(cash_Disbursements_type_nf, completeness, under, 0.750000).

target_assurance(cash_Disbursements_type_nf, occurence, over, 0.750000).

target_assurance(cash_Disbursements_type_nf, measurement_hard, over, 0.750000).

target_assurance(cash_Disbursements_type_nf, measurement_hard, under, 0.750000).

target_assurance(cash_Balances_on_deposit___ns, existence, over, 0.990000).

target_assurance(cash_Balances_on_deposit___ns, completeness, under, 0.990000).

target_assurance(cash_Balances_on_deposit___ns, valuation_hard, over, 0.990000).

target_assurance(cash_Balances_on_deposit___ns, valuation_hard, under, 0.990000).

target_assurance(cash_Balances_on_deposit___s, existence, over, 0.990000).

target_assurance(cash_Balances_on_deposit___s, completeness, under, 0.990000).

target_assurance(cash_Balances_on_deposit___s, valuation_hard, over, 0.990000).

target_assurance(cash_Balances_on_deposit___s, valuation_hard, under, 0.990000).

target_assurance(cash_Receipts_on_Account___1ns, completeness, under, 0.870000).

target_assurance(cash_Receipts_on_Account___1ns, occurence, over, 0.870000).

target_assurance(cash_Receipts_on_Account___1ns, measurement_hard, over, 0.870000).

target_assurance(cash_Receipts_on_Account___1ns, measurement_hard, under, 0.870000).

target_assurance(cash_Receipts_on_Account___1s, completeness, under, 0.870000).
target_assurance(cash_Receipts_on_Account___1s, occurence, over, 0.870000).
target_assurance(cash_Receipts_on_Account___1s, measurement_hard, over, 0.870000).
target_assurance(cash_Receipts_on_Account___1s, measurement_hard, under, 0.870000).
target_assurance(cash_Receipts_cash_sales_1, completeness, under, 0.870000).
target_assurance(cash_Receipts_cash_sales_1, occurence, over, 0.870000).
target_assurance(cash_Receipts_cash_sales_1, measurement_hard, over, 0.870000).
target_assurance(cash_Receipts_cash_sales_1, measurement_hard, under, 0.870000).
target_assurance(sales_Returns_type_nf, completeness, under, 0.750000).
target_assurance(sales_Returns_type_nf, occurence, over, 0.750000).
target_assurance(sales_Returns_type_nf, measurement_hard, over, 0.750000).
target_assurance(sales_Returns_type_nf, measurement_hard, under, 0.950000).
target_assurance(allowance_for_Doubtful_Acc_t, valuation_soft, over, 0.950000).
target_assurance(allowance_for_Doubtful_Acc_t, valuation_soft, under, 0.950000).
target_assurance(cash_Receipts_type_nf, completeness, under, 0.850000).
target_assurance(cash_Receipts_type_nf, occurence, over, 0.900000).
target_assurance(cash_Receipts_type_nf, measurement_hard, over, 0.850000).
target_assurance(cash_Receipts_type_nf, measurement_hard, under, 0.850000).
target_assurance(sales_Revenues___1ns, completeness, under, 0.960000).
target_assurance(sales_Revenues___1ns, occurence, over, 0.950000).
target_assurance(sales_Revenues___1ns, measurement_hard, over, 0.950000).
target_assurance(sales_Revenues___1ns, measurement_hard, under, 0.950000).
target_assurance(cash_Receipts___1ns, completeness, under, 0.850000).
target_assurance(cash_Receipts___1ns, occurence, over, 0.900000).
target_assurance(cash_Receipts___1ns, measurement_hard, over, 0.850000).
target_assurance(cash_Receipts___1ns, measurement_hard, under, 0.850000).

PRIOR ASSURANCE

prior_assurance(cash_Balances_on_hand, existence, over, 0.640000).
prior_assurance(cash_Balances_on_hand, completeness, under, 0.330000).
prior_assurance(cash_Balances_on_hand, valuation_hard, over, 0.640000).
prior_assurance(cash_Balances_on_hand, valuation_hard, under, 0.330000).
prior_assurance(allowance_for_Doubt_Acct___1, valuation_soft, over, 0.640000).
prior_assurance(allowance_for_Doubt_Acct___1, valuation_soft, under, 0.640000).
prior_assurance(sales_on_Account___2ns, completeness, under, 0.580000).
prior_assurance(sales_on_Account___2ns, occurence, over, 0.580000).
prior_assurance(sales_on_Account___2ns, measurement_hard, over, 0.580000).

prior_assurance(sales_on_Account___2ns, measurement_hard, under, 0.580000).
prior_assurance(sales_on_Account___1s, completeness, under, 0.580000).
prior_assurance(sales_on_Account___1s, occurence, over, 0.580000).
prior_assurance(sales_on_Account___1s, measurement_hard, over, 0.580000).
prior_assurance(sales_on_Account___1s, measurement_hard, under, 0.580000).
prior_assurance(sales_on_Account___1ns, completeness, under, 0.580000).
prior_assurance(sales_on_Account___1ns, occurence, over, 0.580000).
prior_assurance(sales_on_Account___1ns, measurement_hard, over, 0.580000).
prior_assurance(sales_on_Account___1ns, measurement_hard, under, 0.580000).
prior_assurance(accounts_Receivable___1ns, existence, over, 0.580000).
prior_assurance(accounts_Receivable___1ns, completeness, under, 0.580000).
prior_assurance(accounts_Receivable___1ns, valuation_hard, over, 0.580000).
prior_assurance(accounts_Receivable___1ns, valuation_hard, under, 0.580000).
prior_assurance(accounts_Receivable___1s, existence, over, 0.580000).
prior_assurance(accounts_Receivable___1s, completeness, under, 0.580000).
prior_assurance(accounts_Receivable___1s, valuation_hard, over, 0.580000).
prior_assurance(accounts_Receivable___1s, valuation_hard, under, 0.580000).
prior_assurance(accounts_Receivable___2ns, existence, over, 0.580000).
prior_assurance(accounts_Receivable___2ns, completeness, under, 0.580000).
prior_assurance(accounts_Receivable___2ns, valuation_hard, over, 0.580000).
prior_assurance(accounts_Receivable___2ns, valuation_hard, under, 0.580000).
prior_assurance(accounts_Receivable___2s, existence, over, 0.580000).
prior_assurance(accounts_Receivable___2s, completeness, under, 0.580000).
prior_assurance(accounts_Receivable___2s, valuation_hard, over, 0.580000).
prior_assurance(accounts_Receivable___2s, valuation_hard, under, 0.580000).
prior_assurance(allowance_for_Doubt_Acct___2, valuation_soft, over, 0.780000).
prior_assurance(allowance_for_Doubt_Acct___2, valuation_soft, under, 0.780000).
prior_assurance(cash_Receipts_on_acct___2ns, completeness, under, 0.580000).
prior_assurance(cash_Receipts_on_acct___2ns, occurence, over, 0.780000).
prior_assurance(cash_Receipts_on_acct___2ns, measurement_hard, over, 0.800000).
prior_assurance(cash_Receipts_on_acct___2ns, measurement_hard, under, 0.580000).
prior_assurance(cash_Receipts_on_acct___2s, completeness, under, 0.580000).
prior_assurance(cash_Receipts_on_acct___2s, occurence, over, 0.800000).
prior_assurance(cash_Receipts_on_acct___2s, measurement_hard, over, 0.800000).
prior_assurance(cash_Receipts_on_acct___2s, measurement_hard, under, 0.580000).
prior_assurance(cash_Sales___1ns, completeness, under, 0.330000).
prior_assurance(cash_Sales___1ns, occurence, over, 0.640000).

prior_assurance(cash_Sales___1ns, measurement_hard, over, 0.640000).
prior_assurance(cash_Sales___1ns, measurement_hard, under, 0.330000).
prior_assurance(cash_Disbursements_type_nf, completeness, under, 0.750000).
prior_assurance(cash_Disbursements_type_nf, occurence, over, 0.750000).
prior_assurance(cash_Disbursements_type_nf, measurement_hard, over, 0.750000).
prior_assurance(cash_Disbursements_type_nf, measurement_hard, under, 0.750000).
prior_assurance(cash_Balances_on_deposit___ns, existence, over, 0.800000).
prior_assurance(cash_Balances_on_deposit___ns, completeness, under, 0.580000).
prior_assurance(cash_Balances_on_deposit___ns, valuation_hard, over, 0.800000).
prior_assurance(cash_Balances_on_deposit___ns, valuation_hard, under, 0.580000).
prior_assurance(cash_Balances_on_deposit___s, existence, over, 0.800000).
prior_assurance(cash_Balances_on_deposit___s, completeness, under, 0.580000).
prior_assurance(cash_Balances_on_deposit___s, valuation_hard, over, 0.800000).
prior_assurance(cash_Balances_on_deposit___s, valuation_hard, under, 0.580000).
prior_assurance(cash_Receipts_on_Account___1ns, completeness, under, 0.580000).
prior_assurance(cash_Receipts_on_Account___1ns, occurence, over, 0.800000).
prior_assurance(cash_Receipts_on_Account___1ns, measurement_hard, over, 0.800000).
prior_assurance(cash_Receipts_on_Account___1ns, measurement_hard, under, 0.580000).
prior_assurance(cash_Receipts_on_Account___1s, completeness, under, 0.580000).
prior_assurance(cash_Receipts_on_Account___1s, occurence, over, 0.800000).
prior_assurance(cash_Receipts_on_Account___1s, measurement_hard, over, 0.800000).
prior_assurance(cash_Receipts_on_Account___1s, measurement_hard, under, 0.580000).
prior_assurance(cash_Receipts_cash_sales_1, completeness, under, 0.330000).
prior_assurance(cash_Receipts_cash_sales_1, occurence, over, 0.640000).
prior_assurance(cash_Receipts_cash_sales_1, measurement_hard, over, 0.640000).
prior_assurance(cash_Receipts_cash_sales_1, measurement_hard, under, 0.330000).
prior_assurance(sales_Returns_type_nf, completeness, under, 0.640000).
prior_assurance(sales_Returns_type_nf, occurence, over, 0.640000).
prior_assurance(sales_Returns_type_nf, measurement_hard, over, 0.640000).
prior_assurance(sales_Returns_type_nf, measurement_hard, under, 0.000000).
prior_assurance(allowance_for_Doubtful_Acc_t, valuation_soft, over, 0.000000).
prior_assurance(allowance_for_Doubtful_Acc_t, valuation_soft, under, 0.000000).
prior_assurance(cash_Receipts_type_nf, completeness, under, 0.000000).
prior_assurance(cash_Receipts_type_nf, occurence, over, 0.000000).
prior_assurance(cash_Receipts_type_nf, measurement_hard, over, 0.000000).
prior_assurance(cash_Receipts_type_nf, measurement_hard, under, 0.000000).
prior_assurance(sales_Revenues___1ns, completeness, under, 0.000000).

prior_assurance(sales_Revenues___1ns, occurence, over, 0.000000).
prior_assurance(sales_Revenues___1ns, measurement_hard, over, 0.000000).
prior_assurance(sales_Revenues___1ns, measurement_hard, under, 0.000000).
prior_assurance(cash_Receipts___1ns, completeness, under, 0.000000).
prior_assurance(cash_Receipts___1ns, occurence, over, 0.000000).
prior_assurance(cash_Receipts___1ns, measurement_hard, over, 0.000000).

Appendix 2.7

PROLOG PROGRAMME FOR GENERATING THE PLAN

GENERATE PLAN.

```
***************************************************************************/
generatePlan :-
   telling(Output_stream),
   tell('plan.did'),
   assert(procedure_completed(none, none, none, none, none, none)),
   assert(direct_assurance(none, none, none, none, none, none)),
   assert(indirect_assurance(none, none, none, none, none, none, none)),
   assert(assuranceNumber(0)),
   applyMandatoryProcedures,
   generatePlanForCriticalAssertions(transaction_stream),
   generatePlanForNonCriticalAssertions(transaction_stream),
   generatePlanForCriticalAssertions(balance_sheet),
   generatePlanForNonCriticalAssertions(balance_sheet),
   retract(indirect_assurance(none, none, none, none, none, none, none)),
   retract(direct_assurance(none, none, none, none, none, none)),
   retract(procedure_completed(none, none, none, none, none, none)),
   tell(Output_stream),
   !.


/****************************************************************************/

generatePlanForCriticalAssertions(Type) :-
   listPrint([nl, nl, 'Generating plan for critical ', Type, ' assertions',
           nl]),
   createListOfCriticalAssertions(Type, List),
   generatePlanForAssertions(List),
   !.
```

```
generatePlanForNonCriticalAssertions(Type) :-
    listPrint([nl, nl, 'Generating plan for non-critical ', Type,
            ' assertions', nl]),
    createListOfNonCriticalAssertions(Type, List),
    generatePlanForAssertions(List),
    !.


generatePlanForAssertions([]).
generatePlanForAssertions([[_, Assertion] | Rest]) :-
    planForAssertion(Assertion, 1),
    generatePlanForAssertions(Rest),
    !.


planForAssertion([Item, Assertion, UnderOver], _) :-
    listPrint([nl, nl, 'Planning for ', Item, ' ', Assertion, ' ', UnderOver,
            nl]),
    getAchievedAssurance(Item, Assertion, UnderOver, Achieved),
    getTargetAssurance(Item, Assertion, UnderOver, Target),
    listPrint(['Target is   ', Target, nl]),
    listPrint(['Achieved is ', Achieved, nl]),
    Achieved >= Target,
    !.
planForAssertion([Item, Assertion, UnderOver], _) :-
    uncompletedDiscretionaryProcedure(Proc, Item, Assertion, UnderOver),
    not(conflictingProcedureCompleted(Proc)),
    applyProcedure(Proc, Item, Assertion, UnderOver),
    fail.
planForAssertion(Assertion, Depth) :-
    recurse_depth(MaxDepth),
    Depth < MaxDepth,
    NewDepth is Depth + 1,
    planForAssertion(Assertion, NewDepth).
planForAssertion(_, _).
```

Appendix 3.1

RELEVANCE MATRIX FOR AUDIT EVIDENCE GATHERING PROCEDURES

	OVER STATEMENT													UNDER STATEMENT												
	A/ R		DA	Ret.		W. offs		Reven.		C.R.		C.Bal		A/R		D A	Ret.		W. offs		Reven.		C.R.		C.Bal	
	E	A	V	O	A	O	A	O	M	O	M	E	M	C	A	V	C	A	C	A	C	M	C	M	C	M
N* M=MANDATORY, MC=MANDATORY CONDITIONAL, D=DISCRETIONARY, DC=DISCRETIONARY CONDITIONAL, S* SAMPLING=S, NON-SAMPLING=NS, R=RECONCILIATION																										
GENERAL																										
Agree supporting schedules to trial balance and subsidiary records																										
Verify mathematical accuracy of all relevant supporting schedules																										
MANUFACTURING																										
Positive confirmation of A/R balance (invoices)	S	S																								
Positive confirmation of A/R balance (balances)	S	S																								
Negative confirmation of A/R balance (invoices) given reasonable conscientious response rate	S	S																								
Negative confirmation of A/R balance (balances) given reasonable conscientious response rate	S	S																								
A/R SUB-LEDGER BY ENTRY TYPE																										
MANDATORY PROCEDURES																										
Review A/R sub-ledger for large or unusual receivables																										
Review credit balances in accounts receivable																										
Reconcile A/R sub-ledger to aged trial balance																										
RECONCILIATION PROCEDURES																										
Reconcile A/R sub-ledger to general ledger*																										

	OVER STATEMENT													UNDER STATEMENT												
	A/ R		DA	Ret.		W. offs		Reven.		C.R.		C.Bal		A/R		D A	Ret.		W. offs		Reven.		C.R.		C.Bal	
	E	**A**	**V**	**O**	**A**	**O**	**A**	**O**	**M**	**O**	**M**	**E**	**M**	**C**	**A**	**V**	**C**	**A**	**C**	**A**	**C**	**M**	**C**	**M**	**C**	**M**
1. SALES																										
Vouch from A/R sub-ledger to sales invoice and support docs. (quantity, price, date, customer)	S	S																								
Trace from shipping invoices to A/R sub-ledger																										
Examine subsequent payments in A/R sub-ledger (customer, invoice no., amount, date)	S	S																								
AGED TRIAL BALANCE																										
MANDATORY PROCEDURES																										
Recomputation of A/R trial balance																										
RECONCILIATION/VERIFICATION PROCEDURES																										
Reconcile aged trial balance with general ledger																										
Verify ageing of the aged trial balance																										
Reconcile aged trial balance to AR sub-ledger																										
Review aged trial balance for large or unusual receivables																										
DISCRETIONARY PROCEDURES																										
Vouch from aged trial balance to sales recording doc. and support doc. (customer, invoice no., amount)	S	S																								
Trace from shipping invoice to aged trail balance																										
PAYMENTS ON ACCOUNT																										
Examine subsequent payments on account in ageing	S		S																							
SALES LEDGER																										
Vouch writeoffs in sales ledger to support docs. (customer, amount, date)						S	S																			
Vouch from sales ledger debits to cash recording doc. (remitt. adv) (customer, invoice no., amount, date)										S	S															
Positive confirmation of sales balances								S	S																	
Reviewing sales contracts								S	S																	
CUTOFF																										
Verify cutoff of sales								S	S																	
Verifying cash receipts cutoff										S	S															
Verify cutoff of returns				S	S																					
Verify cutoff of writeoffs						S	S																			

	OVER STATEMENT													UNDER STATEMENT												
	A/ R		DA	Ret.		W. offs		Reven.		C.R.		C.Bal		A/R		D A	Ret.		W. offs		Reven.		C.R.		C.Bal	
	E	**A**	**V**	**O**	**A**	**O**	**A**	**O**	**M**	**O**	**M**	**E**	**M**	**C**	**A**	**V**	**C**	**A**	**C**	**A**	**C**	**M**	**C**	**M**	**C**	**M**
RECORDED RETURNS																										
Vouch from sales-ledger detail (returns) to recorded returns (customer, invoice no., amount, date)				S	S																					
Trace from sales returns journal to sales ledger/AR details																										
Trace from sales returns journal to aged trial balance																										
CASH RECEIPTS																										
Performing cash count												S	S													
Obtaining bank confirmation of cash balance												S	S													
Vouch from g/l to remittance advice file																										
Vouch from g/l to A/R details																										
REMITTANCE ADVICE FILE																										
Tracing from Remittance advice to A/R details	S	S																								
Tracing from Remittance advice to g/l details										S	S															
CREDIT NOTES FILE																										
Vouch from C/N file to recorded returns																										
Review credit notes subsequent to year end																										
Vouch from C/N file to A/R																										
BAD DEBTS																										
Vouch recovery of bad debts recovered during the year						S	S																			
WRITEOFFS																										
Vouch writeoffs to reasons for writeoffs						S	S																			
ANALYTIC																										
The relevant client specific variables are: 1. Quality of client's records 2. Complexity of client's records 3. Quality of relationship																										

	OVER STATEMENT													UNDER STATEMENT												
	A/ R		DA	Ret.		W. offs		Reven.		C.R.		C.Bal		A/R		D A	Ret.		W. offs		Reven.		C.R.		C.Bal	
	E	A	V	O	A	O	A	O	M	O	M	E	M	C	A	V	C	A	C	A	C	M	C	M	C	M
SALES - Completeness, Existence, Measurement (under/over) One approach in this section is to list the possible relationships between variables and require that the user assesses their strength. It should then be possible to determine the assurance that can be derived from the application of each analytic review procedure for that particular client. There may be a problem here over the frequency of data available, however. There is again the need to consider the reliability of the other variables which may be used in the analytic review procedure. Essentially we look for relationships that have a predictable structure - either in terms of constancy or in terms of constant increase. What variables are reliably related to sales? Consider the following possibilities: Relevant variables: 1. Variability in sales 2. Number of products 3. Variability in product mix If variability in sales (low) and number of products (low) and variability in product mix (low) then trend analysis strong if relationship is strong 1. Sales budgets Compare sales to budgeted sales 2. Inventories and Purchases Compare sales to expected sales using inventory records, prices, purchases 3. Industry averages Compare trend in sales to industry averages 4. Various internal variables Regress sales against relevant internal variables 5. A combination of internal and external variables Regress sales against relevant internal and external variables Profit margin analysis allows for conclusions to be drawn about costs of goods sold given sales figures.																										
PROFIT MARGINS																										
Compare profit margins by product line to industry averages								L	L																	
Regress profit margins by product line against relevant variables								L	L																	

	OVER STATEMENT													UNDER STATEMENT												
	A/ R		DA	Ret.		W. offs		Reven.		C.R.		C.Bal		A/R		D A	Ret.		W. offs		Reven.		C.R.		C.Bal	
	E	**A**	**V**	**O**	**A**	**O**	**A**	**O**	**M**	**O**	**M**	**E**	**M**	**C**	**A**	**V**	**C**	**A**	**C**	**A**	**C**	**M**	**C**	**M**	**C**	**M**
INVENTORY																										
If there is a reliable relationship between inventory figures and sales then sales completeness and existence can be investigated by investigating inventory shrinkage																										
Compare inventory shrinkages to revenue								L	L																	
Compare % inventory shrink to expectation								L	L																	
WRITEOFFS																										
Review writeoffs subsequent to year end (cutoff)			L																							
Compare previous years writeoffs with ageing categories (if an aged trial balance has been used)			L																							
Compare writeoffs to previous years, revenue and trend (this is really to check the appropriateness of the allowance rather than giving any information about writeoffs per se)			L																							
ACCOUNTS RECEIVABLE																										
The main purpose of the following procedures is to determine whether the nature of accounts receivable has changed significantly - if it has then the allowance for doubtful may need to be changed.																										
Review payment record by customer type	L	L								L	L															
ALLOWANCE FOR DOUBTFUL ACCOUNTS																										
This section determines the acceptability of the allowance for doubtful accounts - the procedures applied depend on the type of provision which is used. These types of provision are also used in the financial institutions section.																										
MANDATORY																										
Discuss individually significant non-current A/R with mgt.																										
Check for payments subsequent to year end on non-current A/R (customer, invoice no., amount, date)																										
Review correspondence files for customers with non-current A/R																										

	OVER STATEMENT													UNDER STATEMENT												
	A/ R		DA	Ret.		W. offs		Reven.		C.R.		C.Bal		A/R		D A	Ret.		W. offs		Reven.		C.R.		C.Bal	
	E	**A**	**V**	**O**	**A**	**O**	**A**	**O**	**M**	**O**	**M**	**E**	**M**	**C**	**A**	**V**	**C**	**A**	**C**	**A**	**C**	**M**	**C**	**M**	**C**	**M**
DISCRETIONARY																										
Allocation as % of sales																										
Review average age of receivables (no significant change)																										
Compare bad debt to sales (no significant change)																										
Recompute bad debt provision (no significant difference)																										
Allocation as % of sales by customer category:																										
1. Ageing categories																										
Compare % of A/R in each ageing category with trend																										
Compare trend in w.offs by ageing category (no significant change)																										
Recompute bad debt provision																										
Verify ageing																										
2. Risk classes																										
Review risk class classification (acceptable)																										
Verify classification of receivables (correct)																										
Compare trend in bad debts with risk classes (no s. change)																										
Recompute bad debt provision by risk class (no s. difference)																										
3. Specific sales items																										
Discuss individually material items with client																										
Compare sales to actual bad debts																										
Compare sales to bad debt provision																										
Compare trend in bad debt to sales by customer category																										
Regress bad debt against relevant variables																										
COST OF SALES ASSUMPTIONS																										
Compare ratio of the cost of sales to sales and expectations								L	L																	
Compare regression of cost of sales against relevant variables								L	L																	
SALES ASSUMPTIONS																										
Compare sales by product line to trend	L	L																								
Regress sales by product line with relevant variables	L	L																								
Perform time series analysis of sales	L	L																								

	OVER STATEMENT													UNDER STATEMENT												
	A/ R		DA	Ret.		W. offs		Reven.		C.R.		C.Bal		A/R		D A	Ret.		W. offs		Reven.		C.R.		C.Bal	
	E	**A**	**V**	**O**	**A**	**O**	**A**	**O**	**M**	**O**	**M**	**E**	**M**	**C**	**A**	**V**	**C**	**A**	**C**	**A**	**C**	**M**	**C**	**M**	**C**	**M**
RETURNS ASSUMPTIONS																										
These tests are to establish existence/completeness of returns. Compare returns to previous years, revenue and trend				L	L																					
PRODUCTION RECORDS ASSUMPTIONS																										
Review production records, compare with inventory, sales, returns	L	L		L	L			L	L																	
MISCELLANEOUS																										
Review minutes of board meetings for pledged or factored A/R If consigned items possible then: Examine duplicate invoices for items on consignment	L	L		L	L																					
RETAIL PROCEDURES																										
SALES																										
Trace sales invoices to perpetual inventory records and sales								S	S																	
Trace cash sales to cash balance debits								S	S																	
Trace store charge sales to accounts receivable and sales	S	S						S	S																	
Trace national charge to accounts receivable and sales	S	S						S	S																	
ACCOUNTS RECEIVABLE - CREDIT CARD																										
Confirm credit card receivables with credit card firm	S	S																								
ACCOUNTS RECEIVABLE - STORE CARD																										
Positive confirmation of store credit card receivables	S	S																								
Negative confirmation of store credit card receivables	S	S																								
REGISTER TAPES																										
Verify cash-receipts prelisting with cash balance debits																										
CASH RECEIPTS - GENERAL PROCEDURES																										
RETURNS																										
Review sales returns subsequent to year end (cutoff)				S	S			S	S																	
WRITEOFFS																										
Trace accounts written off to accounts receivable details																										

	OVER STATEMENT													UNDER STATEMENT												
	A/ R		DA	Ret.		W. offs		Reven.		C.R.		C.Bal		A/R		D A	Ret.		W. offs		Reven.		C.R.		C.Bal	
	E	**A**	**V**	**O**	**A**	**O**	**A**	**O**	**M**	**O**	**M**	**E**	**M**	**C**	**A**	**V**	**C**	**A**	**C**	**A**	**C**	**M**	**C**	**M**	**C**	**M**
ANALYTIC																										
SALES																										
Compare expected sales per square foot x # of square feet to book								L	L																	
Compare expected sales by store to other stores and trend								L	L																	
Review margins by product line								L	L																	
CASH RECEIPTS																										
Compare cash receipts per register to other stores and trend										L	L															
Regress cash receipts by store with relevant variables	L	L	L					L	L	L	L	L	L													
RETURNS																										
Compare sales returns by store and trend				L	L																					
BAD DEBTS																										
Compare % of delinquent accounts with trend			L			L	L																			
INVENTORY																										
Compare inventory figures to trend								L	L																	
Compare inventory turnover by store and trend								L	L																	
Compare inventory shrinkage by store and trend								L	L																	
MARKDOWNS																										
Try to determine whether there are any unusual markdowns																										
Compare markdowns by store and trend with expectations								L	L																	

	OVER STATEMENT													UNDER STATEMENT												
	A/ R		DA	Ret.		W. offs		Reven.		C.R.		C.Bal		A/R		D A	Ret.		W. offs		Reven.		C.R.		C.Bal	
	E	**A**	**V**	**O**	**A**	**O**	**A**	**O**	**M**	**O**	**M**	**E**	**M**	**C**	**A**	**V**	**C**	**A**	**C**	**A**	**C**	**M**	**C**	**M**	**C**	**M**
FINANCIAL INSTITUTIONS																										
LOAN BALANCES - GROSS GENERAL																										
EXISTING LOANS - SECURED AND CURRENT Agree beginning balances to prior years working papers Confirm loans (amount, time, rates, security, etc.) Review loan documents for ammendments Review evidence of collateral for changes Evaluate collectibility of loans Verify computation and accounting for accrued loan income Verify computation of interest income Vouch subsequent payments on outstanding loans Vouch and verify accounting for loan payments Vouch additions and charges for allowances for losses																										
NEW AND RENEWED LOANS - CURRENT Confirm loans (amount, time, rates, security, etc.) Inspect loan documents Vouch and verify accounting for new and renewed loans Confirm loan is classified correctly Confirm title documents are in order Confirm validity of legal documentation Confirm valuation of security**																										
EXISTING LOANS - CURRENT PERSONAL Agree beginning balances to prior years working papers Confirm loans (amount, time, rates, security, etc.) Review loan documents for ammendments Review evidence of collateral for changes Review previous loan history, employment and credit rating																										

	OVER STATEMENT													UNDER STATEMENT												
	A/ R		DA	Ret.		W. offs		Reven.		C.R.		C.Bal		A/R		D A	Ret.		W. offs		Reven.		C.R.		C.Bal	
	E	**A**	**V**	**O**	**A**	**O**	**A**	**O**	**M**	**O**	**M**	**E**	**M**	**C**	**A**	**V**	**C**	**A**	**C**	**A**	**C**	**M**	**C**	**M**	**C**	**M**
NEW AND RENEWED LOANS - CURRENT PERSONAL Agree beginning balances to prior years working papers Confirm loans (amount, time rates, security, etc.) Review loan documents for ammendments Review evidence of collateral for changes Review previous loan history, employment and credit rating Review payment history** Review management's classification of loans*** Review correspondence with client**** Review financial statements and business plans** Review previous loan history, employment and credit rating																										
LOANS IN ARREARS Confirm loans (amount, time, rates, security, etc.) Confirm valuation of security** Vouch subsequent payments on outstanding loans																										
LOANS IN DEFAULT Confirm loans (amount, time, rates, security, etc.) Confirm valuation of security** Vouch subsequent payments on outstanding loans Note amount of disbursement																										
CUTOFF - INTEREST REVENUE Note date of disbursement***** Note that disbursement takes place after legal agreement in place Perform surprise inspections of inspection department***** Recompute outstanding principal and accrued interest																										
COLLATERAL Review evidence for legal claim on collateral Review valuation of collateral																										

	OVER STATEMENT													UNDER STATEMENT												
	A/ R		DA	Ret.		W. offs		Reven.		C.R.		C.Bal		A/R		D A	Ret.		W. offs		Reven.		C.R.		C.Bal	
	E	**A**	**V**	**O**	**A**	**O**	**A**	**O**	**M**	**O**	**M**	**E**	**M**	**C**	**A**	**V**	**C**	**A**	**C**	**A**	**C**	**M**	**C**	**M**	**C**	**M**
ALLOWANCE FOR UNCOLLECTIBLE LOANS Discuss collectibility of individually significant loans with mgt. Allocation as % of loans: 1. Risk classes Review risk class classification (acceptable) Verify classification of loans according to risk class (consistent) Compare % of loans in risk classes (change consistent with explns.) Compare w. offs by risk class categories (acceptable) 2. Unique loans Discuss collectibility of loans with mgt.																										
ANALYTICAL GENERAL Analyse and compare yields by risk class Analyse components of loan portfolio																										
INTEREST REVENUE existence and completeness If the risk classes are fairly homogenous and the interest rates are fairly constant - this is probably not appropriate then the following procedure may not provide very much assurance. Calculation of interest income monthly by risk class																										
UNCOLLECTIBLE LOANS Review general provision for bad loans Review planned foreclosures subsequent to year end Review disbursements subsequent to year end Compare trend in early payment penalties Review and verify ageing and delinquency records																										

S = strongly relevant
L = limited relevance

Appendix 3.2

COST & RELIABILITY FACTOR RATINGS

		RELIABILITY													COST								
		Info. Source				Complexity			Source Reliab		Nature		Type		Seniority			Time			Behav. Cost		
	AUDITIING PROCEDURE	D. K	E x	I/ E	I	H	M	L	V R	M R	P	N	O	D	H	M	L	H	M	L	H	M	L
100	Trace from register tape to sales ledger																						
101	Vouch from sales ledger to register tape																						
102	Trace from sales invoices (charge a/c) to sales ledger																						
103	Vouch from sales ledger (charge a/c) to sales invoices																						
104	Trace from sales invoices (national charge a/c) to sales ledger																						
105	Vouch from sales ledger (national charge a/c) to sales invoices (nc a/c)																						
106	Confirm national credit card receivables with credit card firm																						
107	Review subsequent payments on national credit card receivable balance																						
108	Positive confirmation of store credit card receivables																						
109	Negative confirmation of store credit card receivables																						
110	Vouch from A/R sub-ledger (charge a/c) to supporting docs.																						
111	Review subsequent payments on store card receivable balance																						
112	Trace from register tape to cash account debits (cash sales)																						
113	Vouch from cash account debits (cash sales) to register tape																						
114	Trace from remittance advice to cash account debits (sales on account)																						
115	Vouch from cash account debits (sales on account) to remittance advice																						
3	Positive confirmation of A/R balance (invoices)																						

		RELIABILITY													COST								
		Info. Source				Complexity			Source Reliab		Nature		Type		Seniority			Time			Behav. Cost		
	AUDITIING PROCEDURE	D. K	E x	I/ E	I	H	M	L	V R	M R	P	N	O	D	H	M	L	H	M	L	H	M	L
4	Positive confirmation of A/R balance (balances)																						
5	Negative confirmation of A/R balance (invoices)																						
6	Negative confirmation of A/R balance (balances)																						
7	Review A/R sub-ledger for large or unusual receivables																						
8	Review credit balances in accounts receivable																						
9	Reconcile A/R sub-ledger to general ledger																						
10	Vouch from A/R sub-ledger to supporting docs.																						
11	Review subsequent payments to open accounts in A/R sub-ledger at year-end																						
12	Reconcile aged trial balance with general ledger																						
13	Review aged trial balance for large or unusual receivables																						
14	Vouch from aged trial balance to supporting docs.																						
15	Review subsequent payments to accounts in trial balance at year-end																						
16	Discuss individually significant A/R's with mgt.																						
17	Review correspondence files for customers with significant A/R																						
22	Trace from writeoff details to g/l																						
23	Vouch from g/l to writeoff details																						
24	Vouch from sales ledger to supporting docs.																						
25	Trace from shipping docs. to sales ledger																						
26	Positive confirmation of sales balances																						
27	Reviewing sales contracts																						
28	Vouch from sales-ledger detail (returns) to supporting documents																						
29	Trace from sales returns journal to sales ledger																						
30	Vouch from g/l debits (cash) to remittance advice																						

		RELIABILITY													COST								
		Info. Source				Complexity			Source Reliab		Nature		Type		Seniority			Time			Behav. Cost		
	AUDITIING PROCEDURE	D. K	E x	I/ E	I	H	M	L	V R	M R	P	N	O	D	H	M	L	H	M	L	H	M	L
31	Trace from remittance advice to cash account (debits)																						
32	Perform cash count																						
33	Obtain confirmation of cash balance																						
34	Verify cutoff of sales																						
35	Verifying cash receipts cutoff																						
36	Verify cutoff of returns																						
37	Examine subsequent payments in A/R subledger																						
38	Examine subsequent payments on account in ageing																						
39	Review writeoffs subsequent to year end (cutoff)																						

Appendix 4.1

MANUFACTURING PROFILE - 1

This is the first time your office has audited this company. Through audit procedures directed towards the opening numbers on the financial statements, others in your office have determined the figures are accurate, the previous auditors were competent, and they performed sufficient work for you to place reliance on the procedures they performed. The company has changed auditors as a result of the change of ownership of the parent company. The controlling shareholders of the parent company have always been clients of your company. Audited financial results have normally been released by the parent company to the press within 1 month of the year end.

Manufacturing 1 is a company with 7 offices centrally controlled through the company headquarters which is located at a manufacturing location. The company is controlled by Parent, which charges it a management fee and determines the level of dividends to be paid.

The company manufactures two types of heat exchangers which reduce the temperature of natural gas before it is transported via pipeline. Product A is an air cooled exchanger which uses fins to dissipate heat to reduce the temperature of the natural gas. Product B is a water cooled system. Product B is more difficult to build and maintain but it reduces the temperature of the gas more readily than Product A.

The two product lines use totally different engineering concepts although the materials are similar. All of the work completed by the individual locations for Product A is custom work which is bid locally. Product B is built under an agreement with Parent, which allows the use of their patent. Sales are referred by Parent, but are the responsibility of Manufacturing 1.

The overall economy in the natural gas industry has been fairly stable since the significant drop off in 1984. The company has managed to survive in a very competitive industry, where many firms have closed their doors or filed for bankruptcy, by providing excellent follow-up service.

To control costs and revenues, there is a central administration system which controls the accounting, budgeting and purchasing functions. Through stringent quality control guidelines the company has been able to gain a reputation for high quality work and as a result has been able to increase profit margins by two percent over the last year. To maintain this quality control a detailed set of records is maintained to monitor both quality and price of materials used in manufacturing. These records are reviewed on a contract by contract basis and reports of operations, for closed and in progress contracts, are completed monthly and annually.

Cash sales result from the sale of scrap which is readily usable by smaller manufacturers. Each location controls it own scrap sales.

From a review of the prior year's information it appears that the response rate for confirmations was approximately 90% for positive confirmations and 55% for negative confirmations.

Balances for:	**Opening**	**Closing**	**Year to Date**
Accounts receivable - Product A	109,000,000	127,000,000	
Accounts receivable - Product B	153,000,000	205,000,000	
Total	262,000,000	332,000,000	
Cash Sales			*6,500,000
Sales on account - Product A			950,000,000
Sales on account - Product B			1,200,000,000
Total			2,156,500,000
Cash receipts - cash sales			1,500,000
Cash receipts on account - Product A			932,000,000
Cash receipts on account - Product B			1,148,000,000
Total			2,081,500,000
Cash balances - with bank	115,000,000	95,000,000	
Cash balances - on hand	100,000	110,000	
Total	115,100,000	95,110,000	
Doubtful accounts - Product A	2,500,000	2,200,000	
Doubtful accounts - Product B	5,000,000	5,500,000	
Total	7,500,000	7,700,000	
Write-offs - Product A			2,000,000
Write-offs - Product B			4,500,000
Total			6,500,000
Returns			*5,000,000

* Returns are included in cash sales numbers

Average balances for:	**Opening**	**Closing**	**Year to Date**
Accounts receivable - Product A	872,000	1,104,348	
Accounts receivable - Product B	2,040,000	2,562,500	
Average of total	1,310,000	1,702,564	
Cash Sales			6,500
Sales on account - Product A			100,000
Sales on account - Product B			250,000
Average of total			140,948
Cash receipts - cash sales			1,500
Cash receipts on account - Product A			94,141
Cash receipts on account - Product B			273,333
Average of total			137,848
Cash balances - with bank	28,750,000	23,750,000	
Cash balances - on hand	10,000	11,000	
Average of total	8,221,429	6,743,571	
Doubtful accounts - Product A	125,000	122,222	
Doubtful accounts - Product B	200,000	239,130	
Average of total	166,667	187,805	
Write-offs - Product A			117,647
Write-offs - Product B			250,000
Average of total			185,714
Returns			6,667

Percentage of accounts comprising significant items:

	Opening	Closing	YTD	Remainder $	Average $
Accounts receivable - Product A	30	35		30,000,000	401,388
Accounts receivable - Product B	50	50		20,000,000	500,000
Cash Sales			-	1,500,000	1,500
Sales on account - Product A			45	330,000,000	63,158
Sales on account - Product B			30	600,000,000	178,151
Cash receipts - cash sales			-	1,500,000	1,500
Cash receipts on account - Product A			38	400,000,000	65,168
Cash receipts on account - Product B			25	600,000,000	190,476
Cash balances - with bank	25	25		500,000	166,667
Cash balances - on hand	-	-		110,000	11,000
Doubtful accounts - Product A	-	-		2,200,000	122,222
Doubtful accounts - Product B	20	16		2,500,000	129,400
Write-offs - Product A			5	1,500,000	92,879
Write-offs - Product B			8	2,000,000	120,773
Returns			-	5,000,000	6,667

Principal Audit Document for Accounts Receivable:	sub ledger
Clients method for estimating allowance for doubtful accounts:	review of specific accounts
Experience and training level of staff performing analytic review:	moderate

For each financial statement item, target risk and reliance on internal control accomplished through compliance testing of each financial statement item, prior to conducting the substantive phase of the audit are as follows:

	Target Risk	Internal Control
Accounts receivable - Product A	2%	max
Accounts receivable - Product B	2%	max
Cash Sales	25%	max
Sales on account - Product A	25%	max
Sales on account - Product B	25%	max
Cash receipts - cash sales	25%	max
Cash receipts on account - Product A	25%	max
Cash receipts on account - Product B	25%	max
Cash balances - with bank	2%	none
Cash balances - on hand	2%	none
Doubtful accounts - Product A	4%	none
Doubtful accounts - Product B	4%	none
Write-offs - Product A	25%	none
Write-offs - Product B	25%	none
Returns	25%	max

Number of items:	**Opening**	**Closing**	**Year to Date**
Accounts receivable - Product A	125	115	
Accounts receivable - Product B	75	80	
Total	200	195	
Cash Sales			1,000
Sales on account - Product A			9,500
Sales on account - Product B			4,800
Total			15,300
Cash receipts - cash sales			1,000
Cash receipts on account - Product A			9,900
Cash receipts on account - Product B			4,200
Total			15,100
Cash balances - with bank	4	4	
Cash balances - on hand	10	10	
Total	14	14	
Doubtful accounts - Product A	20	18	
Doubtful accounts - Product B	25	23	
Total	45	41	
Write-offs - Product A			17
Write-offs - Product B			18
Total			35
Returns			750

Variability of non-significant item values:	**Opening**	**Closing**	**Year to Date**
Accounts receivable - Product A	significant	significant	
Accounts receivable - Product B	significant	significant	
Cash Sales			moderate
Sales on account - Product A			significant
Sales on account - Product B			significant
Cash receipts - cash sales			moderate
Cash receipts on account - Product A			significant
Cash receipts on account - Product B			significant
Cash balances - with bank	significant	significant	
Cash balances - on hand	significant	significant	
Doubtful accounts - Product A	significant	significant	
Doubtful accounts - Product B	significant	significant	
Write-offs - Product A			significant
Write-offs - Product B			significant
Returns			significant

significant - there is a variability in the account from 10% to 200% of average value, with no significant clusters.
moderate - the account values range from 50% to 150% of the average value.
low - the account values range from 75% to 125% of the average value.

Inherent risk associated with:

	Over Statement	Under Statement
Accounts receivable - Product A	moderate	moderate
Accounts receivable - Product B	high	high
Cash Sales	low	moderate
Sales on account - Product A	low	low
Sales on account - Product B	low	low
Cash receipts - cash sales	low	moderate
Cash receipts on account - Product A	low	moderate
Cash receipts on account - Product B	low	moderate
Cash balances - with bank	low	low
Cash balances - on hand	low	low
Doubtful accounts - Product A	moderate	moderate
Doubtful accounts - Product B	high	high
Write-offs - Product A	low	low
Write-offs - Product B	low	low
Returns	low	moderate

Internal control review has been conducted on the sales/accounts receivable/cash receipts system. However no work has been performed on the cash balances, doubtful accounts or the write-off systems.

Appendix 4.2

MANUFACTURING PROFILE - 2

This is the first time your office has audited this company. Through audit procedures directed towards the opening numbers on the financial statements, others in your office have determined the figures are accurate, the previous auditors were competent, and they performed sufficient work for you to place reliance on the procedures they performed. The company has changed auditors as a result of the merger of the former auditors with another firm with which Manufacturing 2's owner-manager had a bad experience. Audited financial statements have normally been presented to the owner two and one half months after the year end.

Manufacturing 2 is a company with one location. The company builds electrical generation units for remote facilities which do not have access to standard utilities, whether because of their location or because of their significant power needs and continuous power requirements. In the past the client had two distinct products, Product A and Product B, which they built on a custom basis. However over the past two years, because of technology, these products have tended to merge and the distinctions have become less pronounced. There is a manager in charge of each of the product areas and bonuses are determined based on the performance of the area.

The company was built on the expertise of its owner-manager who maintains tight control over the day-to-day operations. There has been a 30% turnover of staff in the accounting area and this may be of concern given an overly complex revenue recording procedure. Generally the business has been good and a major expansion has been financed through a bank loan. As well as providing information for tax purposes, the financial statements must be provided to the bank as a condition of the outstanding loan.

There is a small accounting staff to handle the recording of transactions. Work in progress and final billings are prepared by the managers and approved by the owner before being issued. There are budgets set up for each contract by the manager in the particular area, and a rudimentary cash flow projection prepared by the owner-manager. Budgets are compared to actual results on a contract by contract basis and a month by month basis.

From a review of the prior year's information it appears that the response rate for confirmations was approximately 95% for positive confirmations and 60% for negative confirmations.

Balances for:	**Opening**	**Closing**	**Year to Date**
Accounts receivable - Product A	12,000,000	12,800,000	
Accounts receivable - Product B	9,800,000	13,000,000	
Total	21,800,000	25,800,000	
Cash Sales			*55,000
Sales on account - Product A			100,900,000
Sales on account - Product B			120,000,000
Total			220,955,000
Cash receipts - cash sales			5,000
Cash receipts on account - Product A			100,100,000
Cash receipts on account - Product B			116,800,000
Total			216,905,000
Cash balances - with bank	1,000,000	900,000	
Cash balances - on hand	5,000	5,000	
Total	1,005,000	905,000	
Doubtful accounts - Product A	100,000	95,000	
Doubtful accounts - Product B	90,000	90,000	
Total	190,000	185,000	
Write-offs - Product A			80,000
Write-offs - Product B			75,000
Total			155,000
Returns			*50,000

* Returns are included in cash sales numbers

Average balances for:	**Opening**	**Closing**	**Year to Date**
Accounts receivable - Product A	266,667	320,000	
Accounts receivable - Product B	280,000	325,000	
Average of total	272,500	322,500	
Cash Sales			500
Sales on account - Product A			366,909
Sales on account - Product B			533,333
Average of total			433,138
Cash receipts - cash sales			500
Cash receipts on account - Product A			566,111
Cash receipts on account - Product B			778,667
Average of total			637,956
Cash balances - with bank	333,333	300,000	
Cash balances - on hand	2,500	2,500	
Average of total	201,000	181,000	
Doubtful accounts - Product A	33,333	300,000	
Doubtful accounts - Product B	45,000	45,000	
Average of total	38,000	37,000	
Write-offs - Product A			26,667
Write-offs - Product B			37,500
Average of total			31,000
Returns			5,000

Percentage of accounts containing significant items:

	Opening	Closing	YTD	Remainder $	Average $
Accounts receivable - Product A	40	35		4,000,000	153,846
Accounts receivable - Product B	40	45		5,000,000	227,273
Cash Sales			-	5,000	500
Sales on account - Product A			32	50,000,000	267,380
Sales on account - Product B			24	45,000,000	263,158
Cash receipts - cash sales			-	5,000	500
Cash receipts on account - Product A			25	60,000,000	444,444
Cash receipts on account - Product B			24	50,000,000	438,596
Cash balances - with bank	33	33		800,000	400,000
Cash balances - on hand	-	-		5,000	2,500
Doubtful accounts - Product A	-	-		95,000	31,667
Doubtful accounts - Product B	-	-		90,000	45,000
Write-offs - Product A			-	80,000	26,667
Write-offs - Product B			-	75,000	37,500
Returns			-	50,000	5,000

Principal Audit Document for Accounts Receivable:	aged trail balance
Clients method for estimating allowance for doubtful accounts:	review of specific accounts
Experience and training of staff performing analytic review:	moderate

For each financial statement item, target risk and reliance on internal control accomplished through compliance testing of each financial statement item, prior to conducting the substantive phase of the audit are as follows:

	Target Risk	Internal Control
Accounts receivable - Product A	2%	none
Accounts receivable - Product B	2%	none
Cash Sales	25%	none
Sales on account - Product A	25%	none
Sales on account - Product B	25%	none
Cash receipts - cash sales	25%	none
Cash receipts on account - Product A	25%	none
Cash receipts on account - Product B	25%	none
Cash balances - with bank	2%	none
Cash balances - on hand	2%	none
Doubtful accounts - Product A	4%	none
Doubtful accounts - Product B	4%	none
Write-offs - Product A	25%	none
Write-offs - Product B	25%	none
Returns	25%	none

Number of items:	**Opening**	**Closing**	**Year to Date**
Accounts receivable - Product A	45	40	
Accounts receivable - Product B	35	40	
Total	80	80	
Cash Sales			10
Sales on account - Product A			275
Sales on account - Product B			225
Total			510
Cash receipts - cash sales			10
Cash receipts on account - Product A			180
Cash receipts on account - Product B			150
Total			340
Cash balances - with bank	3	3	
Cash balances - on hand	2	2	
Total	5	5	
Doubtful accounts - Product A	3	3	
Doubtful accounts - Product B	2	2	
Total	5	5	
Write-offs - Product A			3
Write-offs - Product B			2
Total			5
Returns			10

Variability of non-significant item values:	**Opening**	**Closing**	**Year to Date**
Accounts receivable - Product A	significant	significant	
Accounts receivable - Product B	significant	significant	
Cash Sales			moderate
Sales on account - Product A			significant
Sales on account - Product B			significant
Cash receipts - cash sales			moderate
Cash receipts on account - Product A			significant
Cash receipts on account - Product B			significant
Cash balances - with bank	significant	significant	
Cash balances - on hand	moderate	moderate	
Doubtful accounts - Product A	significant	significant	
Doubtful accounts - Product B	significant	significant	
Write-offs - Product A			significant
Write-offs - Product B			significant
Returns			moderate

significant - there is a variability in the account from 20% to 150% of average value, with no significant clusters.
moderate - the account values range from 55% to 140% of the average value.
low - the account values range from 70% to 120% of the average value.

Inherent risk associated with:

	Over Statement	Under Statement
Accounts receivable - Product A	moderate	moderate
Accounts receivable - Product B	moderate	moderate
Cash Sales	low	moderate
Sales on account - Product A	moderate	moderate
Sales on account - Product B	moderate	moderate
Cash receipts - cash sales	low	moderate
Cash receipts on account - Product A	low	moderate
Cash receipts on account - Product B	low	moderate
Cash balances - with bank	low	moderate
Cash balances - on hand	low	moderate
Doubtful accounts - Product A	low	low
Doubtful accounts - Product B	low	low
Write-offs - Product A	low	moderate
Write-offs - Product B	low	moderate
Returns	low	moderate

Because of the lack of documented controls over the system no review of internal control has been performed.

Appendix 4.3

RETAIL PROFILE - 1

This is the first time your office has audited this company. Through audit procedures directed towards the opening numbers on the financial statements, others in your office have determined the figures are accurate, the previous auditors were competent, and they performed sufficient work for you to place reliance on the procedures they performed. The company has changed auditors as a result of excellent tax services provided in your office. Audited financial statements have normally been presented to the owner three months after the year end.

Retail 1 is a local retailer which has built a reputation for high quality, lower priced hardware items. The centrally located store has a wide variety of lower-priced merchandise. The store is a very steady performer in that profits have been reasonably consistent over the years with no spectacular growth or decline. The local economy is reasonably buoyant but this should not add or detract from the normal performance.

Customers are able to open an account with the store by producing two pieces of identification and submitting to a credit check.

The store has five sales registers, which are controlled through a reconciliation of receipts to the cash register tape completed by the cashier and approved by the accounting department before the cashier leaves each day. Overall the accounting records are not complicated and the accounting staff will provide the majority of the schedules required for the audit.

The financial statements are provided to the bank as a condition of a revolving loan agreement, the balance of which is secured by a general assignment of receivables. The client does not prepare any budgets other than an informal cash flow projection. Performance of the various departments within the store is monitored by the owner who has an intimate knowledge of the purchasing and sales information. Monthly statements showing items purchased and sold by department are available, but are only given a cursory review by the owner.

From a review of the prior year's information it appears that the response rate for confirmations was approximately 85% for positive confirmations and 60% for negative confirmations.

Balances for:	Opening	Closing	Year to Date
Accounts receivable - national credit card	100,200	120,100	
Accounts receivable - store credit	75,500	90,400	
Accounts receivable - wholesale	88,000	110,000	
Total	263,700	320,500	
Cash Sales			*733,500
Sales on account - national credit card			975,000
Sales on account - store credit			600,000
Sales on account - wholesale			700,000
Total			3,008,500
Cash receipts - cash sales			555,000
Cash receipts on account - national credit card			955,100
Cash receipts on account - store credit			590,100
Cash receipts on account - wholesale			690,000
Total			2,790,200
Cash balances - with bank	200,000	150,000	
Cash balances - on hand	9,000	10,000	
Total	209,000	160,000	
Doubtful accounts - store credit	15,000	20,000	
Doubtful accounts - wholesale	18,000	30,000	
Total	33,000	50,000	
Write-offs - store credit			12,000
Write-offs - wholesale			16,500
Total			28,500
Returns			*28,500
Mark downs			*150,000

* Returns are included in cash sales numbers

Average balances for:	Opening	Closing	Year to Date
Accounts receivable - national credit card	133	145	
Accounts receivable - store credit	94	96	
Accounts receivable - wholesale	3,826	4,400	
Average of total	146	178	
Cash Sales			45
Sales on account - national credit card			107
Sales on account - store credit			75
Sales on account - wholesale			3,889
Average of total			96
Cash receipts - cash sales			45
Cash receipts on account - national credit card			26,531
Cash receipts on account - store credit			143
Cash receipts on account - wholesale			2,464
Average of total			167
Cash balances - with bank	66,667	37,500	
Cash balances - on hand	1,500	1,429	
Average of total	23,222	14,545	
Doubtful accounts - store credit	-	-	
Doubtful accounts - wholesale	-	-	
Average of total	-	-	
Write-offs - store credit			75
Write-offs - wholesale			8,250
Average of total			176
Returns			25
Mark downs			71

Number of items:	**Opening**	**Closing**	**Year to Date**
Accounts receivable - national credit card	754	827	
Accounts receivable - store credit	805	942	
Accounts receivable - wholesale	23	25	
Total	1,582	1,794	
Cash Sales			12,225
Sales on account - national credit card			9,125
Sales on account - store credit			7,950
Sales on account - wholesale			180
Total			29,480
Cash receipts - cash sales			12,225
Cash receipts on account - national credit card			36
Cash receipts on account - store credit			4,125
Cash receipts on account - wholesale			280
Total			16,666
Cash balances - with bank	3	4	
Cash balances - on hand	6	7	
Doubtful accounts - store credit	-	-	
Doubtful accounts - wholesale	-	-	
Write-offs - store credit			160
Write-offs - wholesale			2
Returns			1,125
Markdowns			2,100

Variability of non-significant item values:	**Opening**	**Closing**	**Year to Date**
Accounts receivable - national credit card	low	low	
Accounts receivable - store credit	low	low	
Accounts receivable - wholesale	low	low	
Cash Sales			low
Sales on account - national credit card			low
Sales on account - store credit			low
Sales on account - wholesale			low
Cash receipts - cash sales			low
Cash receipts on account - national credit card			low
Cash receipts on account - store credit			low
Cash receipts on account - wholesale			low
Cash balances - with bank	significant	significant	
Cash balances - on hand	moderate	moderate	
Doubtful accounts - store credit	low	low	
Doubtful accounts - wholesale	low	low	
Write-offs - store credit			low
Write-offs - wholesale			low
Returns			low
Mark downs			low

significant - there is a variability in the account from 10% to 1,000% of average value, with no significant clusters.
moderate - the account balances vary from 50% to 150% of the average value.
low - the value of the accounts do vary from 85% to 115% of the average value of the items included in the balance.

Percentage of accounts comprising significant items:

	Opening	Closing	YTD	Remainder $	Average $
Accounts receivable - national credit card	-	-			
Accounts receivable - store credit	-	-			
Accounts receivable - wholesale	-	-			
Cash Sales			-		
Sales on account - national credit card			-		
Sales on account - store credit			-		
Sales on account - wholesale			-		
Cash receipts - cash sales			-		
Cash receipts on account - nat'l credit card			-		
Cash receipts on account - store credit			-		
Cash receipts on account - wholesale			-		
Cash balances - with bank	33	50		10,000	5,000
Cash balances - on hand	-	-			
Doubtful accounts - store credit	-	-			
Doubtful accounts - wholesale	-	-			
Write-offs - store credit			-		
Write-offs - wholesale			-		
Returns			-		
Mark downs			-		

Principal Audit Document for Accounts Receivable:	aged trail balance
Clients method for estimating allowance for doubtful accounts:	% of sales
Experience and training level of staff performing analytic review:	moderate

For each financial statement item, target risk and reliance on internal control accomplished through compliance testing of each financial statement item, prior to conducting the substantive phase of the audit are as follows:

	Target Risk	Internal Control
Accounts receivable - national credit card	4%	little
Accounts receivable - store credit	4%	little
Accounts receivable - wholesale	4%	little
Cash Sales	10%	little
Sales on account - national credit card	10%	little
Sales on account - store credit	10%	little
Sales on account - wholesale	10%	little
Cash receipts - cash sales	10%	little
Cash receipts on account - nat'l credit card	10%	little
Cash receipts on account - store credit	10%	little
Cash receipts on account - wholesale	10%	little
Cash balances - with bank	2%	none
Cash balances - on hand	2%	none
Doubtful accounts - store credit	4%	none
Doubtful accounts - wholesale	4%	none
Write-offs - store credit	4%	none
Write-offs - wholesale	4%	none
Returns	10%	little
Mark downs	10%	little

Inherent risk associated with:

	Over Statement	Under Statement
Accounts receivable - national credit card	low	low
Accounts receivable - store credit	moderate	moderate
Accounts receivable - wholesale	low	low
Cash Sales	low	moderate
Sales on account - national credit card	low	low
Sales on account - store credit	low	low
Sales on account - wholesale	low	low
Cash receipts - cash sales	low	moderate
Cash receipts on account - nat'l credit card	low	moderate
Cash receipts on account - store credit	low	moderate
Cash receipts on account - wholesale	low	moderate
Cash balances - with bank	low	low
Cash balances - on hand	low	low
Doubtful accounts - store credit	moderate	moderate
Doubtful accounts - wholesale	low	low
Write-offs - store credit	low	low
Write-offs - wholesale	low	low
Returns	low	moderate
Mark downs	low	low

Internal control review has been conducted on the sales/accounts receivable/cash receipts system. However no work has been performed on the cash balances, doubtful accounts or the write-off systems.

Appendix 4.4

RETAIL PROFILE - 2

This is the first time your office has audited this company. Through audit procedures directed towards the opening numbers on the financial statements, others in your office have determined the figures are accurate, the previous auditors were competent, and they performed sufficient work for you to place reliance on the procedures they performed. The company has changed auditors as a result of the death of the former engagement partner, and the lack of confidence in the remaining partners by the owners of Retail 2. Audited financial statements have normally been presented one month after the year end.

Retail 2 is a clothing company with four local stores. The company was started at the turn of the century and has become a local institution. The local economy is buoyant and this should affect profits favorably, if selections remain consistent with prior years.

Each of the four stores has a manager in charge of the quantity of purchases and credit policies within predetermined guidelines. Compensation for the managers is determined as a percentage of store profitability and manager's ability to meet or exceed individual department and store wide budgets. Mark ups and mark downs are centrally established, and central marketing campaigns are carried out.

Tight controls are maintained over recording of transactions and a monthly report of performance by department is available for each manager. These reports include unit sales, purchases, and inventory levels, as well as operating results by product line. As part of the annual audit reporting, calculations of individual store profitability and the ultimate compensation of the managers are verified.

From a review of the prior year's information it appears that the response rate for confirmations was approximately 80% for positive confirmations and 50% for negative confirmations.

Balances for:	**Opening**	**Closing**	**Year to Date**
Accounts receivable - national credit card	15,975,000	17,150,000	
Accounts receivable - store credit	16,925,000	18,675,000	
Accounts receivable - wholesale	3,320,000	4,340,000	
Total	36,220,000	40,165,000	
Cash Sales			*16,840,000
Sales on account - national credit card			165,250,000
Sales on account - store credit			106,975,000
Sales on account - wholesale			42,750,000
Total			331,815,000
Cash receipts - cash sales			6,050,000
Cash receipts on account - national credit card			164,075,000
Cash receipts on account - store credit			105,225,000
Cash receipts on account - wholesale			41,730,000
Total			317,080,000
Cash balances - with bank	10,500,000	9,750,000	
Cash balances - on hand	2,000,000	2,100,000	
Total	12,500,000	11,850,000	
Doubtful accounts - store credit	600,000	615,000	
Doubtful accounts - wholesale	25,000	40,000	
Total	625,000	655,000	
Write-offs - store credit			510,000
Write-offs - wholesale			15,000
Total			525,000
Returns			*1,250,000
Mark downs			*9,540,000

* Returns are included in cash sales numbers

Average balances for:	**Opening**	**Closing**	**Year to Date**
Accounts receivable - national credit card	178	168	
Accounts receivable - store credit	308	328	
Accounts receivable - wholesale	1,328	1,699	
Average of total	246	249	
Cash Sales			134
Sales on account - national credit card			178
Sales on account - store credit			97
Sales on account - wholesale			1,336
Average of total			152
Cash receipts - cash sales			134
Cash receipts on account - national credit card			4,557,639
Cash receipts on account - store credit			877
Cash receipts on account - wholesale			2,087
Average of total			1,714
Cash balances - with bank	1,750,000	1,625,000	
Cash balances - on hand	100,000	84,000	
Average of total	480,769	382,258	
Doubtful accounts - store credit	-	-	
Doubtful accounts - wholesale	-	-	
Average of total	-	-	
Write-offs - store credit			128
Write-offs - wholesale			125
Average of total			127
Returns			60
Mark downs			20

Number of items:	**Opening**	**Closing**	**Year to Date**
Accounts receivable - national credit card	90,000	102,000	
Accounts receivable - store credit	55,000	57,000	
Accounts receivable - wholesale	2,500	2,600	
Total	147,500	161,600	
Cash Sales			45,000
Sales on account - national credit card			930,000
Sales on account - store credit			1,100,000
Sales on account - wholesale			32,000
Total			2,107,000
Cash receipts - cash sales			45,000
Cash receipts on account - national credit card			36
Cash receipts on account - store credit			120,000
Cash receipts on account - wholesale			20,000
Total			185,036
Cash balances - with bank	6	6	
Cash balances - on hand	20	25	
Doubtful accounts - store credit	-	-	
Doubtful accounts - wholesale	-	-	
Write-offs - store credit			4,000
Write-offs - wholesale			120
Returns			21,000
Markdowns			475,000

Variability of non-significant item values:	**Opening**	**Closing**	**Year to Date**
Accounts receivable - national credit card	moderate	moderate	
Accounts receivable - store credit	moderate	moderate	
Accounts receivable - wholesale	moderate	moderate	
Cash Sales			moderate
Sales on account - national credit card			moderate
Sales on account - store credit			moderate
Sales on account - wholesale			moderate
Cash receipts - cash sales			moderate
Cash receipts on account - national credit card			significant
Cash receipts on account - store credit			moderate
Cash receipts on account - wholesale			moderate
Cash balances - with bank	significant	significant	
Cash balances - on hand	moderate	moderate	
Doubtful accounts - store credit	moderate	moderate	
Doubtful accounts - wholesale	moderate	moderate	
Write-offs - store credit			moderate
Write-offs - wholesale			significant
Returns			moderate
Mark downs			low

significant - there is a variability in the account from 10% to 180% of average value, with no significant clusters.
moderate - the itmes tend to be from 50% to 130% of the average value.
low - the items tend to be from 90% to 110% of the average value.

Percentage of accounts comprising significant items:

	Opening	**Closing**	**YTD**	**Remainder $**	**Average $**
Accounts receivable - national credit card	-	-			
Accounts receivable - store credit	-	-			
Accounts receivable - wholesale	-	-			
Cash Sales			-		
Sales on account - national credit card			-		
Sales on account - store credit			-		
Sales on account - wholesale			-		
Cash receipts - cash sales			-		
Cash receipts on account - nat'l credit card			-		
Cash receipts on account - store credit			-		
Cash receipts on account - wholesale			-		
Cash balances - with bank	33	33		100,000	25,000
Cash balances - on hand	-	-			
Doubtful accounts - store credit	-	-			
Doubtful accounts - wholesale	-	-			
Write-offs - store credit			-		
Write-offs - wholesale			-		
Returns			-		
Mark downs			-		

Principal Audit Document for Accounts Receivable:	sub ledger
Clients method for estimating allowance for doubtful accounts:	age of receivables
Experience and training of staff performing analytic review:	moderate

For each financial statement item, target risk and reliance on internal control accomplished through compliance testing of each financial statement item, prior to conducting the substantive phase of the audit are as follows:

	Target Risk	Internal Control
Accounts receivable - national credit card	4%	moderate
Accounts receivable - store credit	4%	moderate
Accounts receivable - wholesale	4%	moderate
Cash Sales	25%	moderate
Sales on account - national credit card	25%	moderate
Sales on account - store credit	25%	moderate
Sales on account - wholesale	25%	moderate
Cash receipts - cash sales	25%	moderate
Cash receipts on account - nat'l credit card	25%	moderate
Cash receipts on account - store credit	25%	moderate
Cash receipts on account - wholesale	25%	moderate
Cash balances - with bank	2%	none
Cash balances - on hand	2%	none
Doubtful accounts - store credit	4%	none
Doubtful accounts - wholesale	4%	none
Write-offs - store credit	4%	none
Write-offs - wholesale	4%	none
Returns	25%	moderate
Mark downs	25%	moderate

Inherent risk associated with:

	Over Statement	Under Statement
Accounts receivable - national credit card	moderate	moderate
Accounts receivable - store credit	moderate	moderate
Accounts receivable - wholesale	moderate	moderate
Cash Sales	moderate	high
Sales on account - national credit card	moderate	moderate
Sales on account - store credit	moderate	moderate
Sales on account - wholesale	moderate	moderate
Cash receipts - cash sales	moderate	high
Cash receipts on account - nat'l credit card	moderate	moderate
Cash receipts on account - store credit	moderate	high
Cash receipts on account - wholesale	moderate	high
Cash balances - with bank	moderate	moderate
Cash balances - on hand	moderate	moderate
Doubtful accounts - store credit	moderate	moderate
Doubtful accounts - wholesale	moderate	moderate
Write-offs - store credit	moderate	high
Write-offs - wholesale	moderate	moderate
Returns	moderate	high
Mark downs	moderate	moderate

Internal control review has been conducted on the sales/accounts receivable/cash receipts system. However no work has been performed on the cash balances, doubtful accounts or the write-off systems.

Appendix 4.5

AFB BANK CANADA

AFB Bank Canada (AFB or the "Bank") is a small bank and a wholly-owned subsidiary of Another Bank Corporation of New York. It is headquartered in Toronto, Ontario, and has a lending office in Vancouver, British Columbia. The Bank was incorporated on July 16, 19W5 under the provisions of the Bank Act of Canada (1980). The Canadian and US banking environments are quite similar.

This is the first time audit of this bank by your firm. Through audit procedures directed towards the opening numbers on the financial statements, others in your office have determined that these numbers are accurate, the previous auditors were competent, and that the previous auditors performed sufficient and appropriate audit work for you to place the reliance on the procedures they performed. The bank has changed auditors as a result of the change of ownership of the parent. The recovery on this engagement (as with the parent) is expected to be good as the previous auditors had no fee pressures.

A review of the prior year's files by your manager and partner indicated that the Bank was very control conscious, and that adequate information and control systems were in place. Other information regarding the new client was obtained by the previous in charge who began planning this engagement, and supervised the control testing. You are to complete the audit risk assessment and substantive planning.

AFB is a moderate-sized bank, with total assets of C$1.4 billion at October 31, 19X1. As the enclosed exhibit indicates, the Bank's assets are fairly evenly distributed between the various types of income producing assets. It does not conduct retail personal banking. Its leverage ratio is 18.3, compared with an industry average of 19.6 and a regulatory limit of 22.

The Bank offers general corporate banking services to businesses, including working capital financing (operating lines of credit), medium-term project financing and short- and medium-term financing for the development of resources in the forest products and mining industries. Operating lines are always at interest rates that float with prime, while regular bank loans have either fixed or floating rates of interest.

The Bank has also developed a portfolio of retail mortgages which offer basic residential mortgages at competitive rates. Mortgages are offered for terms of three to five years, at fixed rates.

Funding is principally in the form of deposits with other banks and market investors.

The banking industry in Canada and the United States has been relatively stable after some difficult years. The Bank has no sovereign risk loans to countries in financial difficulty and the risk is generally Canadian, with some further guarantees from parent companies in other industrialized countries.

The accounting and administration functions are located in Toronto, with all documents located there. While the Vancouver office can grant loans, larger advances require credit approval from Toronto. Actual disbursements and receipts are in Toronto, generally through inter bank transfers.

Excess funds are held in the form of cash and liquid securities (government treasury bills). Minimum liquidity is required by banking regulators. The Bank has always met regulatory requirements. Balances of cash and cash equivalents are as follows ($000s):

October 31, 19X0	27
October 31, 19X1	37

Overall risk for all financial statement assertions is planned at 2%.

Mortgage loans are generally for similar amounts. Business loans vary more, while operating lines change on a daily basis and can range from zero to the customer's credit limit.

Records are kept in Lender Sub-ledger, a software package bought from and tailored by a major software house. This sub-ledger details the total credit limit, outstanding balance, interest rate, accrued interest and other loan/mortgage agreement details.

Loan loss provisions are made on a specific item basis for business loans, and on an historic formula basis for mortgages. The client also has a general loss provision which covers unforeseen circumstances and the general risk of the portfolios. According to the prior auditors' working papers, the formula method for mortgages has appeared to be adequate in prior years.

Prior risk levels (i.e., after inherent risk and control risk evaluation, but before any substantive audit work) are listed in Table 1.

Detailed financial information is provided in Tables 2 and 3.

Audit work on internal controls on the loan/mortgage/receipts cycle has been done.

TABLE 1

Levels of Risk

	Balance					Accrued Interest					Revenue/Expense			
	C	E	A over	A under	V	C	E	A over	A under	V	C	E	A over	A under
Inherent Risk														
Fixed balance, fixed rate	50	40	50	30	100	40	30	60	40	100	50	50	50	40
Fixed balance, floating rate	60	50	60	40	100	50	40	50	30	100	60	60	60	50
Operating line of credit	70	60	70	50	100	n/a	n/a	n/a	n/a	n/a	60	60	60	50
Mortgages	50	40	50	30	100	40	40	40	20	100	50	50	50	40
Cash - balances	20	10	10	10	n/a	n/a	n/a	n/a	n/a	n/a	n/a	n/a	n/a	n/a
Cash - receipts	30	30	60	40	n/a	n/a	n/a	n/a	n/a	n/a	n/a	n/a	n/a	n/a
Cash - disbursements	30	30	40	60	n/a	n/a	n/a	n/a	n/a	n/a	n/a	n/a	n/a	n/a
Control Risk														
Fixed balance, fixed rate	60	60	60	60	100	100	100	100	100	100	70	70	70	70
Fixed balance, floating rate	70	70	70	70	100	100	100	100	100	100	80	80	80	80
Operating line of credit	80	80	80	80	100	n/a	n/a	n/a	n/a	n/a	90	90	90	90
Mortgages	60	60	60	60	100	100	100	100	100	100	70	70	70	70
Cash - balances	20	10	10	10	n/a	n/a	n/a	n/a	n/a	n/a	n/a	n/a	n/a	n/a
Cash - receipts	30	30	60	60	n/a	n/a	n/a	n/a	n/a	n/a	n/a	n/a	n/a	n/a
Cash - disbursements	30	30	60	60	n/a	n/a	n/a	n/a	n/a	n/a	n/a	n/a	n/a	n/a
Risk Prior to Substantive Work														
Fixed balance, fixed rate	30	24	30	18	100	40	30	60	40	100	35	35	35	28
Fixed balance, floating rate	42	35	42	28	100	50	40	50	30	100	48	48	48	40
Operating line of credit	56	48	56	40	100	n/a	n/a	n/a	n/a	n/a	54	54	54	45
Mortgages	30	24	30	18	100	40	40	40	20	100	35	35	35	28
Cash - balances	4	1	1	1	n/a	n/a	n/a	n/a	n/a	n/a	n/a	n/a	n/a	
Cash - receipts	9	9	36	24	n/a	n/a	n/a	n/a	n/a	n/a	n/a	n/a	n/a	
Cash - disbursements	9	9	24	36	n/a	n/a	n/a	n/a	n/a	n/a	n/a	n/a	n/a	

Key to Assertions

C	completeness
E	existence/ occurrence
A	accuracy
V	valuation

TABLE 2

Financial Information

Number of Items

	Business Loans				
	Term Balance, Fixed Interest	Term Balance, Floating Interest	Operating Line of Credit	Mortgages	Total
Paid down in current period	50	40	8	1,200	1,298
Existing from prior period	170	120	70	3,500	3,860
Advances during current period	80	66	12	1,450	1,608
Period end	250	186	12	4,950	5,468
	Aggregate business loans →		448		

Operating lines of credit relate to numbers of customers with approved lines of credit

Average Dollar Value of Items

	Business Loans			
	Term Balance, Fixed Interest	Term Balance, Floating Interest	Operating Line of Credit	Mortgages
Paid down in current period	2,400	1,100	200	60
Existing from prior period	2,250	1,550	300	85
Advances during current period	2,600	1,300	75	95
Period end	2,362	1,461	1,825	88

Total Dollar Value of Items

	Business Loans				
	Term Balance, Fixed Interest	Term Balance, Floating Interest	Operating Line of Credit	Mortgages	Total
Paid down in current period	120,000	44,000	1,600	72,000	237,600
Existing from prior period	382,500	186,000	21,000	297,500	887,000
Advances during current period	208,000	85,800	900	137,750	432,450
	590,500	271,800	21,900	435,250	1,319,450
Period end	Aggregate business loans →		884,200		

Operating lines are advanced and paid down on a daily basis. The above balances represent the net transactions. Further information is as follows:

Total advances	123,200
Total repayments	123,900

Number of Significant Items

	Business Loans				
	Term Balance, Fixed Interest	Term Balance, Floating Interest	Operating Line of Credit	Mortgages	Total
Paid down in current period	20	16	1	4	41
Existing from prior period	60	42	14	13	129
Advances during current period	24	20	3	5	52
Period end	84	62	17	18	181
	Aggregate business loans →		163		

Percentage of Significant Items

	Business Loans			
	Term Balance, Fixed Interest	Term Balance, Floating Interest	Operating Line of Credit	Mortgages
Paid down in current period	85%	80%	40%	7%
Existing from prior period	85%	75%	40%	7%
Advances during current period	80%	65%	40%	7%

Total Dollar Value of Significant Items

	Business Loans				
	Term Balance, Fixed Interest	Term Balance, Floating Interest	Operating Line of Credit	Mortgages	Total
Paid down in current period	102,000	35,200	640	5,040	142,880
Existing from prior period	325,125	139,500	8,400	20,825	493,850
Advances during current period	166,400	55,770	360	9,643	232,173
	491,525	195,270	8,760	30,468	726,023
	Aggregate business loans →		695,555		

Total Dollar Value of Non-Significant Items

	Business Loans				
	Term Balance, Fixed Interest	Term Balance, Floating Interest	Operating Line of Credit	Mortgages	Total
Paid down in current period	18,000	8,800	960	66,960	94,720
Existing from prior period	57,375	46,500	12,600	276,675	393,150
Advances during current period	41,600	30,030	540	128,107	200,277
	98,975	76,530	13,140	404,782	593,427
	Aggregate business loans →		188,645		

Total Dollar Value of Interest Revenue

	Business Loans				
	Term Balance, Fixed Interest	Term Balance, Floating Interest	Operating Line of Credit	Mortgages	Total
Paid down in current period	7,200	2,640	96	4,320	9,936
Existing from prior period	42,075	20,460	2,310	38,675	64,845
Advances during current period	12,480	5,148	54	9,643	17,682
	61,755	28,248	2,460	52,638	92,463
	Aggregate business loans →		92,463		

Total Dollar Value of Interest Receipts

	Business Loans				
	Term Balance, Fixed Interest	Term Balance, Floating Interest	Operating Line of Credit	Mortgages	Total
Paid down in current period	9,696	2,983	96	4,963	17,738
Existing from prior period	39,971	20,119	2,310	38,030	62,400
Advances during current period	11,856	5,062	54	9,482	16,972
	61,523	28,164	2,460	52,475	97,110
	Aggregate business loans →		92,147		

Total Dollar Value of Accrued Interest Receivable

	Business Loans				
	Term Balance, Fixed Interest	Term Balance, Floating Interest	Operating Line of Credit	Mortgages	Total
Paid down in current period	n/a	n/a	n/a	n/a	n/a
Existing from prior period	10,519	1,705	n/a	3,223	15,447
Advances during current period	3,120	429	n/a	804	4,353
	13,639	2,134	n/a	4,027	19,800

Interest Yield

	Business Loans			
	Term Balance, Fixed Interest	Term Balance, Floating Interest	Operating Line of Credit	Mortgages
Paid down in current period	12.00%	12.00%	13.00%	12.00%
Existing from prior period	11.00%	11.00%	12.00%	13.00%
Advances during current period	12.00%	12.00%	13.00%	14.00%

TABLE 3

Loan Characteristics

	Based on size:					
	Individually Significant		Individually Non-significant			
			Upper Strata		Lower Strata	
	#	$	#	$	#	$
Mortgages						
Current	15	25,409	651	169,237	3,958	164,125
Arrears						
1-30 days	1	1,211	149	34,542	84	4,426
31-90 days	0	0	33	12,658	18	1,658
over 90 days	1	2,200	18	8,157	2	268
Collection/litigation						
secured	1	1,648	13	9,352	6	359
non-secured	n/a	n/a	n/a	n/a	n/a	n/a
Total	18	30,468	864	233,946	4,068	170,836
		Total non-significant			4,932	404,782
		Total mortgages			4,950	435,250
Business loans						
Current	128	611,916	99	86,451	112	52,378
Arrears						
1-30 days	14	35,689	22	20,528	18	7,456
31-90 days	9	23,385	12	9,493	7	3,252
over 90 days	7	12,560	2	1,666	4	1,854
Collection/litigation						
secured	3	6,381	5	3,467	2	815
non-secured	2	5,624	1	950	1	335
Total	163	695,555	141	122,555	144	66,090
		Total non-significant			285	188,645
		Total business loans			448	884,200

Appendix 4.6

WESTERN FINANCIAL CORPORATION

Western Financial Corporation (WFC) is a small financial institution. Its shares are listed on the Alberta Stock Exchange, and they trade over the counter in many other jurisdictions. It is headquartered in Edmonton, Alberta, and has lending offices in 24 western Canadian cities and towns. WFC began as a farming cooperative almost 100 years ago, and was reconstituted as a lending company. The Canadian and US lending environments are quite similar.

This is the first time that this financial institution has been audited by your firm. Through audit procedures directed towards the opening numbers on the financial statements, others in your office have determined that the opening numbers are accurate, the previous auditors were competent, and that the previous auditors performed sufficient and appropriate audit work for you to place reliance on the procedures they carried out. The financial institution has changed auditors as a result of the change of ownership of the parent. The recovery on this engagement (as with the parent) is expected to be good as the previous auditors had no fee pressures.

A review of the prior year's file by your manager and partner indicated that the financial institution was very control conscious, and that adequate information and control systems were in place. Other information regarding the new client was obtained by the previous in charge who began planning this engagement, and supervised the control testing. You are to complete the audit risk assessment and substantive planning.

WFC is a small financial institution, with total assets of C$75 million at October 31, 19X1. As the enclosed exhibits indicates, the financial institution's assets are fairly evenly distributed between the various types of income producing assets. It does not conduct retail personal banking. Its leverage ratio is 21.3, compared with an industry average of 19.6 and a regulatory limit of 22.

WFC offers general corporate banking services to businesses, including working capital financing (operating lines of credit). While it is trying to gain a bigger share of loans to the resource and manufacturing industries, its principal market is still the agricultural sector. Most agricultural loans are recorded in the Prairies, while some non-agricultural loans are booked in the Toronto office which is still only a few years old. Operating lines are always at interest rates that float with prime, while other business loans have either fixed or floating rates of interest. The balances of business loans vary significantly, while operating lines of credit vary more dramatically. Operating lines are often changed on a daily basis.

In recent years, WFC has also developed a portfolio of retail mortgages which offer basic residential mortgages at competitive rates. Mortgages are offered for terms of three to five years, at fixed rates. Many of these are with farmers who also have business loans. Mortgage loans do not vary significantly in amounts compared to the average.

Funding is principally in the form of deposits with other financial institutions and market investors.

The lending industry in Canada and the United States has been relatively stable after some difficult years. WFC has no loans to non-Canadian residents. All loans are in Canadian dollars.

WFC's accounting and administration functions are located in Edmonton, with all documentation located in all branches where the credit approval is granted. All offices can grant loans, issue disbursements and accept receipts.

Excess funds are held in the form of cash and liquid securities (government treasury bills). Minimum liquidity is required by regulators. WFC has always met regulatory requirements. Balances of cash and cash equivalents are as follows ($000s):

October 31, 19X0	12
October 32, 19X1	16

Overall audit risk for all financial statement assertions is planned at 2%.

Records are kept by a sub-ledger, a software package bought from and tailored by a major software house. This sub-ledger details the total loan/mortgage limit, outstanding balance, interest rate, accrued interest and other loan agreement details.

Loan loss provisions are made on a specific item basis for business loans, and on an historic formula basis for mortgages. The client also has a general loss provision which covers unforeseen circumstances and the general risk of the portfolios. According to the prior auditors' working papers, the formula method for mortgages has appeared to be adequate in prior years.

Prior risk levels (i.e., after inherent risk and control risk evaluation, but before any substantive audit work) are listed in Table 1.

Detailed financial information is provided in the other tables.

Audit work on internal controls on the loan/mortgage/receipts cycle has been done.

TABLE 1

Levels of Risk

	Balance					Accrued Interest					Revenue/Expense			
	C	E	A over	A under	V	C	E	A over	A under	V	C	E	A over	A under
Inherent Risk														
Fixed balance, fixed rate	60	45	50	30	100	45	30	60	40	100	55	50	50	40
Fixed balance, floating rate	65	55	60	40	100	55	40	50	30	100	65	60	60	50
Operating line of credit	75	65	70	50	100	n/a	n/a	n/a	n/a	n/a	65	60	60	50
Mortgages	60	45	50	30	100	45	40	40	20	100	55	50	50	40
Cash - balances	30	20	10	10	n/a	n/a	n/a	n/a	n/a	n/a	n/a	n/a	n/a	n/a
Cash - receipts	40	35	65	45	n/a	n/a	n/a	n/a	n/a	n/a	n/a	n/a	n/a	n/a
Cash - disbursements	40	35	45	65	n/a	n/a	n/a	n/a	n/a	n/a	n/a	n/a	n/a	n/a
Control Risk														
Fixed balance, fixed rate	65	65	65	65	100	100	100	100	100	100	70	70	70	70
Fixed balance, floating rate	75	75	75	75	100	100	100	100	100	100	80	80	80	80
Operating line of credit	85	85	85	85	100	n/a	n/a	n/a	n/a	n/a	90	90	90	90
Mortgages	65	65	65	65	100	100	100	100	100	100	70	70	70	70
Cash - balances	20	10	10	10	n/a	n/a	n/a	n/a	n/a	n/a	n/a	n/a	n/a	n/a
Cash - receipts	30	30	60	60	n/a	n/a	n/a	n/a	n/a	n/a	n/a	n/a	n/a	n/a
Cash - disbursements	30	30	60	60	n/a	n/a	n/a	n/a	n/a	n/a	n/a	n/a	n/a	n/a
Risk Prior to Substantive Work														
Fixed balance, fixed rate	39	29	33	20	100	45	30	60	40	100	39	35	35	28
Fixed balance, floating rate	49	41	45	30	100	55	40	50	30	100	52	48	48	40
Operating line of credit	64	55	60	43	100	n/a	n/a	n/a	n/a	n/a	59	54	54	45
Mortgages	39	29	33	20	100	45	40	40	20	100	39	35	35	28
Cash - balances	6	2	1	1	n/a	n/a	n/a	n/a	n/a	n/a	n/a	n/a	n/a	n/a
Cash - receipts	12	11	39	27	n/a	n/a	n/a	n/a	n/a	n/a	n/a	n/a	n/a	n/a
Cash - disbursements	12	11	27	39	n/a	n/a	n/a	n/a	n/a	n/a	n/a	n/a	n/a	n/a

Key to Assertions

- C completeness
- E existence/ occurrence
- A accuracy
- V valuation

TABLE 2

Financial Information

Number of Items

	Business Loans				
	Term Balance, Fixed Interest	Term Balance, Floating Interest	Operating Line of Credit	Mortgages	Total
Paid down in current period	30	55	5	266	356
Existing from prior period	119	140	17	458	734
Advances during current period	50	75	6	301	432
Period end	169	215	6	759	1,166
	Aggregate business loans →		390		

Operating lines of credit relate to numbers of customers with approved lines of credit.

Average Dollar Value of Items

	Business Loans			
	Term Balance, Fixed Interest	Term Balance, Floating Interest	Operating Line of Credit	Mortgages
Paid down in current period	70	50	20	45
Existing from prior period	83	72	23	50
Advances during current period	97	77	15	60
Period end	87	74	80	54
	Aggregate business loans →		80	

Total Dollar Value of Items

	Business Loans				
	Term Balance, Fixed Interest	Term Balance, Floating Interest	Operating Line of Credit	Mortgages	Total
Paid down in current period	21,000	2,750	100	11,970	16,920
Existing from prior period	9,877	10,077	391	22,967	43,312
Advances during current period	4,850	5,775	90	18,060	28,775
Period end	14,727	15,852	481	41,027	72,087
	Aggregate business loans →		31,060		

Operating lines are advanced and paid down on a daily basis. The above balances represent the net transactions. Further information is as follows:

Total advances	2,151
Total repayments	2,161

Number of Significant Items

	Business Loans				
	Term Balance, Fixed Interest	Term Balance, Floating Interest	Operating Line of Credit	Mortgages	Total
Paid down in current period	4	2	1	4	11
Existing from prior period	6	5	1	12	12
Advances during current period	3	2	0	6	5
Period end	9	7	1	18	17
	Aggregate business loans →		17		

Percentage of Significant Items

	Business Loans			
	Term Balance, Fixed Interest	Term Balance, Floating Interest	Operating Line of Credit	Mortgages
Paid down in current period	40%	25%	60%	4%
Existing from prior period	52%	34%	64%	6%
Advances during current period	43%	28%	70%	4%

Total Dollar Value of Significant Items

	Business Loans				
	Term Balance, Fixed Interest	Term Balance, Floating Interest	Operating Line of Credit	Mortgages	Total
Paid down in current period	840	688	60	479	2,067
Existing from prior period	5,175	3,409	252	1,354	10,190
Advances during current period	2,083	1,641	63	698	4,485
	7,258	5,050	315	2,052	14,675
	Aggregate business loans →		12,623		

Total Dollar Value of Non-Significant Items

	Business Loans				
	Term Balance, Fixed Interest	Term Balance, Floating Interest	Operating Line of Credit	Mortgages	Total
Paid down in current period	1,260	2,062	40	11,491	14,853
Existing from prior period	4,702	6,668	139	21,613	92,106
Advances during current period	2,767	4,134	27	17,362	116,372
	7,469	10,802	166	38,975	208,478
	Aggregate business loans →		18,437		

Total Dollar Value of Interest Revenue

	Business Loans				
	Term Balance, Fixed Interest	Term Balance, Floating Interest	Operating Line of Credit	Mortgages	Total
Paid down in current period	126	165	6	718	297
Existing from prior period	1,086	1,108	43	2,986	2,237
Advances during current period	291	347	5	1,264	643
	1,503	1,620	54	4,968	3,177
	Aggregate business loans →		3,177		

Total Dollar Value of Interest Receipts

	Business Loans				
	Term Balance, Fixed Interest	Term Balance, Floating Interest	Operating Line of Credit	Mortgages	Total
Paid down in current period	184	188	6	802	1,180
Existing from prior period	1,032	1,090	43	2,936	2,165
Advances during current period	276	341	5	1,243	622
	1,492	1,619	54	4,981	3,967
	Aggregate business loans →		3,165		

Total Dollar Value of Accrued Interest Receivable

	Business Loans				
	Term Balance, Fixed Interest	Term Balance, Floating Interest	Operating Line of Credit	Mortgages	Total
Paid down in current period	n/a	n/a	n/a	n/a	n/a
Existing from prior period	272	92	n/a	249	613
Advances during current period	73	29	n/a	105	207
	345	121	n/a	354	820

Interest Yield

	Business Loans			
	Term Balance, Fixed Interest	Term Balance, Floating Interest	Operating Line of Credit	Mortgages
Paid down in current period	12.00%	12.00%	13.00%	12.00%
Existing from prior period	11.00%	11.00%	12.00%	13.00%
Advances during current period	12.00%	12.00%	13.00%	14.00%

TABLE 3

Loan Characteristics

	Based on size:					
	Individually Significant		Individually Non-significant			
			Upper Strata		Lower Strata	
	#	$	#	$	#	$
Mortgages						
Current	15	1,684	225	13,848	246	9,934
Arrears						
1-30 days	1	122	114	6,908	66	2,443
31-90 days	0	0	33	2,332	18	764
over 90 days	1	130	14	1,162	4	154
Collection/litigation						
secured	1	116	15	1,250	6	180
non-secured	n/a	n/a	n/a	n/a	n/a	n/a
Total	18	2,052	401	25,500	340	13,475
		Total non-significant			741	38,975
		Total mortgages			759	41,027
Business loans						
Current	13	10,503	74	9,290	106	4,724
Arrears						
1-30 days	2	1,114	9	959	13	506
31-90 days	0	0	7	1,246	7	374
over 90 days	1	434	2	325	3	188
Collection/litigation						
secured	1	572	3	456	2	180
non-secured	0	0	1	156	1	33
Total	17	12,623	96	12,432	132	6,005
		Total non-significant			228	18,437
		Total business loans			245	31,060

Appendix 4.7

AUDIT PLANNING CASES - INSTRUCTIONS AND ADDITIONAL INFORMATION

MANUFACTURING CLIENTS

GENERAL INSTRUCTIONS

You are asked to review a previously-prepared substantive audit program plan for each of the clients profiled. Please consider the client information provided and evaluate the audit program by completing the attached questionnaire for each client.

Appendix A contains a reference list of procedures which was available to the plan preparer as well.

Manufacturing Client 1

Consider that ALL financial statement items are material.

Assume that the procedures constituting the solution plan are applied and that there are no indications of material error in the evidence they provide.

One of your staff has conducted audit procedures directed towards cash disbursements. You assess that the remaining risk of a material misstatement for all cash disbursement assertions is 25%. At the present time you do not plan to obtain any further direct evidence concerning cash disbursements.

PLANNING QUESTIONNAIRE

QUESTION 1 - PLAN EFFECTIVENESS

Part 1

Please assess the effectiveness of the attached plan with respect to each financial statement item assertion on a scale of 1 to 5 by filling out the worksheet on this page. The interpretation of scale values is given below the worksheet.

Note: When assessing the effectiveness of any procedure, or set of procedures please take into account the impact of evidence provided by all the other procedures which constitute the plan.

	Existence/ Occurrence	Completeness	Accuracy	Valuation
Accounts receivable - Product A				
Accounts receivable - Product B				
Cash Sales				
Cash Receipts on Account - Product A				
Cash Receipts on Account - Product B				
Cash balances				
Sales on Account - Product A				
Sales on Account - Product B				
Allowance for Doubtful Accounts - Product A				
Allowance for Doubtful Accounts - Product B				
Writeoffs - Product A				
Writeoffs - Product B				
Returns				

1 = The actual risk of a material error remaining undetected with respect to the financial statement item assertion in question is significantly greater than the target risk.

2 = The actual risk of a material error remaining undetected with respect to the financial statement item assertion in question is slightly greater than the target risk.

3 = The actual risk of a material error remaining undetected with respect to the financial statement item assertion in question is equal to the target risk.

4 = The actual risk of a material error remaining undetected with respect to the financial statement item assertion in question is slightly less than the target risk.

5 = The actual risk of a material error remaining undetected with respect to the financial statement item assertion in question is significantly less than the target risk.

Part 2

Please assess the effectiveness of the plan with respect to each financial statement item using the worksheet on this page. Please use a scale of 1 to 5. The interpretation of the scale values is given below the worksheet.

Accounts receivable - Product A
Accounts receivable - Product B

Cash Sales
Cash Receipts on Account - Product A
Cash Receipts on Account - Product B

Cash balances

Sales on Account - Product A
Sales on Account - Product B

Allowance for Doubtful Accounts - Product A
Allowance for Doubtful Accounts - Product B

Writeoffs - Product A
Writeoffs - Product B

Returns

1 = Target risks would not be achieved for any of the financial statement item assertions.

2 = Target risks would not be achieved for most critical and most non-critical financial statement item assertions.

3 = Target risks would be achieved for most critical and some non-critical financial statement item assertions.

4 = Target risks would be achieved for all critical and most non-critical financial statement item assertions.

5 = Target risks would be achieved (or reduced below target) for all financial statement item assertions.

Part 3

Please indicate you assessment of the overall effectiveness of the plan by choosing the statement which best describes the plan's effectiveness at the financial statement level.

1 = Target risks would not be achieved for any financial statement item assertions.

2 = Target risks would not be achieved for most financial statement item assertions.

3 = Target risks would be achieved for some critical and some non-critical financial statement item assertions.

4 = Target risks would be achieved for all critical and most non-critical financial statement item assertions.

5 = Target risks would be achieved (or reduced below target) for all financial statement item assertions.

QUESTION 2 - PLAN EFFICIENCY

Part 1

Please assess the efficiency of the plan with respect to each financial statement item assertion on a scale of 1 to 5 by filling out the worksheet on this page. The interpretation of the scale values is given below the worksheet.

	Existence/ Occurrence	Completeness	Accuracy	Valuation
Accounts receivable - Product A				
Accounts receivable - Product B				
Cash Sales				
Cash Receipts on Account - Product A				
Cash Receipts on Account - Product B				
Cash balances				
Sales on Account - Product A				
Sales on Account - Product B				
Allowance for Doubtful Accounts - Product A				
Allowance for Doubtful Accounts - Product B				
Writeoffs - Product A				
Writeoffs - Product B				
Returns				

1 = There are other sets of procedures which would result in the achievement of the same level of risk with respect to the financial statement item assertion in question as that achieved by the plan at a significantly lower cost than that of the plan.

2 = There are other sets of procedures which would result in the achievement of the same level of risk with respect to the financial statement item assertion in question as that achieved by the plan at a slightly lower cost than that of the plan.

3 = Any alternative set of procedures which would result in the achievement of the same level of risk with respect to the financial statement item assertion in question as that achieved by the plan would have the approximately the same cost as that of the plan.

4 = Any alternative set of procedures which would result in the achievement of the same level of risk with respect to the financial statement item assertion in question as that achieved by the plan would have a cost slightly greater than that of the plan.

5 = Any alternative set of procedures which would result in the achievement of the same level of risk with respect to the financial statement item assertion in question as that achieved by the plan would have a cost which was significantly greater than that of the plan.

Part 2

Please assess the efficiency of the plan with respect to each financial statement item on a scale of 1 to 5 by filling out the worksheet on this page. The interpretation of the scale values is given below the worksheet.

Accounts receivable - Product A
Accounts receivable - Product B

Cash Sales
Cash Receipts on Account - Product A
Cash Receipts on Account - Product B

Cash balances

Sales on Account - Product A
Sales on Account - Product B
Allowance for Doubtful Accounts - Product A
Allowance for Doubtful Accounts - Product B

Writeoffs - Product A
Writeoffs - Product B

Returns

1 = There are other sets of procedures which would result in the achievement of the same level of risk with respect to all financial statement item assertions as that achieved by the plan at a significantly lower cost than that of the plan.

2 = There are other sets of procedures which would result in the achievement of the same level of risk with respect to all financial statement item assertions as that achieved by the plan at a slightly lower cost than that of the plan.

3 = Any alternative set of procedures which would result in the achievement of the same level of risk with respect to all financial statement item assertions as that achieved by the plan would have approximately the same cost as that of the plan.

4 = Any alternative set of procedures which would result in the achievement of the same level of risk with respect to all financial statement item assertions as that achieved by the plan would have a cost slightly greater than that of the plan.

5 = Any alternative set of procedures which would result in the achievement of the same level of risk with respect to all financial statement item assertions as that achieved by the plan would have a cost which was significantly greater than that of the plan.

Part 3

Please indicate you assessment of the overall efficiency of the solution plan by choosing the statement listed below which best describes the efficiency of the plan at the financial statement level.

1 = There are other sets of procedures which would result in the achievement of the same level of overall risk as that achieved by the plan at a significantly lower cost than that of the plan.

2 = There are other sets of procedures which would result in the achievement of the same level of overall risk as that achieved by the plan at a slightly lower cost than of the plan.

3 = Any alternative set of procedures which would result in the achievement of the same level of overall risk as that achieved by the plan would have approximately the same cost as that of the plan.

4 = Any alternative set of procedures which would result in the achievement of the same level of overall risk as that achieved by the plan would have a cost slightly greater than that of the plan.

5 = Any alternative set of procedures which would result in the achievement of the same level of overall risk as that achieved by the plan would have a cost which was significantly greater than that of the plan.

QUESTION 3 - PLAN ACCEPTABILITY

Part 1

Please assess the acceptability of the solution plan by choosing a statement which best describes the overall acceptability of the plan to you.

1 = The plan is fundamentally unacceptable and even major revisions cannot change this conclusion.

2 = The plan is unacceptable and can only be made acceptable through major revisions.

3 = The plan is generally acceptable but some significant revisions are necessary.

4 = The plan is generally acceptable but some minor revisions are necessary.

5 = The plan is acceptable without any revisions being required.

Part 2

If you have chosen statement 2,3, or 4 in the above assessment please indicate below the revisions that you would make to the solution plan to make it acceptable. Beside each revision please indicate the reason(s) for making it.

Revision	Reason(s)

QUESTION 4 - THE COMPETENCE OF THE PLAN PREPARER

Please assess the competence of the preparer of the plan by checking the cell in the matrix below which best describes your assessment of the seniority and experience of the preparer of the plan.

	Seniority	Partner	Manager	Staff	Junior
Experience					
Extensive Industry but not this client					
No experience of this industry					

QUESTION 5 - MISSING AND REDUNDANT PROCEDURES

Please list any procedures which are missing from the solution plan and that you believe should be included in any solution plan for the client in question.

Please list any procedures which are included in the solution plan which you consider to be redundant.

Please indicate any procedures which are included in the solution plan that you would consider necessary but should be carried out with smaller sample sizes (smaller confidence factors).

Please indicate any procedures which are included in the solution plan that you would consider necessary but should be carried out with larger sample sizes (larger confidence factors).

Appendix 4.8

AUDIT PLANNING CASES - INSTRUCTIONS AND ADDITIONAL INFORMATION

MANUFACTURING CLIENTS

GENERAL INSTRUCTIONS

You are asked to review a previously-prepared substantive audit program plan for each of the clients profiled. Please consider the client information provided and evaluate the audit program by completing the attached questionnaire for each client.

Appendix A contains a reference list of procedures which was available to the plan preparer as well.

Manufacturing Profile 2

All items WITH THE EXCEPTION OF the following are material:

Cash Sales
Cash balances - on hand

Doubtful accounts - product A
Doubtful accounts - product B

Writeoffs - product A
Writeoffs - product B

Assume that the procedures constituting the solution plan are applied and that there are no indications of material error in the evidence they provide.

One of your staff has conducted audit procedures directed towards cash disbursements. You assess that the remaining risk of a material misstatement for all cash disbursement assertions is 25%. At the present time you do not plan to obtain any further direct evidence concerning cash disbursements.

PLANNING QUESTIONNAIRE

QUESTION 1 - PLAN EFFECTIVENESS

Part 1

Please assess the effectiveness of the attached plan with respect to each financial statement item assertion on a scale of 1 to 5 by filling out the worksheet on this page. The interpretation of scale values is given below the worksheet.

Note: When assessing the effectiveness of any procedure, or set of procedures please take into account the impact of evidence provided by all the other procedures which constitute the plan.

	Existence/ Occurrence	Completeness	Accuracy	Valuation
Accounts receivable - Product A				
Accounts receivable - Product B				
Cash Receipts on Account - Product A				
Cash Receipts on Account - Product B				
Cash balances				
Sales on Account - Product A				
Sales on Account - Product B				
Returns				

1 = The actual risk of a material error remaining undetected with respect to the financial statement item assertion in question is significantly greater than the target risk.

2 = The actual risk of a material error remaining undetected with respect to the financial statement item assertion in question is slightly greater than the target risk.

3 = The actual risk of a material error remaining undetected with respect to the financial statement item assertion in question is equal to the target risk.

4 = The actual risk of a material error remaining undetected with respect to the financial statement item assertion in question is slightly less than the target risk.

5 = The actual risk of a material error remaining undetected with respect to the financial statement item assertion in question is significantly less than the target risk.

Part 2

Please assess the effectiveness of the plan with respect to each financial statement item using the worksheet on this page. Please use a scale of 1 to 5. The interpretation of the scale values is given below the worksheet.

Accounts receivable - Product A
Accounts receivable - Product B

Cash Receipts on Account - Product A
Cash Receipts on Account - Product B

Cash balances

Sales on Account - Product A
Sales on Account - Product B

Returns

1 = Target risks would not be achieved for any of the financial statement item assertions.

2 = Target risks would not be achieved for most critical and most non-critical financial statement item assertions.

3 = Target risks would be achieved for most critical and some non-critical financial statement item assertions.

4 = Target risks would be achieved for all critical and most non-critical financial statement item assertions.

5 = Target risks would be achieved (or reduced below target) for all financial statement item assertions.

Part 3

Please indicate you assessment of the overall effectiveness of the plan by choosing the statement which best describes the plan's effectiveness at the financial statement level.

1 = Target risks would not be achieved for any financial statement item assertions.

2 = Target risks would not be achieved for most financial statement item assertions.

3 = Target risks would be achieved for some critical and some non-critical financial statement item assertions.

4 = Target risks would be achieved for all critical and most non-critical financial statement item assertions.

5 = Target risks would be achieved (or reduced below target) for all financial statement item assertions.

QUESTION 2 - PLAN EFFICIENCY

Part 1

Please assess the efficiency of the plan with respect to each financial statement item assertion on a scale of 1 to 5 by filling out the worksheet on this page. The interpretation of the scale values is given below the worksheet.

	Existence/ Occurrence	Completeness	Accuracy	Valuation
Accounts receivable - Product A				
Accounts receivable - Product B				
Cash Receipts on Account - Product A				
Cash Receipts on Account - Product B				
Cash balances				
Sales on Account - Product A				
Sales on Account - Product B				
Returns				

1 = There are other sets of procedures which would result in the achievement of the same level of risk with respect to the financial statement item assertion in question as that achieved by the plan at a significantly lower cost than that of the plan.

2 = There are other sets of procedures which would result in the achievement of the same level of risk with respect to the financial statement item assertion in question as that achieved by the plan at a slightly lower cost than that of the plan.

3 = Any alternative set of procedures which would result in the achievement of the same level of risk with respect to the financial statement item assertion in question as that achieved by the plan would have the approximately the same cost as that of the plan.

4 = Any alternative set of procedures which would result in the achievement of the same level of risk with respect to the financial statement item assertion in question as that achieved by the plan would have a cost slightly greater than that of the plan.

5 = Any alternative set of procedures which would result in the achievement of the same level of risk with respect to the financial statement item assertion in question as that achieved by the plan would have a cost which was significantly greater than that of the plan.

Part 2

Please assess the efficiency of the plan with respect to each financial statement item on a scale of 1 to 5 by filling out the worksheet on the next page. The interpretation of the scale values is given below the worksheet.

Accounts receivable - Product A
Accounts receivable - Product B

Cash Receipts on Account - Product A
Cash Receipts on Account - Product B

Cash balances

Sales on Account - Product A
Sales on Account - Product B

Returns

1 = There are other sets of procedures which would result in the achievement of the same level of risk with respect to all financial statement item assertions as that achieved by the plan at a significantly lower cost than that of the plan.

2 = There are other sets of procedures which would result in the achievement of the same level of risk with respect to all financial statement item assertions as that achieved by the plan at a slightly lower cost than that of the plan.

3 = Any alternative set of procedures which would result in the achievement of the same level of risk with respect to all financial statement item assertions as that achieved by the plan would have approximately the same cost as that of the plan.

4 = Any alternative set of procedures which would result in the achievement of the same level of risk with respect to all financial statement item assertions as that achieved by the plan would have a cost slightly greater than that of the plan.

5 = Any alternative set of procedures which would result in the achievement of the same level of risk with respect to all financial statement item assertions as that achieved by the plan would have a cost which was significantly greater than that of the plan.

Part 3

Please indicate you assessment of the overall efficiency of the solution plan by choosing the statement listed below which best describes the efficiency of the plan at the financial statement level.

1 = There are other sets of procedures which would result in the achievement of the same level of overall risk as that achieved by the plan at a significantly lower cost than that of the plan.

2 = There are other sets of procedures which would result in the achievement of the same level of overall risk as that achieved by the plan at a slightly lower cost than of the plan.

3 = Any alternative set of procedures which would result in the achievement of the same level of overall risk as that achieved by the plan would have approximately the same cost as that of the plan.

4 = Any alternative set of procedures which would result in the achievement of the same level of overall risk as that achieved by the plan would have a cost slightly greater than that of the plan.

5 = Any alternative set of procedures which would result in the achievement of the same level of overall risk as that achieved by the plan would have a cost which was significantly greater than that of the plan.

QUESTION 3 - PLAN ACCEPTABILITY

Part 1

Please assess the acceptability of the solution plan by choosing a statement which best describes the overall acceptability of the plan to you.

1 = The plan is fundamentally unacceptable and even major revisions cannot change this conclusion.

2 = The plan is unacceptable and can only be made acceptable through major revisions.

3 = The plan is generally acceptable but some significant revisions are necessary.

4 = The plan is generally acceptable but some minor revisions are necessary.

5 = The plan is acceptable without any revisions being required.

Part 2

If you have chosen statement 2,3, or 4 in the above assessment please indicate below the revisions that you would make to the solution plan to make it acceptable. Beside each revision please indicate the reason(s) for making it.

Revision	Reason(s)

QUESTION 4 - THE COMPETENCE OF THE PLAN PREPARER

Please assess the competence of the preparer of the plan by checking the cell in the matrix below which best describes your assessment of the seniority and experience of the preparer of the plan.

	Seniority	Partner	Manager	Staff	Junior
Experience					
Extensive Industry but not this client					
No experience of this industry					

QUESTION 5 - MISSING AND REDUNDANT PROCEDURES

Please list any procedures which are missing from the solution plan and that you believe should be included in any solution plan for the client in question.

Please list any procedures which are included in the solution plan which you consider to be redundant.

Please indicate any procedures which are included in the solution plan that you would consider necessary but should be carried out with smaller sample sizes (smaller confidence factors).

Please indicate any procedures which are included in the solution plan that you would consider necessary but should be carried out with larger sample sizes (larger confidence factors).

Appendix 4.9

AUDIT PLANNING CASES - INSTRUCTIONS AND ADDITIONAL INFORMATION

RETAIL CLIENTS

GENERAL INSTRUCTIONS

You are asked to review a previously-prepared substantive audit program plan for each of the clients profiled. Please consider the client information provided and evaluate the audit program by completing the attached questionnaire for each client.

Appendix A contains a reference list of procedures which was available to the plan preparer as well.

Retail Profile 1

All items WITH THE EXCEPTION OF the following are material:

Cash balances - on hand

Writeoffs - store credit card

Writeoffs - wholesale

Assume that the procedures constituting the solution plan are applied and that there are no indications of material error in the evidence they provide.

One of your staff has conducted audit procedures directed towards cash disbursements. You assess that the remaining risk of a material misstatement for all cash disbursement assertions is 25%. At the present time you do not plan to obtain any further direct evidence concerning cash disbursements.

PLANNING QUESTIONNAIRE

QUESTION 1 - PLAN EFFECTIVENESS

Part 1

Please assess the effectiveness of the attached plan with respect to each financial statement item assertion on a scale of 1 to 5 by filling out the worksheet on this page. The interpretation of scale values is given below the worksheet.

Note: When assessing the effectiveness of any procedure, or set of procedures please take into account the impact of evidence provided by all the other procedures which constitute the plan.

	Existence/ Occurrence	Completeness	Accuracy	Valuation
Accounts receivable - National Credit Card				
Accounts receivable - Store Credit Card				
Accounts receivable - Wholesale Credit				
Cash Sales				
Cash Receipts on Account - National Credit Card				
Cash Receipts on Account - Store Credit Card				
Cash Receipts on Account - Wholesale Credit				
Cash balances				
Sales on Account - National Credit Card				
Sales on Account - Store Credit Card				
Sales on Account - Wholesale Credit				
Allowance for Doubtful Accounts - Store Credit Card				
Allowance for Doubtful Accounts - Wholesale Credit				
Writeoffs - Store Credit Card				
Writeoffs -Wholesale Credit				
Returns				
Markdowns				

1 = The actual risk of a material error remaining undetected with respect to the financial statement item assertion in question is significantly greater than the target risk.

2 = The actual risk of a material error remaining undetected with respect to the financial statement item assertion in question is slightly greater than the target risk.

3 = The actual risk of a material error remaining undetected with respect to the financial statement item assertion in question is equal to the target risk.

4 = The actual risk of a material error remaining undetected with respect to the financial statement item assertion in question is slightly less than the target risk.

5 = The actual risk of a material error remaining undetected with respect to the financial statement item assertion in question is significantly less than the target risk.

Part 2

Please assess the effectiveness of the plan with respect to each financial statement item using the worksheet on this page. Please use a scale of 1 to 5. The interpretation of the scale values is given below the worksheet.

Accounts receivable - National Credit Card
Accounts receivable - Store Credit Card
Accounts receivable - Wholesale Credit

Cash Sales
Cash Receipts on Account - National Credit Card
Cash Receipts on Account - Store Credit Card
Cash Receipts on Account - Wholesale Credit

Cash balances

Sales on Account - National Credit Card
Sales on Account - Store Credit Card
Sales on Account - Wholesale Credit

Allowance for Doubtful Accounts - Store Credit Card
Allowance for Doubtful Accounts - Wholesale Credit

Writeoffs - Store Credit Card
Writeoffs -Wholesale Credit

Returns
Markdowns

1 = Target risks would not be achieved for any of the financial statement item assertions.

2 = Target risks would not be achieved for most critical and most non-critical financial statement item assertions.

3 = Target risks would be achieved for most critical and some non-critical financial statement item assertions.

4 = Target risks would be achieved for all critical and most non-critical financial statement item assertions.

5 = Target risks would be achieved (or exceeded) for all financial statement item assertions.

Part 3

Please indicate you assessment of the overall effectiveness of the plan by choosing the statement which best describes the plan's effectiveness at the financial statement level.

1 = Target risks would not be achieved for any financial statement item assertions.

2 = Target risks would not be achieved for most financial statement item assertions.

3 = Target risks would be achieved for some critical and some non-critical financial statement item assertions.

4 = Target risks would be achieved for all critical and most non-critical financial statement item assertions.

5 = Target risks would be achieved (or exceeded) for all financial statement item assertions.

QUESTION 2 - PLAN EFFICIENCY

Part 1

Please assess the efficiency of the plan with respect to each financial statement item assertion on a scale of 1 to 5 by filling out the worksheet on this page. The interpretation of the scale values is given below the worksheet.

	Existence/ Occurrence	Completeness	Accuracy	Valuation
Accounts receivable - National Credit Card				
Accounts receivable - Store Credit Card				
Accounts receivable - Wholesale Credit				
Cash Sales				
Cash Receipts on Account - National Credit Card				
Cash Receipts on Account - Store Credit Card				
Cash Receipts on Account - Wholesale Credit				
Cash balances				
Sales on Account - National Credit Card				
Sales on Account - Store Credit Card				
Sales on Account - Wholesale Credit				
Allowance for Doubtful Accounts - Store Credit Card				
Allowance for Doubtful Accounts - Wholesale Credit				
Writeoffs - Store Credit Card				
Writeoffs -Wholesale Credit				
Returns				
Markdowns				

1 = There are other sets of procedures which would result in the achievement of the same level of risk with respect to the financial statement item assertion in question as that achieved by the plan at a significantly lower cost than that of the plan.

2 = There are other sets of procedures which would result in the achievement of the same level of risk with respect to the financial statement item assertion in question as that achieved by the plan at a slightly lower cost than that of the plan.

3 = Any alternative set of procedures which would result in the achievement of the same level of risk with respect to the financial statement item assertion in question as that achieved by the plan would have the approximately the same cost as that of the plan.

4 = Any alternative set of procedures which would result in the achievement of the same level of risk with respect to the financial statement item assertion in question as that achieved by the plan would have a cost slightly greater than that of the plan.

5 = Any alternative set of procedures which would result in the achievement of the same level of risk with respect to the financial statement item assertion in question as that achieved by the plan would have a cost which was significantly greater than that of the plan.

Part 2

Please assess the efficiency of the plan with respect to each financial statement item on a scale of 1 to 5 by filling out the worksheet on this page. The interpretation of the scale values is given below the worksheet.

Accounts receivable - National Credit Card
Accounts receivable - Store Credit Card
Accounts receivable - Wholesale Credit

Cash Sales
Cash Receipts on Account - National Credit Card
Cash Receipts on Account - Store Credit Card
Cash Receipts on Account - Wholesale Credit

Cash balances

Sales on Account - National Credit Card
Sales on Account - Store Credit Card
Sales on Account - Wholesale Credit

Allowance for Doubtful Accounts - Store Credit Card
Allowance for Doubtful Accounts - Wholesale Credit

Writeoffs - Store Credit Card
Writeoffs -Wholesale Credit

Returns
Markdowns

1 = There are other sets of procedures which would result in the achievement of the same level of risk with respect to all financial statement item assertions as that achieved by the plan at a significantly lower cost than that of the plan.

2 = There are other sets of procedures which would result in the achievement of the same level of risk with respect to all financial statement item assertions as that achieved by the plan at a slightly lower cost than that of the plan.

3 = Any alternative set of procedures which would result in the achievement of the same level of risk with respect to all financial statement item assertions as that achieved by the plan would have approximately the same cost as that of the plan.

4 = Any alternative set of procedures which would result in the achievement of the same level of risk with respect to all financial statement item assertions as that achieved by the plan would have a cost slightly greater than that of the plan.

5 = Any alternative set of procedures which would result in the achievement of the same level of risk with respect to all financial statement item assertions as that achieved by the plan would have a cost which was significantly greater than that of the plan.

Part 3

Please indicate you assessment of the overall efficiency of the solution plan by choosing the statement listed below which best describes the efficiency of the plan at the financial statement level.

1 = There are other sets of procedures which would result in the achievement of the same level of overall risk as that achieved by the plan at a significantly lower cost than that of the plan.

2 = There are other sets of procedures which would result in the achievement of the same level of overall risk as that achieved by the plan at a slightly lower cost than of the plan.

3 = Any alternative set of procedures which would result in the achievement of the same level of overall risk as that achieved by the plan would have approximately the same cost as that of the plan.

4 = Any alternative set of procedures which would result in the achievement of the same level of overall risk as that achieved by the plan would have a cost slightly greater than that of the plan.

5 = Any alternative set of procedures which would result in the achievement of the same level of overall risk as that achieved by the plan would have a cost which was significantly greater than that of the plan.

QUESTION 3 - PLAN ACCEPTABILITY

Part 1

Please assess the acceptability of the solution plan by choosing a statement which best describes the overall acceptability of the plan to you.

1 = The plan is fundamentally unacceptable and even major revisions cannot change this conclusion.

2 = The plan is unacceptable and can only be made acceptable through major revisions.

3 = The plan is generally acceptable but some significant revisions are necessary.

4 = The plan is generally acceptable but some minor revisions are necessary.

5 = The plan is acceptable without any revisions being required.

Part 2

If you have chosen statement 2,3, or 4 in the above assessment please indicate below the revisions that you would make to the solution plan to make it acceptable. Beside each revision please indicate the reason(s) for making it.

Revision	Reason(s)

QUESTION 4 - THE COMPETENCE OF THE PLAN PREPARER

Please assess the competence of the preparer of the plan by checking the cell in the matrix below which best describes your assessment of the seniority and experience of the preparer of the plan.

Experience \ Seniority	Partner	Manager	Staff	Junior
Extensive Industry but not this client				
No experience of this industry				

QUESTION 5 - MISSING AND REDUNDANT PROCEDURES

Please list any procedures which are missing from the solution plan and that you believe should be included in any solution plan for the client in question.

Please list any procedures which are included in the solution plan which you consider to be redundant.

Please indicate any procedures which are included in the solution plan that you would consider necessary but should be carried out with smaller sample sizes (smaller confidence factors).

Please indicate any procedures which are included in the solution plan that you would consider necessary but should be carried out with larger sample sizes (larger confidence factors).

Appendix 4.10

AUDIT PLANNING CASES - INSTRUCTIONS AND ADDITIONAL INFORMATION

RETAIL CLIENTS

GENERAL INSTRUCTIONS

You are asked to review a previously-prepared substantive audit program plan for each of the clients profiled. Please consider the client information provided and evaluate the audit program by completing the attached questionnaire for each client.

Appendix A contains a reference list of procedures which was available to the plan preparer as well.

Retail Profile 2

All items WITH THE EXCEPTION OF the following are material:

Doubtful accounts - wholesale
Writeoffs - wholesale

Assume that the procedures constituting the solution plan are applied and that there are no indications of material error in the evidence they provide.

One of your staff has conducted audit procedures directed towards cash disbursements. You assess that the remaining risk of a material misstatement for all cash disbursement assertions is 25%. At the present time you do not plan to obtain any further direct evidence concerning cash disbursements.

PLANNING QUESTIONNAIRE

QUESTION 1 - PLAN EFFECTIVENESS

Part 1

Please assess the effectiveness of the attached plan with respect to each financial statement item assertion on a scale of 1 to 5 by filling out the worksheet on this page. The interpretation of scale values is given below the worksheet.

Note: When assessing the effectiveness of any procedure, or set of procedures please take into account the impact of evidence provided by all the other procedures which constitute the plan.

	Existence/ Occurrence	Completeness	Accuracy	Valuation
Accounts receivable - National Credit Card				
Accounts receivable - Store Credit Card				
Accounts receivable - Wholesale Credit				
Cash Sales				
Cash Receipts on Account - National Credit Card				
Cash Receipts on Account - Store Credit Card				
Cash Receipts on Account - Wholesale Credit				
Cash balances				
Sales on Account - National Credit Card				
Sales on Account - Store Credit Card				
Sales on Account - Wholesale Credit				
Allowance for Doubtful Accounts - Store Credit Card				
Writeoffs - Store Credit Card				
Returns				
Markdowns				

1 = The actual risk of a material error remaining undetected with respect to the financial statement item assertion in question is significantly greater than the target risk.

2 = The actual risk of a material error remaining undetected with respect to the financial statement item assertion in question is slightly greater than the target risk.

3 = The actual risk of a material error remaining undetected with respect to the financial statement item assertion in question is equal to the target risk.

4 = The actual risk of a material error remaining undetected with respect to the financial statement item assertion in question is slightly less than the target risk.

5 = The actual risk of a material error remaining undetected with respect to the financial statement item assertion in question is significantly less than the target risk.

Part 2

Please assess the effectiveness of the plan with respect to each financial statement item using the worksheet on this page. Please use a scale of 1 to 5. The interpretation of the scale values is given below the worksheet.

Accounts receivable - National Credit Card
Accounts receivable - Store Credit Card
Accounts receivable - Wholesale Credit

Cash Sales
Cash Receipts on Account - National Credit Card
Cash Receipts on Account - Store Credit Card
Cash Receipts on Account - Wholesale Credit

Cash balances

Sales on Account - National Credit Card
Sales on Account - Store Credit Card
Sales on Account - Wholesale Credit

Allowance for Doubtful Accounts - Store Credit Card

Writeoffs - Store Credit Card

Returns
Markdowns

1 = Target risks would not be achieved for any of the financial statement item assertions.

2 = Target risks would not be achieved for most critical and most non-critical financial statement item assertions.

3 = Target risks would be achieved for most critical and some non-critical financial statement item assertions.

4 = Target risks would be achieved for all critical and most non-critical financial statement item assertions.

5 = Target risks would be achieved (or exceeded) for all financial statement item assertions.

Part 3

Please indicate you assessment of the overall effectiveness of the plan by choosing the statement which best describes the plan's effectiveness at the financial statement level.

1 = Target risks would not be achieved for any financial statement item assertions.

2 = Target risks would not be achieved for most financial statement item assertions.

3 = Target risks would be achieved for some critical and some non-critical financial statement item assertions.

4 = Target risks would be achieved for all critical and most non-critical financial statement item assertions.

5 = Target risks would be achieved (or exceeded) for all financial statement item assertions.

QUESTION 2 - PLAN EFFICIENCY

Part 1

Please assess the efficiency of the plan with respect to each financial statement item assertion on a scale of 1 to 5 by filling out the worksheet on this page. The interpretation of the scale values is given below the worksheet.

	Existence/ Occurrence	Completeness	Accuracy	Valuation
Accounts receivable - National Credit Card				
Accounts receivable - Store Credit Card				
Accounts receivable - Wholesale Credit				
Cash Sales				
Cash Receipts on Account - National Credit Card				
Cash Receipts on Account - Store Credit Card				
Cash Receipts on Account - Wholesale Credit				
Cash balances				
Sales on Account - National Credit Card				
Sales on Account - Store Credit Card				
Sales on Account - Wholesale Credit				
Allowance for Doubtful Accounts - Store Credit Card				
Writeoffs - Store Credit Card				
Returns				
Markdowns				

1 = There are other sets of procedures which would result in the achievement of the same level of risk with respect to the financial statement item assertion in question as that achieved by the plan at a significantly lower cost than that of the plan.

2 = There are other sets of procedures which would result in the achievement of the same level of risk with respect to the financial statement item assertion in question as that achieved by the plan at a slightly lower cost than that of the plan.

3 = Any alternative set of procedures which would result in the achievement of the same level of risk with respect to the financial statement item assertion in question as that achieved by the plan would have the approximately the same cost as that of the plan.

4 = Any alternative set of procedures which would result in the achievement of the same level of risk with respect to the financial statement item assertion in question as that achieved by the plan would have a cost slightly greater than that of the plan.

5 = Any alternative set of procedures which would result in the achievement of the same level of risk with respect to the financial statement item assertion in question as that achieved by the plan would have a cost which was significantly greater than that of the plan.

Part 2

Please assess the efficiency of the plan with respect to each financial statement item on a scale of 1 to 5 by filling out the worksheet on the next page. The interpretation of the scale values is given below the worksheet.

Accounts receivable - National Credit Card
Accounts receivable - Store Credit Card
Accounts receivable - Wholesale Credit

Cash Sales
Cash Receipts on Account - National Credit Card
Cash Receipts on Account - Store Credit Card
Cash Receipts on Account - Wholesale Credit

Cash balances

Sales on Account - National Credit Card
Sales on Account - Store Credit Card
Sales on Account - Wholesale Credit

Allowance for Doubtful Accounts - Store Credit Card

Writeoffs - Store Credit Card

Returns
Markdowns

1 = There are other sets of procedures which would result in the achievement of the same level of risk with respect to all financial statement item assertions as that achived by the plan at a significantly lower cost than that of the plan.

2 = There are other sets of procedures which would result in the achievement of the same level of risk with respect to all financial statement item assertions as that achived by the plan at a slightly lower cost than that of the plan.

3 = Any alternative set of procedures which would result in the achievement of the same level of risk with respect to all financial statement item assertions as that achieved by the plan would have approximately the same cost as that of the plan.

4 = Any alternative set of procedures which would result in the achievement of the same level of risk with respect to all financial statement item assertions as that achieved by the plan would have a cost slightly greater than that of the plan.

5 = Any alternative set of procedures which would result in the achievement of the same level of risk with respect to all financial statement item assertions as that achieved by the plan would have a cost which was significantly greater than that of the plan.

Part 3

Please indicate you assessment of the overall efficiency of the solution plan by choosing the statement listed below which best describes the efficiency of the plan at the financial statement level.

1 = There are other sets of procedures which would result in the achievement of the same level of overall risk as that achived by the plan at a significantly lower cost than that of the plan.

2 = There are other sets of procedures which would result in the achievement of the same level of overall risk as that achived by the plan at a slightly lower cost than of the plan.

3 = Any alternative set of procedures which would result in the achievement of the same level of overall risk as that achieved by the plan would have approximately the same cost as that of the plan.

4 = Any alternative set of procedures which would result in the achievement of the same level of overall risk as that achieved by the plan would have a cost slightly greater than that of the plan.

5 = Any alternative set of procedures which would result in the achievement of the same level of overall risk as that achieved by the plan would have a cost which was significantly greater than that of the plan.

QUESTION 3 - PLAN ACCEPTABILITY

Part 1

Please assess the acceptability of the solution plan by choosing a statement which best describes the overall acceptability of the plan to you.

1 = The plan is fundamentally unacceptable and even major revisions cannot change this conclusion.

2 = The plan is unacceptable and can only be made acceptable through major revisions.

3 = The plan is generally acceptable but some significant revisions are necessary.

4 = The plan is generally acceptable but some minor revisions are necessary.

5 = The plan is acceptable without any revisions being required.

Part 2

If you have chosen statement 2,3, or 4 in the above assessment please indicate below the revisions that you would make to the solution plan to make it acceptable. Beside each revision please indicate the reason(s) for making it.

Revision	Reason(s)

QUESTION 4 - THE COMPETENCE OF THE PLAN PREPARER

Please assess the competence of the preparer of the plan by checking the cell in the matrix below whch best describes your assessment of the senority and experience of the preparer of the plan.

	Senority	Partner	Manager	Staff	Junior
Experience					
Extensive Industry but not this client					
No experience of this industry					

QUESTION 5 - MISSING AND REDUNDANT PROCEDURES

Please list any procedures which are missing from the solution plan and that you believe should be included in any solution plan for the client in question.

Please list any procedures which are included in the solution plan which you consider to be redundant.

Please indicate any procedures which are included in the solution plan that you would consider necessary but should be carried out with smaller sample sizes (smaller confidence factors).

Please indicate any procedures which are included in the solution plan that you would consider necessary but should be carried out with larger sample sizes (larger confidence factors).

Appendix 4.11

AUDIT PLANNING CASES - INSTRUCTIONS AND ADDITIONAL INFORMATION

BANKING CLIENTS

GENERAL INSTRUCTIONS

You are asked to develop a substantive audit program plan for each of the clients profiled. You are asked to identify the procedures that you would plan to perform assuming that each procedure selected does not indicate the presence of a material error. For each selected procedure you are asked to specify a **planned extent, sample size, or sample size factor.** Please provide a list of the procedures and their matching extents on the sheets provided.

SUBSTANTIVE AUDIT PLAN

Name ________________

Case ________________

Part 1 The Plan

Please identify below the substantive audit evidence gathering procedures that you would plan to carry out to collect sufficient evidence to reduce the risk that a material error has occurred, but not been detected, to the target level of risk defined in the cases.

Each procedure that you plan to carry out should have an **extent, sample size**, or **sample size factor** associated with it. Please identify each procedure with a number so that you can refer to it in Part 2.

Procedure Extent

Part 2 - Analysis of Evidential Support

Please indicate which procedures provide **direct** evidence for which financial statement item assertions by entering the appropriate number(s) in the matrix below. If you expect more than one procedure to provide direct evidence concerning a particular financial statement item please write the number of the procedure providing the strongest evidence at the left side of the appropriate column and order the other procedure number(s) from left to right in decreasing order of evidential support.

	Existence/ Occurrence	Completeness	Accuracy	Valuation
Fixed balance, fixed rate loan balances				
Fixed balance, floating rate loan balances				
Operating line of credit loan balances				
Mortgages loan balances				
Fixed balance, fixed rate revenue				
Fixed balance, floating rate revenue				
Operating line of credit revenue				
Mortgages loan revenue				
Fixed balance, fixed rate accrued interest				
Fixed balance, floating rate accrued interest				
Operating line of credit accrued interest				
Mortgages loan revenue				
Cash receipts				
Cash disbursements				
Cash balances				
Loan loss provision - Mortgages				
Loan loss provision - other business loans				

SUBSTANTIVE AUDIT PLAN REVISIONS?

Name ________________

Case : ______________

Please inspect the target levels of risk which are provided on the attached revised page of the case. In the light of these target levels of risk would you revise the plan that you generated for this case initially.

If you consider that revisions are necessary please indicate them below giving your reasons for each revision.

Revision   Reason

PLANNING QUESTIONNAIRE

QUESTION 1 - PLAN EFFECTIVENESS

Part 1

Please assess the effectiveness of the attached plan with respect to each financial statement item assertion on a scale of 1 to 5 by filling out the worksheet on the next page. The interpretation of scale values in given below.

Note: When assessing the effectiveness of any procedure, or set of procedures please take into account the impact of evidence provided by all the other procedures which constitute the plan.

	Existence/ Occurrence	Completeness	Accuracy	Valuation
Fixed balance, fixed rate loan balances				
Fixed balance, floating rate loan balances				
Operating line of credit loan balances				
Mortgages loan balances				
Fixed balance, fixed rate revenue				
Fixed balance, floating rate revenue				
Operating line of credit revenue				
Mortgages loan revenue				
Fixed balance, fixed rate accrued interest				
Fixed balance, floating rate accrued interest				
Operating line of credit accrued interest				
Mortgages loan revenue				
Cash receipts				
Cash disbursements				
Cash balances				
Loan loss provision - Mortgages				
Loan loss provision - other business loans				

Effectiveness scale at the financial statement item assertion level. Assume that the procedures constituting the solution plan are applied and that there are no indications of material error in the evidence they provide.

1 = The actual risk of a material error remaining undetected with respect to the financial statement item assertion in question is significantly greater than the target risk.

2 = The actual risk of a material error remaining undetected with respect to the financial statement item assertion in question is slightly greater than the target risk.

3 = The actual risk of a material error remaining undetected with respect to the financial statement item assertion in question is equal to the target risk.

4 = The actual risk of a material error remaining undetected with respect to the financial statement item assertion in question is slightly less than the target risk.

5 = The actual risk of a material error remaining undetected with respect to the financial statement item assertion in question is significantly less than the target risk.

Part 2

Please assess the effectiveness of the plan with respect to each financial statement item using the worksheet on the next page. Please use a scale of 1 to 5. The interpretation of the scale values is given below the worksheet.

Fixed balance, fixed rate loan balances
Fixed balance, floating rate loan balances
Operating line of credit loan balances
Mortgages loan balances

Fixed balance, fixed rate revenue
Fixed balance, floating rate revenue
Operating line of credit revenue
Mortgages loan revenue

Fixed balance, fixed rate accrued interest
Fixed balance, floating rate accrued interest
Operating line of credit accrued interest
Mortgages loan revenue

Cash receipts
Cash disbursements
Cash balances

Loan loss provision - Mortgages
Loan loss provision - other business loans

1 = Target risks would not be achieved for any of the financial statement item assertions.

2 = Target risks would not be achieved for most critical and most non-critical financial statement item assertions.

3 = Target risks would be achieved for most critical and some non-critical financial statement item assertions.

4 = Target risks would be achieved for all critical and most non-critical financial statement item assertions.

5 = Target risks would be achieved (or exceeded) for all financial statement item assertions.

Part 3

Please indicate you assessment of the overall effectiveness of the plan by choosing the statement which best describes the plan's effectiveness at the financial statement level.

1 = Target risks would not be achieved for any financial statement item assertions.

2 = Target risks would not be achieved for most financial statement item assertions.

3 = Target risks would be achieved for some critical and some non-critical financial statement item assertions.

4 = Target risks would be achieved for all critical and most non-critical financial statement item assertions.

5 = Target risks would be achieved (or exceeded) for all financial statement item assertions.

QUESTION 2 - PLAN EFFICIENCY

Part 1

Please assess the efficiency of the plan with respect to each financial statement item assertion on a scale of 1 to 5 by filling out the worksheet on the next page. The interpretation of the scale values is given below the worksheet.

	Existence/ Occurrence	Completeness	Accuracy	Valuation
Fixed balance, fixed rate loan balances				
Fixed balance, floating rate loan balances				
Operating line of credit loan balances				
Mortgages loan balances				
Fixed balance, fixed rate revenue				
Fixed balance, floating rate revenue				
Operating line of credit revenue				
Mortgages loan revenue				
Fixed balance, fixed rate accrued interest				
Fixed balance, floating rate accrued interest				
Operating line of credit accrued interest				
Mortgages loan revenue				
Cash receipts				
Cash disbursements				
Cash balances				
Loan loss provision - Mortgages				
Loan loss provision - other business loans				

1 = There are other sets of procedures which would result in the achievement of the same level of risk with respect to the financial statement item assertion in question as that achieved by the plan at a significantly lower cost than that of the plan.

2 = There are other sets of procedures which would result in the achievement of the same level of risk with respect to the financial statement item assertion in question as that achieved by the plan at a slightly lower cost than that of the plan.

3 = Any alternative set of procedures which would result in the achievement of the same level of risk with respect to the financial statement item assertion in question as that achieved by the plan would have the approximately the same cost as that of the plan.

4 = Any alternative set of procedures which would result in the achievement of the same level of risk with respect to the financial statement item assertion in question as that achieved by the plan would have a cost slightly greater than that of the plan.

5 = Any alternative set of procedures which would result in the achievement of the same level of risk with respect to the financial statement item assertion in question as that achieved by the plan would have a cost which was significantly greater than that of the plan.

Part 2

Please assess the efficiency of the plan with respect to each financial statement item on a scale of 1 to 5 by filling out the worksheet on the next page. The interpretation of the scale values is given below the worksheet.

Fixed balance, fixed rate loan balances
Fixed balance, floating rate loan balances
Operating line of credit loan balances
Mortgages loan balances

Fixed balance, fixed rate revenue
Fixed balance, floating rate revenue
Operating line of credit revenue
Mortgages loan revenue

Fixed balance, fixed rate accrued interest
Fixed balance, floating rate accrued interest
Operating line of credit accrued interest
Mortgages loan revenue

Cash receipts
Cash disbursements

Cash balances

Loan loss provision - Mortgages
Loan loss provision - other business loans

1 = There are other sets of procedures which would result in the achievement of the same level of risk with respect to all financial statement item assertions as that achieved by the plan at a significantly lower cost than that of the plan.

2 = There are other sets of procedures which would result in the achievement of the same level of risk with respect to all financial statement item assertions as that achieved by the plan at a slightly lower cost than that of the plan.

3 = Any alternative set of procedures which would result in the achievement of the same level of risk with respect to all financial statement item assertions as that achieved by the plan would have approximately the same cost as that of the plan.

4 = Any alternative set of procedures which would result in the achievement of the same level of risk with respect to all financial statement item assertions as that achieved by the plan would have a cost slightly greater than that of the plan.

5 = Any alternative set of procedures which would result in the achievement of the same level of risk with respect to all financial statement item assertions as that achieved by the plan would have a cost which was significantly greater than that of the plan.

Part 3

Please indicate you assessment of the overall efficiency of the solution plan by choosing the statement listed below which best describes the efficiency of the plan at the financial statement level.

1 = There are other sets of procedures which would result in the achievement of the same level of overall risk as that achieved by the plan at a significantly lower cost than that of the plan.

2 = There are other sets of procedures which would result in the achievement of the same level of overall risk as that achieved by the plan at a slightly lower cost than of the plan.

3 = Any alternative set of procedures which would result in the achievement of the same level of overall risk as that achieved by the plan would have approximately the same cost as that of the plan.

4 = Any alternative set of procedures which would result in the achievement of the same level of overall risk as that achieved by the plan would have a cost slightly greater than that of the plan.

5 = Any alternative set of procedures which would result in the achievement of the same level of overall risk as that achieved by the plan would have a cost which was significantly greater than that of the plan.

QUESTION 3 - PLAN ACCEPTABILITY

Part 1

Please assess the acceptability of the solution plan by choosing a statement which best describes the overall acceptability of the plan to you.

1 = The plan is fundamentally unacceptable and even major revisions cannot change this conclusion.

2 = The plan is unacceptable and can only be made acceptable through major revisions.

3 = The plan is generally acceptable but some significant revisions are necessary.

4 = The plan is generally acceptable but some minor revisions are necessary.

5 = The plan is acceptable without any revisions being required.

Part 2

If you have chosen statement 2,3, or 4 in the above assessment please indicate below the revisions that you would make to the solution plan to make it acceptable. Beside each revision please indicate the reason(s) for making it.

Revision	Reason(s)

QUESTION 4 - THE COMPETENCE OF THE PLAN PREPARER

Please assess the competence of the preparer of the plan by checking the cell in the matrix below which best describes your assessment of the seniority and experience of the preparer of the plan.

Seniority	Partner	Manager	Staff	Junior
Experience				
Extensive Industry but not this client				
No experience of this industry				

QUESTION 5 - MISSING AND REDUNDANT PROCEDURES

Please list any procedures which are missing from the solution plan and that you believe should be included in any solution plan for the client in question.

Please list any procedures which are included in the solution plan which you consider to be redundant.

Please indicate any procedures which are included in the solution plan that you would consider necessary but should be carried out with smaller sample sizes (smaller confidence factors).

Please indicate any procedures which are included in the solution plan that you would consider necessary but should be carried out with larger sample sizes (larger confidence factors).

SUBSTANTIVE AUDIT PLAN REVISIONS?

Name _______________

Case : _____________

In the light of the plan you have just assessed would you revise the plan that you generated for this case initially.

If you consider that revisions are necessary please indicate them below giving your reasons for each revision.

Revision Reason

Appendix 4.12

AUDIT PLANNING CASES - INSTRUCTIONS AND ADDITIONAL INFORMATION

BANKING CLIENTS

GENERAL INSTRUCTIONS

You are asked to develop a substantive audit program plan for each of the clients profiled. You are asked to identify the procedures that you would plan to perform assuming that each procedure selected does not indicate the presence of a material error. For each selected procedure you are asked to specify a **planned extent, sample size, or sample size factor.** Please provide a list of the procedures and their matching extents on the sheets provided.

SUBSTANTIVE AUDIT PLAN

Name ________________

Case ________________

Part 1 The Plan

Please identify below the substantive audit evidence gathering procedures that you would plan to carry out to collect sufficient evidence to reduce the risk that a material error has occurred, but not been detected, to the target level of risk defined in the cases.

Each procedure that you plan to carry out should have an **extent, sample size**, or **sample size factor** associated with it. Please identify each procedure with a number so that you can refer to it in Part 2.

Procedure	Extent

Part 2 - Analysis of Evidential Support

Please indicate which procedures provide **direct** evidence for which financial statement item assertions by entering the appropriate number(s) in the matrix below. If you expect more than one procedure to provide direct evidence concerning a particular financial statement item please write the number of the procedure providing the strongest evidence at the left side of the appropriate column and order the other procedure number(s) from left to right in decreasing order of evidential support.

	Existence/ Occurrence	Completeness	Accuracy	Valuation
Fixed balance, fixed rate loan balances				
Fixed balance, floating rate loan balances				
Operating line of credit loan balances				
Mortgages loan balances				
Fixed balance, fixed rate revenue				
Fixed balance, floating rate revenue				
Operating line of credit revenue				
Mortgages loan revenue				
Fixed balance, fixed rate accrued interest				
Fixed balance, floating rate accrued interest				
Operating line of credit accrued interest				
Mortgages loan accrued interest				
Cash receipts				
Cash disbursements				
Cash balances				
Loan loss provision - Mortgages				
Loan loss provision - other business loans				

SUBSTANTIVE AUDIT PLAN REVISIONS?

Name _______________

Case : _____________

Please inspect the target levels of risk which are provided on the attached revised page of the case. In the light of these target levels of risk would you revise the plan that you generated for this case initially.

If you consider that revisions are necessary please indicate them below giving your reasons for each revision.

Revision	Reason

PLANNING QUESTIONNAIRE

QUESTION 1 - PLAN EFFECTIVENESS

Part 1

Please assess the effectiveness of the attached plan with respect to each financial statement item assertion on a scale of 1 to 5 by filling out the worksheet on the next page. The interpretation of scale values in given below.

Note: When assessing the effectiveness of any procedure, or set of procedures please take into account the impact of evidence provided by all the other procedures which constitute the plan.

	Existence/ Occurrence	Completeness	Accuracy	Valuation
Fixed balance, fixed rate loan balances				
Fixed balance, floating rate loan balances				
Operating line of credit loan balances				
Mortgages loan balances				
Fixed balance, fixed rate revenue				
Fixed balance, floating rate revenue				
Operating line of credit revenue				
Mortgages loan revenue				
Fixed balance, fixed rate accrued interest				
Fixed balance, floating rate accrued interest				
Operating line of credit accrued interest				
Mortgages loan revenue				
Cash receipts				
Cash disbursements				
Cash balances				
Loan loss provision - Mortgages				
Loan loss provision - other business loans				

Effectiveness scale at the financial statement item assertion level. Assume that the procedures constituting the solution plan are applied and that there are no indications of material error in the evidence they provide.

1 = The actual risk of a material error remaining undetected with respect to the financial statement item assertion in question is significantly greater than the target risk.

2 = The actual risk of a material error remaining undetected with respect to the financial statement item assertion in question is slightly greater than the target risk.

3 = The actual risk of a material error remaining undetected with respect to the financial statement item assertion in question is equal to the target risk.

4 = The actual risk of a material error remaining undetected with respect to the financial statement item assertion in question is slightly less than the target risk.

5 = The actual risk of a material error remaining undetected with respect to the financial statement item assertion in question is significantly less than the target risk.

Part 2

Please assess the effectiveness of the plan with respect to each financial statement item using the worksheet on the next page. Please use a scale of 1 to 5. The interpretation of the scale values is given below the worksheet.

Fixed balance, fixed rate loan balances
Fixed balance, floating rate loan balances
Operating line of credit loan balances
Mortgages loan balances

Fixed balance, fixed rate revenue
Fixed balance, floating rate revenue
Operating line of credit revenue
Mortgages loan revenue

Fixed balance, fixed rate accrued interest
Fixed balance, floating rate accrued interest
Operating line of credit accrued interest
Mortgages loan revenue

Cash receipts
Cash disbursements
Cash balances

Loan loss provision - Mortgages
Loan loss provision - other business loans

1 = Target risks would not be achieved for any of the financial statement item assertions.

2 = Target risks would not be achieved for most critical and most non-critical financial statement item assertions.

3 = Target risks would be achieved for most critical and some non-critical financial statement item assertions.

4 = Target risks would be achieved for all critical and most non-critical financial statement item assertions.

5 = Target risks would be achieved (or exceeded) for all financial statement item assertions.

Part 3

Please indicate you assessment of the overall effectiveness of the plan by choosing the statement which best describes the plan's effectiveness at the financial statement level.

1 = Target risks would not be achieved for any financial statement item assertions.

2 = Target risks would not be achieved for most financial statement item assertions.

3 = Target risks would be achieved for some critical and some non-critical financial statement item assertions.

4 = Target risks would be achieved for all critical and most non-critical financial statement item assertions.

5 = Target risks would be achieved (or exceeded) for all financial statement item assertions.

QUESTION 2 - PLAN EFFICIENCY

Part 1

Please assess the efficiency of the plan with respect to each financial statement item assertion on a scale of 1 to 5 by filling out the worksheet on the next page. The interpretation of the scale values is given below the worksheet.

	Existence/ Occurrence	Completeness	Accuracy	Valuation
Fixed balance, fixed rate loan balances				
Fixed balance, floating rate loan balances				
Operating line of credit loan balances				
Mortgages loan balances				
Fixed balance, fixed rate revenue				
Fixed balance, floating rate revenue				
Operating line of credit revenue				
Mortgages loan revenue				
Fixed balance, fixed rate accrued interest				
Fixed balance, floating rate accrued interest				
Operating line of credit accrued interest				
Mortgages loan revenue				
Cash receipts				
Cash disbursements				
Cash balances				
Loan loss provision - Mortgages				
Loan loss provision - other business loans				

1 = There are other sets of procedures which would result in the achievement of the same level of risk with respect to the financial statement item assertion in question as that achieved by the plan at a significantly lower cost than that of the plan.

2 = There are other sets of procedures which would result in the achievement of the same level of risk with respect to the financial statement item assertion in question as that achieved by the plan at a slightly lower cost than that of the plan.

3 = Any alternative set of procedures which would result in the achievement of the same level of risk with respect to the financial statement item assertion in question as that achieved by the plan would have the approximately the same cost as that of the plan.

4 = Any alternative set of procedures which would result in the achievement of the same level of risk with respect to the financial statement item assertion in question as that achieved by the plan would have a cost slightly greater than that of the plan.

5 = Any alternative set of procedures which would result in the achievement of the same level of risk with respect to the financial statement item assertion in question as that achieved by the plan would have a cost which was significantly greater than that of the plan.

Part 2

Please assess the efficiency of the plan with respect to each financial statement item on a scale of 1 to 5 by filling out the worksheet on the next page. The interpretation of the scale values is given below the worksheet.

Fixed balance, fixed rate loan balances
Fixed balance, floating rate loan balances
Operating line of credit loan balances
Mortgages loan balances

Fixed balance, fixed rate revenue
Fixed balance, floating rate revenue
Operating line of credit revenue
Mortgages loan revenue

Fixed balance, fixed rate accrued interest
Fixed balance, floating rate accrued interest
Operating line of credit accrued interest
Mortgages loan revenue

Cash receipts
Cash disbursements

Cash balances

Loan loss provision - Mortgages
Loan loss provision - other business loans

1 = There are other sets of procedures which would result in the achievement of the same level of risk with respect to all financial statement item assertions as that achieved by the plan at a significantly lower cost than that of the plan.

2 = There are other sets of procedures which would result in the achievement of the same level of risk with respect to all financial statement item assertions as that achieved by the plan at a slightly lower cost than that of the plan.

3 = Any alternative set of procedures which would result in the achievement of the same level of risk with respect to all financial statement item assertions as that achieved by the plan would have approximately the same cost as that of the plan.

4 = Any alternative set of procedures which would result in the achievement of the same level of risk with respect to all financial statement item assertions as that achieved by the plan would have a cost slightly greater than that of the plan.

5 = Any alternative set of procedures which would result in the achievement of the same level of risk with respect to all financial statement item assertions as that achieved by the plan would have a cost which was significantly greater than that of the plan.

Part 3

Please indicate you assessment of the overall efficiency of the solution plan by choosing the statement listed below which best describes the efficiency of the plan at the financial statement level.

1 = There are other sets of procedures which would result in the achievement of the same level of overall risk as that achieved by the plan at a significantly lower cost than that of the plan.

2 = There are other sets of procedures which would result in the achievement of the same level of overall risk as that achieved by the plan at a slightly lower cost than of the plan.

3 = Any alternative set of procedures which would result in the achievement of the same level of overall risk as that achieved by the plan would have approximately the same cost as that of the plan.

4 = Any alternative set of procedures which would result in the achievement of the same level of overall risk as that achieved by the plan would have a cost slightly greater than that of the plan.

5 = Any alternative set of procedures which would result in the achievement of the same level of overall risk as that achieved by the plan would have a cost which was significantly greater than that of the plan.

QUESTION 3 - PLAN ACCEPTABILITY

Part 1

Please assess the acceptability of the solution plan by choosing a statement which best describes the overall acceptability of the plan to you.

1 = The plan is fundamentally unacceptable and even major revisions cannot change this conclusion.

2 = The plan is unacceptable and can only be made acceptable through major revisions.

3 = The plan is generally acceptable but some significant revisions are necessary.

4 = The plan is generally acceptable but some minor revisions are necessary.

5 = The plan is acceptable without any revisions being required.

Part 2

If you have chosen statement 2,3, or 4 in the above assessment please indicate below the revisions that you would make to the solution plan to make it acceptable. Beside each revision please indicate the reason(s) for making it.

Revision	Reason(s)

QUESTION 4 - THE COMPETENCE OF THE PLAN PREPARER

Please assess the competence of the preparer of the plan by checking the cell in the matrix below which best describes your assessment of the seniority and experience of the preparer of the plan.

	Seniority	Partner	Manager	Staff	Junior
Experience					
Extensive Industry but not this client					
No experience of this industry					

QUESTION 5 - MISSING AND REDUNDANT PROCEDURES

Please list any procedures which are missing from the solution plan and that you believe should be included in any solution plan for the client in question.

Please list any procedures which are included in the solution plan which you consider to be redundant.

Please indicate any procedures which are included in the solution plan that you would consider necessary but should be carried out with smaller sample sizes (smaller confidence factors).

Please indicate any procedures which are included in the solution plan that you would consider necessary but should be carried out with larger sample sizes (larger confidence factors).

<u>SUBSTANTIVE AUDIT PLAN REVISIONS?</u>

Name _______________

Case : _____________

In the light of the plan you have just assessed would you revise the plan that you generated for this case initially.

If you consider that revisions are necessary please indicate them below giving your reasons for each revision.

Revision Reason

BIBLIOGRAPHY

Abdolmohammadi, M.J., and A. Wright . "An Examination of the Effects of Task Complexity on Audit Judgments." *he Accounting Review,* January 1987, pp. 1-13.

Aldersley, S.J. "Comments on "The Structuring of Audit Evidence: An Expert Systems Approach." by J.E. Boritz and A.K.P. Wensley," *Auditing: A Journal of Practice and Theory*, vol. 9, supplement, 1990, pp. 95-102.

Anderson, J.R. "Acquisition of Proof Skills in Geometry." In *Machine Learning: An Artificial Intelligence Approach.* Ed. J.G. Carbonell, R. Michalski, and T. Mitchell. San Fransisco: Tioga, 1983.

Anderson, R.J. *The External Audit.* 2nd. ed., Toronto: Copp Clark Pitman, 1984.

Ashton, J.H. "Experience and Error Frequency Knowledge as Potential Determinants of Audit Expertise." *The Accounting Review*, April 1991, pp. 218-239.

Bailey, A.D. Jr., G.L. Duke, J. Gerlach, C. Ko, R.D. Meservy, and A.B. Whinston. "TICOM and the Analysis of Internal Controls." *The Accounting Review*, April 1985, pp. 186-201.

Bédard, J. "Expertise in Auditing: Myth or Reality." *Accounting, Organizations and Society*, 1989, pp. 113-131.

Bharadwaj, A., R.K. Mahapatra, A.S. Vinze, V. Karan, and U.S. Murthy. APX-An Expert System for Audit Planning. Working Paper, Texas A&M University, College Station, TX, 1992.

Biggs, S.F., and J.J Wild. "An Investigation of Auditor Judgment in Analytical Review." *The Accounting Review*, vol. LX, no. 4, 1985, pp. 607-633.

_____, W.F. Messier, and J.V. Hansen. "A Descriptive Analysis of Computer Audit Specialist's Decision-Making Behavior in Advanced Computer Environments." *Auditing: A Journal of Theory and Practice*, vol. 6, no. 2, Spring 1987, pp. 1-21.

Blocher, E.J., and J.J. Willingham. *Analytical Review: A Guide to Evaluating Financial Statements*. New York: McGraw Hill, 1985.

Bonnet, A., Haton, J.P., and J.M. Truong-Ngoc. *Expert Systems*. New York: Prentice Hall, 1988.

Boritz, J.E. "The Effect of Information Presentation Structures on Audit Planning and Review Judgments." *Contemporary Accounting Research*, vol. 1, no. 2, 1987, pp. 193-218.

_____. "Audit Risk and Financial Statement Assertions: A Spreadsheet Based Decision Aid." Unpublished Manuscript. Accounting Group, University of Waterloo, Ontario, Canada, 1986.

_____. "Audit Risk and Financial Statement Assertions: A Spreadsheet-Based Decision Aid." Unpublished Manuscript. School of Accountancy, University of Waterloo, Ontario, Canada, July 1985a.

_____. "Audit Judgement, Decision Support and Expert Systems." *Internal Audit Handbook.* vol II, Department of Finance and Treasury Board of Canada, 1985b.

_____. *Planning and Coordination of Audit Activities*. The Institute of Internal Auditors Research Foundation, 1983.

_____, and R.E. Jensen. "An Hierarchical Assertion-Oriented Approach to Planning Audit Evidence-Gathering Procedures." Paper presented at the *Symposium on Audit Judgment and Evidence Evaluation,* University of Southern California, Los Angeles, CA, February 1985.

_____, and A.K.P.Wensley. "Structuring the Assessment of Audit Evidence - An Expert Systems Approach." Unpublished Manuscript. School of Accountancy, University of Waterloo, Ontario, Canada, 1987.

_____, C. Ditner, and A.K.P. Wensley, "An Expert System for Assertion-Based Audit Planning." Unpublished Manuscript. School of Accountancy, University of Waterloo, Ontario, Canada, 1986.

Brinberg, D., and J.E. McGrath. "A Network of Validity Concepts Within the Research Process." In *Forms of Validity in Research.* Ed. D. Brinberg, and L.H. Kidder. San Fransisco: Jossey-Bass Inc., 1982, pp.5-22.

_____. *Validity and the Research Process*. London, England: Sage, 1985.

Brown, J.S., and P. Duguid. "Organizational Learning and Communities-in-Practice: Toward a Unified View of Working, Learning, and Innovation. *Organization Science*, vol. 2, no. 1, 1991, pp. 40-57.

Chandrasekaran, B., and S.Mittal. "Deep Versus Compiled Knowledge Approaches to Diagnostic Problem Solving." *International Journal of Man-Machine Studies,* vol. 19, 1983, pp. 425-436.

Coakley, J.R. "Analytical Review: A comparison of procedures and techniques used in auditing." Unpublished Ph.D. Thesis. University of Utah, 1982.

Cohen, P.R. *Heuristic Reasoning about Uncertainty: An Artificial Intelligence Approach.* Boston: Pitman Publishing Inc., 1985.

Cordingley, E.S. "Knowledge Elicitation Techniques for Knowledge-based Systems." In *Knowledge Elicitation.* Ed. D. Diaper. Chichester, UK: Ellis Horwood, 1988, pp. 89-175.

Dawes, R. *Rational Choice in an Uncertain World.* New York: Harcourt, Brace, Jovanovich, 1988.

Dungan, C.W. "A Model of Audit Judgement in the Form of an Expert System" Ph.D. Dissertation. Department of Accountancy, University of Illinois at Urbana, 1983.

Edelson, M. *Hypothesis and Evidence in Psychoanalysis.* Chicago: The University of Chicago Press, 1984.

Eden, C. "Managing Strategic Ideas: The Role of the Computer." *The ICL Technical Journal*, vol. 5, issue 2, November 1986, pp. 173-183.

_____, and J. Harris. *Management Decisions and Decision Analysis*. London: Macmillan, 1975.

_____, and D. Sims. *Problem Definition Between Clients and Consultants*. Centre for the Study of Organizational Change and Development, University of Bath, United Kingdom, 1977.

_____, S. Jones, and D.Sims. *Messing About in Problems*. Oxford: Pergammon Press, 1983.

_____, S. Jones, and D. Sims. *Thinking in Organizations*. London: Macmillan, 1979.

_____, T. Smithin, and J.Wiltshire. *COPE User Guide and Reference Manual*. Bristol: Bath Software Research, 1985.

Edwards, W., and D. von Winterfeldt. *Decision Analysis and Behavioral Research*. Cambridge: Cambridge University Press, 1986.

Einhorn, H.J., and R.M. Hogarth. "Behavioral Decision Theory: Processes of Judgement and Choice." *Annual Review of Psychology*, 32, 1981, pp. 53-88.

Elstein, A.S. and G. Bordage. "Psychology of Clinical Reasoning." In *Professional Judgment*. Ed. J. Dowie and A. Elstein. Cambridge: Cambridge University Press, 1988, pp. 109-129.

Elster, J. *Sour Grapes*. Cambridge: Cambridge University Press, 1985.

_____. *Ulysses and the Sirens*. Cambridge: Cambridge University Press, 1984.

Ericsson, K.A. and H.A. Simon. *Protocol Analysis: Verbal Reports as Data*. Cambridge, MA: MIT Press, 1984.

Feigenbaum, E.A., and P. McCorduck. *The Fifth Generation*. London: Pan Books, 1984.

_____, B. Buchanan, and J. Lederberg. "On Generality and Problem Solving: A Case Study Using the DENDRAL Program." *Machine Intelligence*. New York: Elsevier, vol. 6, 1971, pp. 165-190.

Feltovich, P.J. "Knowledge Based Components of Expertise in Medical Diagnosis." Unpublished Doctoral Dissertation. University of Minnesota, 1981.

Fikes, R and T. Kehler. "The Role of Frame-Based Representation in Reasoning." *Communications of the ACM*, vol. 28, no. 9, September 1985, pp. 904-920.

Fischhoff, B. "Judgmental Aspects of Risk Analysis." In *Handbook of Risk Assessment*, National Science Foundation and Office of Management and Budget, 1986.

_____. "Debiasing." In *Judgement Under Uncertainty: Heuristics and Biases*. Ed. D. Kahneman, P. Slovic, and A. Tversky. Cambridge: Cambridge University Press, 1982a, pp. 335-351.

_____. "For Those Condemned to Study the Past: Heuristics and Biases in Hindsight." In *Judgement Under Uncertainty: Heuristics and Biases*. Ed. D. Kahneman,

P. Slovic and A. Tversky. Cambridge: Cambridge University Press, 1982b, pp. 335-351.

_____. "Hindsight = Foresight: The Effect of Outcome Knowledge of Judgement under Uncertainty." *Journal of Experimental Psychology: Human Perception and Performance*, 1, 1975, pp. 288-299.

_____. "Hindsight: Thinking Backwards." *Psychology Today*, August 1975b.

_____. S. Lichtenstein, P. Slovic, S.C. Derby, and R.L. Keeney. *Acceptable Risk*. Cambridge: Cambridge University Press, 1981.

Fishburn, P.C. *Mathematics of Decision Theory*. The Hague: UNESCO, 1972.

_____. *Decision and Value Theory*. New York: John Wiley, 1964.

Fishman, G.S., and P.J. Kiviat. "The Analysis of Simulation Generated Time Series." *Management Science*, vol. 13, no. 7, March 1967, pp. 525-557.

Fjeldstad, O.D., and B.R. Konsynski. "The Role of Cognitive Apportionment in Information Systems Design of Group Decision Making." *Proceedings of the 7th. International Conference on Information Systems*. San Diego, CA, 1986, pp. 84-98.

Fodor, J.A. *Modularity of Mind*. Cambridge, MA: MIT Press, 1983.

Fox, M. personal interviews, 1989.

Fox, J. "Formal and Knowledge-based Methods in Decision Technology." In *Professional Judgment*. Ed. J. Dowie and A. Elstein. Cambridge: Cambridge University Press, 1988, pp.226-252.

_____. "Knowledge, Decision Making and Uncertainty." *Artificial Intelligence and Statistics*. Reading, MA: Addison Wesley, 1986a, pp. 57-76.

_____. "Three Arguments for Extending the Framework of Probability." In *Uncertainty in Artificial Intelligence*. Ed. L.N. Kanal, and J.F. Lemmer. New York: Elsevier, North-Holland, 1986b, pp. 447-458.

Freedman, D.P., and G.M. Weinberg. *Handbook of Walkthroughs, Inspections, and Technical Reviews*. Boston: Little Brown and Co., 1982.

French, S. *Decision Theory*. New York: John Wiley, 1986.

Frost, R.A. *Introduction to Knowledge Base Systems*. London: Collins, 1986.

Fu, L. "Integration of Phenomenological and Fundamental Knowledge in Diagnostic Expert Systems." *Proceedings of the IEEE International Conference on Systems, Man and Cybernetics*, Atlanta, Georgia, 1986, pp.552-556.

Fung, R.M., and C.Y. Chong. "Metaprobability and Dempster-Shafer in Evidential Reasoning." In *Uncertainty in Artificial Intelligence*. Ed. L.N. Kanal and J.F. Lemmer. New York: Elsevier North-Holland, 1986, pp. 295-302.

Gaines, B.R. "Knowledge Acquisition Systems." In *Knowledge Engineering*. Ed. H. Adelli,. New York: McGraw-Hill, pp. 52-102.

_____, and M.L.G.Shaw. "Logical Foundations of Expert Systems." *Proceedings of the IEEE International Conference on Systems, Man and Cybernetics*, New York, New York, 1984, pp. 238-247.

Gal, G. "Using Auditor Knowledge to Formulate Data Model Constraints: Expert Systems for Internal Control Evaluation." Ph.D. Dissertation. Michigan State University, 1985.

_____, and P.Steinbart. "Artificial Intelligence and Research in Accounting Information Systems: Opportunities and Issues." *Journal of Information Systems*, vol. 2, no. 1, Fall 1987, pp. 54-64.

_____, et al. "The Use of Rule-Based Expert Systems to Investigate the Effects of Experience on Audit Judgments." *Proceedings of the 7th. International Conference on Information Systems*, San Diego, CA, 1986, pp. 206-213.

Gardner, H. *Frames of Mind.* New York: Basic Books, 1983.

Garvey, T.D., J.D. Lowrance, and M.A. Fischler. "An Inference Technique for Integrating Knowledge from Disparate Sources," *Proceedings of the 7th International Joint Conference on Artificial Intelligence*, Vancouver, 1981, pp. 319-325.

Gaschnig, J., P. Klahr, H. Pople, E. Shortliffe, and A. Terry. "Evaluation of Expert Systems: Issues and Case Studies." In *Building Expert Systems.* Ed. F. Hayes-Roth, D.A. Waterman, and D.B. Lenat. Reading, MA: Addison-Wesley Inc., 1983, pp. 241-280.

Geissman, J.R., and R.D. Schultz. "Verification and Validation of Expert Systems." *AI Expert*, vol. 3, no. 2, February 1988, pp. 26-35.

Gettier, E. "Is Justified True Belief Knowledge?" *Analysis*, 23, pp. 121-123.

Gillett, P. "Automated Dynamic Programme Tailoring: An Expert System Approach." *Auditing: A Journal of Practice and Theory*, vol. 12, Supplement, 1993, pp. 173-189.

Gordon, J., and E.H.Shortliffe. "A Method of Managing Evidential Reasoning in a Hierarchical Hypothesis Space." *Artificial Intelligence*, 26, 1985, pp. 323-357.

Graham, L.E. and D. Shpilberg. "Developing an ES for Auditing." *Symposium on Expert Systems and Audit Judgments*, University of Southern California, February 1986.

Grammack, J.G. "Different Techniques and Different Aspects of Declarative Knowledge." In *Knowledge Acquisition for Expert Systems.* Ed. A.L. Kidd. London: Plenum, 1987, pp. 137-164.

_____, and R.M. Young. "Psychological Techniques for Eliciting Expert Knowledge." In *Research and Development in Expert Systems.* Ed. M.A. Braemer. Cambridge: Cambridge University Press, 1985, pp. 105-112.

Greenwell, M. *Knowledge Engineering for Expert Systems.* Chichester, UK: Ellis Horwood, 1988.

Grosof, B.N. "An Inequality Paradigm for Probabilistic Knowledge." In *Uncertainty in Artificial Intelligence.* Ed. L.N. Kanal and J.F. Lemmer. New York: Elsevier North-Holland, 1986a, pp. 259-275.

_____. "Evidential Confirmation as Transformed Probability." In *Uncertainty in Artificial Intelligence*. L.N. Kanal and J.F Lemmer. New York: Elsevier North-Holland, 1986b, pp. 153-166.

Hacking, I. *Logic and Statistical Inference*. Cambridge: Cambridge University Press, 1965.

Haddawy, P. "Implementation of and Experiments with a Variable Precision Logic Inference System." *Proceedings of AAAI-86*, Philadelphia, PA, 1986, pp. 238-242.

Hall, H.K., J.C Moore, and A.B. Whinston. "An Economic Basis for Expert Systems." Unpublished Manuscript. Krannert Graduate School of Management, Purdue University, West Lafayette, 1985.

Ham, J., D. Losell, and W. Smieliauskas. "An Empirical Study of Error Characteristics in Accounting Populations." *The Accounting Review*, vol. LX, no. 3, July 1985, pp. 387-406.

Hamm, R.M. "Clinical Intuition and Clinical Analysis: Expertise and the Cognitive Continuum." In *Professional Judgment*. Ed. J. Dowie and A. Elstein. Cambridge: Cambridge University Press, 1988, pp.78-108.

Hammond, K.R. "Toward a Unified Approach to the Study of Expert Systems." In *Expert Judgment and Expert Systems*. Ed. J. Mumpower, *et al*. New York: Springer Verlag, 1987, pp. 1-16.

Hampden-Turner, C. *Maps of the Mind*. New York: Macmillan, 1981.

Hansen, J.V. and W.F. Messier Jr. "Continued Development of a Knowledge-Based System for Auditing Advanced Computer Systems." Preliminary Report submitted to Peat, Marwick, Mitchell Foundation, Montvale, NJ, 1984.

Hansen, J., and W. Messier. "Preliminary Testing of EDP-XPERT." *Symposium on Expert Systems and Audit Judgement*, University of Southern California, February, 1986a.

_____, et al. "A Preliminary Investigation of EDP-XPERT." *Auditing: A Journal of Practice and Theory*, vol. 6, no. 1, Fall 1986, pp. 109-123.

Harman, G. *Change in View: Principle of Reasoning*. Cambridge, MA: MIT Press, 1986.

Harmon, P., and D. King. *Expert Systems: Artificial Intelligence in Business*. New York: Wiley, 1985.

Harris, L. "Brain Waves." *AI Expert*, vol. 3, no. 7, July 1988, pp. 70-80.

Hart, A. *Expert Systems: An Introduction for Managers*. London: Kogan Page, 1988.

_____. *Knowledge Acquisition for Expert Systems*. New York: Plenum, 1987.

Hartigan, J.A. *Bayes Theory*. New York: Springer-Verlag, 1983.

Hayes-Roth, B. "Evolution of Cognitive Structures and Processes." *Psychological Review*, vol. 84, no. 3, 1977, pp. 260-278.

Hayes-Roth, F., D. Waterman, and D. Lenat, eds. *Building Expert Systems*. Don Mills: Addison-Wesley, 1983.

Hayes-Roth, F. "Rule Based Systems." *Communications of the ACM*, volume 28, number 9, September 1985, pp. 933-941.

Heckerman, D. "Probabilistic Interpretations of MYCIN's Certainty Factors." In *Uncertainty in Artificial Intelligence*. Ed. L.N. Kanal and J.F. Lemmer. New York: Elsevier North-Holland, 1986, pp. 167-196.

Heckerman, D.E., and E.J. Horvitz. "On the Expressiveness of Rule-based Systems for Reasoning with Uncertainty." *Proceedings of the American Association for Artificial Intelligence Sixth National Conference on Artificial Intelligence*. Seattle, 1987, pp. 121-126.

Hedberg, B., and S. Jonsson. "Designing Semi-confusing Information Systems for Organizations in Changing Environments." In *Information Analysis: Selected Readings*. Ed. R. Galliers. Reading, Mass: Addison-Wesley, 1987, pp. 179-202.

Henrion, M. "Uncertainty in Artificial Intelligence: Is Probability Epistemologically and Heuristically Adequate." In *Expert Judgment and Expert Systems*. Ed. J. Mumpower, et al. New York: Springer Verlag, 1987, pp. 105-130.

Hink, R.F., and D.L. Woods. "How Humans Process Uncertain Knowledge: An Introduction for Knowledge Engineers." *AI Magazine*, Fall 1987, pp. 41-53.

Hoare, C.A.R., and J.C. Shepherdson, eds. *Mathematical Logic and Programming Languages*. New York: Prentice-Hall International, 1985.

Hoffman, R.R. "The Problem of Extracting the Knowledge of Experts." *The AI Magazine*, vol. 8, no. 2, Summer 1987, pp. 53-67.

Hogarth, R.M. and S. Makridakis. "Forecasting and Planning: an evaluation." *Management Science*, vol. 27, no. 2, 1981, pp.115-138.

Holder, W.W. "Analytical Review Procedures in Planning the Audit: An Application Study." *Auditing: A Journal of Practice and Theory*, vol. 2, no 2, Spring 1983, pp. 100-108.

Holland, J.R., K.J. Holyoak, R.E. Nisbett, and P.R. Thagard. *Induction: Processes of Inference, Learning, and Discovery*. Cambridge, MA: MIT Press, 1986.

Holtzman, S. and J. Breese. "Exact Reasoning about Uncertainty: On the Design if Expert Systems for Expert Support." In *Uncertainty in Artificial Intelligence*. Ed. L.N. Kanal and J.F. Lemmer. New York: Elsevier North-Holland, 1986, pp. 339-345.

Hooper, G. "A Calculation of the Credibility of Human Testimony." *Philosophical Transactions of the Royal Society*, 21, 1699, pp. 359-365.

Horvitz, E.J., D.E. Heckerman, and C.P. Langlotz. "A Framework for Comparing Alternative Formalisms for Plausible Reasoning." *Proceedings of AAAI-86*, Philadelphia, PA, 1986, pp. 210-214.

Horwich, P. *Asymmetries in Time*. Cambridge, MA: MIT Press, 1987.

Howard, R.A., and J.E. Matheson. "Influence Diagrams." In *Readings on the Principles and Applications of Decision Analysis*. Ed. R.A. Howard and J.E. Matheson. Menlo Park, CA: Strategic Decision Group. 1981, pp. 721-762.

Howe, J. "Learning Through Model Building." In *Expert Systems in the Micro-electronics Age*. Ed. D. Michie. Edinburgh: Edinburgh University Press, 1979, pp. 215-225.

Hubbard, T.D. and J.D. Ballington. "Positive and Negative Confirmation Requests - A Test." *Journal of Accountancy*, March 1972, pp. 48-56.

Humphreys, P. "Decision Aids: Aiding Decisions." In *Human Decision Making*. Ed. L. Sjoberg, T. Tyszka, and J.A.Wise. Bodafors, Sweden: Doxa, pp. 14-44.

_____—. "Levels of Representation in Structuring Decision Problems." *Journal of Applied Systems Analysis*, vol. 11, April 1984, pp. 3-22.

_____, and D. Berkeley. "Problem Structuring Calculi and Levels of Knowledge Representation in Decision Making." In *Decision Making Under Uncertainty*. Ed. R. Scholz. New York: Elsevier North-Holland, 1983, pp. 121-157.

_____, and W. McFadden. "Experiences with MAUD: Aiding Decision Structuring versus Bootstrapping the Decision Maker." *Acta Psychologica*, 45, 1980, pp. 51-69.

_____, and A. Wishuda. *MAUD4. Decision Analysis Unit. Technical Report 82-5*. London: London School of Economics and Political Science, 1982.

_____, S. Wooler, and L.D. Phillips. *Structuring Decisions: The Role of Structuring Heuristics. Decision Analysis Unit. Technical Report 80-1.* Uxbridge, England: Brunel University, 1980.

Hunter, D. "Uncertain Reasoning using Maximum Entropy Inference." In *Uncertainty in Artificial Intelligence*. Ed. L.N. Kanal and J.F. Lemmer. New York: Elsevier North-Holland, 1986, pp. 203-209.

Jeffrey, R.C. *The Logic of Decision*. 2nd ed. Chicago: University of Chicago Press, 1983.

Johnson, E.N. "Auditor Memory for Audit Evidence: Effects of Group Assistance, Time Delay, and Memory Tasks." *Auditing: A Journal of Practice and Theory*, vol. 13, no. 1, Spring 1994, pp. 36-56.

Johnson, J., R. Leitch, and J. Neter. "Characteristics of Errors in Accounts Receivable and Inventory Audits." *The Accounting Review*, April 1981, pp. 270-293.

Johnson, L. "The Need for Competence Models in the Design of Expert Consultant Systems." *International Journal of Systems Research and Information Science*, vol. 1, no. 1, 1985, pp. 23-36.

Johnson, N.E. "Mediating Representations in Knowledge Elicitation." In *Knowledge Elicitation*. Ed. D. Diaper. Chichester: Ellis Horwood, 1989, pp. 179-194.

Johnson, P.E. "Cognitive Models of Expertise." Paper presented at the *USC Conference on Audit Judgment*, University of Southern California, February, 1986.

_____. "The expert mind: A new challenge for the information scientist." In *Beyond productivity: Information systems development for organizational effectiveness*. Ed. Th. M.A. Bemelmans. New York: Elsevier North-Holland, 1983, pp. 367-386.

_____. "What Kind of Expert Should a System Be?" *Journal of Medicine and Philosophy*, vol. 8, pp. 77-97, 1983.

_____, K. Jamal, and R.G. Berryman. "Audit Judgment Research: Cognition, Memory and Knowledge Representation." Paper presented at the *USC Conference on Audit Judgement*, University of Southern California, February 1987.

Johnson, R.W. "Independence and Bayesian Updating Methods." *Artificial Intelligence*, 29, 1986, pp. 217-222.

Johnson-Laird, P.N. *Mental Models*. Cambridge: Cambridge University Press, 1983.

Joyce, E.J. "Expert Judgement in Audit Program Planning." *Studies in Human Information Processing in Accounting*, Supplement to the *Journal of Accounting Research*, volume 14, 1976, pp. 29-60.

_____, and R. Libby. "Behavioral Studies of Audit Decision Making." *Journal of Accounting Literature*, vol. 1, 1982, pp. 102-123.

Kadesch, R.R. "Subjective Inference with Multiple Evidence." *Artificial Intelligence*, 28, 1986, pp. 333-341.

Kahneman, D., and A. Tversky. "Judgment Under Uncertainty: Heuristics and Biases." In *Judgment Under Uncertainty: Heuristics and Biases*. Ed. D. Kahneman, P. Slovic, and A. Tversky. Cambridge: Cambridge University Press, 1982, pp. 1-20.

Kaplan, R.S. "A Financial Planning Model for an Analytic Review: The Case of a Savings and Loan Association." *Auditing: A Journal of Theory and Practice*, vol. 2, no. 2, Spring 1983, pp. 52-65.

_____. "Developing a Financial Planning Model for an Analytic Review: A Feasibility Study." *Symposium on Auditing Research III*, University of Illinois, Urbana Champaign, 1978, pp. 3-37.

Kavrakoglu, I. "Interactive Decision Support Systems for Enhancing Expert Judgment." In *Expert Judgment and Expert Systems*. Ed. J. Mumpower, *et al.* New York: Springer Verlag, 1987, pp. 147-154.

Keeney, R., and H. Raiffa. *Decisions with Multiple Objectives: Preferences and Value Tradeoffs*. New York: Wiley, 1976.

Kelly, K.P., G.S. Ribar, and J.J. Willingham. "Interim Report on the Development of an Expert System for the Auditor's Loan Loss Evaluation." *Auditing Symposium VIII*, University of Kansas, Lawrence, KA, 1986, 167-181.

Kent, S. "Words of Estimated Probability." *Studies in Intelligence*, 8, 1964, pp. 49-65.

Keravnou, E.T., and L.Johnson. *Competent Expert Systems*. London: Kogan Page, 1986.

Kessel, K.L. "Methodological Tools for Knowledge Acquisition." *Proceedings of the IEEE International Conference on Systems, Man and Cybernetics*, Atlanta, GA, 1986, pp. 541-546.

Kidd, A.L. "Knowledge Acquisition - An Introductory Framework." In *Knowledge Acquisition for Expert Systems*. Ed. A.L. Kidd. London: Plenum, 1987, pp. 1-16.

_____, and M.B.Cooper. "Man-Machine Interface Issues in the Construction and Use of an Expert System." *International Journal of Man-Machine Studies*, 22, 1985, pp. 91-102.

Kielstra, R.G. "A Prototype Expert System for the Assessment of Inherent Risk." Unpublished Manuscript. School of Accountancy, University of Waterloo, Ontario, Canada, July 1986.

Kim, J.H., and J. Pearl. "A Computational Model for Causal and Diagnostic Reasoning in Inference Systems." *Proceedings of the 8th International Joint Conference on Artificial Intelligence*, Karlsruhe, West Germany, 1983, pp. 190-193.

Kinney, W.R. "Attention-Directing Analytical Review Using Accounting Ratios: A Case Study." *Auditing: A Journal of Practice and Theory*, vol. 6, no. 2, Spring 1987, pp. 59-73.

_____. "A Note on the Compounding of Probabilities in Auditing." *Auditing: A Journal of Practice and Theory*, vol. 2, no. 2, Spring 1983, pp. 13-22.

_____. "The Predictive Power of Limited Information in Preliminary Analytical Review: An Empirical Study." *Journal of Accounting Research*, Supplement 1979, pp. 148-165.

_____. "ARIMA and Regression in Analytical Review: An Empirical Test." *The Accounting Review*, January 1978, pp. 48-60.

Kissinger, J.N. "A General Theory of Evidence as the Conceptual Foundation in Auditing Theory: Some Comments and Extensions." *The Accounting Review*, vol. LII, no. 2, April 1977, pp. 322-339.

Kjaergaard, D. "What is Knowledge? And What is Management Support." Working Paper. Copenhagen School of Business, Informatics and Management Accounting, 1987.

Klein, H.K., and R.Hirschheim. "Fundamental Issues of Decision Support: A Consequentialist Approach." *Decision Support Systems*, vol. 1, no. 1, 1985, pp. 5-24.

Klir, G.J., and T.A. Folger. *Fuzzy Sets, Uncertainty, and Information*. New York: Prentice Hall, 1988.

Knechel, W.R. "The Effectiveness of Statistical Analytical Review as a Substantive Auditing Procedure: A Simulation Analysis." *The Accounting Review*, vol. LXIII, no. 1, January 1988, pp. 74-95.

_____. "A Simulation Study of the Effectiveness of Alternative Analytical Review Procedures." *Decision Sciences*, vol 17, Summer 1986, pp. 376-394.

Kolmogorov, A.N. *Foundations of a Theory of Probability* . New York: Chelsea, 1956.

Kolodner, J.L. "Towards an understanding of the role of experience in the evolution from novice to expert." In *Developments in Expert Systems*. Ed. M.J. Coombs. London: Academic Press, 1985, pp. 95-116.

_____. "The Role of Experience in the Development of Expertise." *Proceedings of AAAI-82*, Pittsburg, PA, 1982, pp. 284-289.

_____, and R.L. Simpson, Jr. "Problem Solving and Dynamic Memory." In *Experience, Memory and Reasoning*. Ed. J.L. Kolodner and C.K. Riesbeck. Hillsdale, NJ: Lawrence Erlbaum, 1986, pp. 99-114.

Kong, A., G.O. Barnett, F. Mosteller, and C. Youtz. "How Medical Professionals Evaluate Expressions of Probability." *The New England Journal of Medicine*, 315, September 1986, pp. 740-744.

Kowalski, R. *Logic for Problem Solving*. New York: Elsevier, 1983.

Landry, M., D. Pascot, and D. Briolat. "Can DSS Evolve Without Changing Our View of the Concept of 'Problem'." *Decision Support Systems*, vol. 1, no. 1, 1985, pp. 25-36.

Lane, N.E. "Global Issues in Evaluation of Expert Systems." *Proceedings of the IEEE Conference on Systems, Man and Cybernetics*, New York, NY, 1986, pp. 121-125.

Langley, P. "Rediscovering Physics with BACON-3," *IJCAI-79*, Tokyo, 1979, pp. 505-507.

_____. "BACON1: A General Discovery System." *Proceedings of the Second National Conference of the Canadian Society for Computational Studies*, Toronto, ONT, Canada, 1978.

_____, and J.G. Carbonell. "Approaches to Machine Learning." *Journal of the American Society for Information Science*, 35, 1984, pp. 304-316.

_____, H.A. Simon, G.L. Bradshaw, and J.M. Zytkow. *Scientific Discovery: Computational Explorations of the Creative Process*. Cambridge, MA: MIT Press, 1987.

Langlotz, C.P., and E.H. Shortliffe. "Logical and Decision-Theoretic Methods for Planning under Uncertainty." *AI Magazine*, vol 10, no. 1, Spring 1989, pp. 39-48.

_____, et al. "Using Decision Theory to Justify Heuristics." *Proceedings of AAAI-86*, Philadelphia, PA, 1986, pp. 215-219.

_____, et al. "Adapting a Consulting System to Critique User Plans." In *Developments in Expert Systems*. Ed. M.J. Coombs. London: Academic Press, 1984, pp. 77-94.

_____, et al. "Adapting a Consultation System to Critique User Plans." *International Journal of Man-Machine Studies*, vol. 19, 1983, pp. 479-496.

Larkin, J.H. "The Role of Problem Representation in Physics." In *Mental Models*.. Ed. D. Gentner and A.L. Stevens. Hillsdale, NJ: Erlbaum, 1983, pp. 75-98.

_____. "Enriching Formal Knowledge: A Model for Learning to Solve Textbook Problems." In *Cognitive Skills and Their Acquisition*. Ed. J.R. Anderson. Hillsdale, NJ: Erlbaum, 1981, pp. 311-334.

_____, D. McDermott, D. Simon, and H. Simon. "Expert and Novice Performance in Solving Physics Problems." *Science*, June 1980, pp. 1335-1342.

Larsson, S., and G.R. Chesley. "An Analysis of the Auditor's Uncertainty about Probabilities." *Contemporary Accounting Research*, vol. 2, no. 2, Spring 1986, pp. 259-282.

Laudan, L. *Science and Values*. Berkeley, CA: University of California Press, 1984.

Lee, R.M. "Bureaucracy as Artificial Intelligence." Paper presented at *IFIP Working Group TC 8.3*. Durham, England, 1984.

_____. "Epistemological Aspects of Knowledge-Base Decision Support Systems." In *Processes and Tools for Decision Support*. Ed. H.G. Sol. Amsterdam: North-Holland, 1983, pp. 25-36.

Lehner, P.N., M.A. Probus, and M.L. Donnell. "Building Decision Aids: Exploiting the Synergy Between Decision Analysis and Artificial Intelligence." *IEEE Transactions on Systems, Man and Cybernetics*, vol. SMC15, no. 4, July/August 1985, pp. 469-474.

Lemmer, J.F., and S.W. Barth. "Efficient Minimum Information Updating for Bayesian Inferencing in Expert Systems." *Proceedings of the National Conference on Artificial Intelligence*. Pittsburg, 1982, pp. 424-427.

Lemon, W.M., A.A. Arens, and J.K. Loebbecke. *Auditing: An Integrated Approach*. Canadian 4th ed. Scarborough, Ontario, Canada: Prentice-Hall, 1987.

Leslie, D.A. "An Analysis of the Audit Framework Focusing on Inherent Risk and the Role of Statistical Sampling in Compliance Testing." *Auditing Symposium VIII*. University of Kansas, Lawrence, KA, 1984, pp. 31-64.

_____. "Audit of Accounting Estimates." *CA Magazine*, January 1978, pp. 34-44.

_____, S.J. Aldersley, D.J. Cockburn, and C.J. Reiter. "An Assertion Based Approach to Auditing." *Research on Auditing Symposium VIII*, The University of Kansas, Lawrence, Kansas, 1986.

Levi, I. *The Enterprise of Knowledge*. Cambridge, MA: MIT Press, 1983.

Libby, R. *Accounting and Human Information Processing: Theory and Applications*. Englewood Cliffs, NJ: Prentice Hall, 1981.

Libby, R., J.T. Artman, and J.T. Willingham. "Process Susceptibility, Control Risk, and Audit Planning." *The Accounting Review*, vol. LX, no. 2, April 1985, pp. 212-230.

Lin, W.T., T.J. Mock, and A.Wright. "The Use of the Analytic Hierarchy Process as an Aid in Planning the Nature and Extent of Audit Procedures." Working Paper No. 53, Center for Accounting Research, University of Southern California, 1983.

Lind, J.H. "Downloading the Expert: Knowledge Acquisition for Expert Systems." *Proceedings of the IEEE International Conference on Systems, Man and Cybernetics*, Atlanta, GA, 1986, pp.547-550.

Lindley, D.V. *Introduction to Probability and Statistics, Parts 1 and 2*. New York: Cambridge University Press, 1980.

Loebbecke, J.K., and P.J. Steinbart. "An Investigation of the Use of Preliminary Analytical Review to Provide Substantive Audit Evidence." *Auditing: A Journal of Theory and Practice*, vol. 6, no. 2, Spring 1987, pp. 74-79.

Loui, R.P. "Interval-Based Decisions for Reasoning Systems." In *Uncertainty in*

Artificial Intelligence. Ed. L.N. Kanal and J.F. Lemmer. New York: Elsevier North-Holland, 1986, pp. 459-472.

Lowrance, J.D., and T.D. Garvey. "Evidential Reasoning: A Developing Concept." *Proceedings of the International Conference on Cybernetics and Society*. Seattle, Washington, 1982, pp. 6-9.

Lu, S.Y., and H.E. Stephanou. "A Set-Theoretic Framework for the Processing of Uncertain Knowledge." *Proceedings of the National Conference on Artificial Intelligence*. Pittsburg, 1982, pp. 216-221.

Lucas, H.C. *Why Information Systems Fail*. New York: Columbia, 1975.

Makridakis, S., and R. Winkler. "Averages of Forecasts: Some Empirical Results." *Management Science*, vol. 29, no. 9, September 1983, pp. 987-996.

Malone, T.W., K.R. Grant, F.A. Turbak, S.A. Brobst, and M.D. Cohen. "Intelligent Information-sharing Systems." *Communications of the ACM*, vol. 30, no. 5, May 1987, pp. 390-402.

_____, J. Yates, and R.J. Benjamin. "Electronic Markets and Electronic Hierarchies." *Communications of the ACM*, vol. 30, no. 6, June 1987, pp. 484-498.

Mandler, J.M. *Stories, Scripts, and Scenes: Aspects of Schema Theory*. Hillsdale, NJ: Lawrence Erlbaum, 1984.

Marcot, B. "Testing your Knowledge Base." *AI Expert*, vol 2, no. 8, August 1987, pp. 42-47.

Margolis, H. *Patterns, Thinking, and Cognition: A Theory of Judgment*. Chicago: University of Chicago Press, 1987.

Markus, M.L., and N. Bjorn-Andersen. "Power over Users: Its Exercise by System Professionals." *Communications of the ACM*, vol. 30, no. 6, June 1987, pp. 498-504.

Martin, J., and C. McClure. *Structured Techniques for Computing*. Englewood Cliffs, NJ: Prentice-Hall, 1985.

Mattersich, R. *Instrumental Reasoning and Systems Methodology*. Boston: D.Reidel Publishing Company, 1978.

Mautz, R.K. "Evidence, Judgment and the Auditor's Opinion." *The Journal of Accountancy*, April 1959, pp. 40-44.

_____. "The Nature and Reliability of Audit Evidence." *The Journal of Accountancy*, May 1958, pp. 40-47.

_____, and H.A.Sharaf. *The Philosophy of Auditing*. Sarasota, FL: American Accounting Association, 1961.

McCarthy, J. and P.J.Hayes. "Some Philosophical Problems from the Standpoint of Artificial Intelligence." In *Machine Intelligence 4*. Ed. D. Michie and B. Meltzer. Edinburgh: Edinburgh University Press, 1969.

McDermott, J. "R1: An Expert System in Computer System Domains." *AAAI-80*, 1980, pp. 269-271.

McKeithen, K.B., J.S. Reitman, H.H. Rueter, and S.C. Hirtle. "Knowledge Organization and Skill Differences in Computer Programmers." *Cognitive Psychology*, 13, 1981, pp. 307-325.

McTear, M.F. *Understanding Cognitive Science*. Chichester, UK: Ellis Horwood, 1988.

Meservy, R.D., A.D. Bailey, and P.E. Johnson. "Internal Control Evaluation: A Computational Model of the Review Process." *Auditing: A Journal of Practice and Theory*, vol. 6, no. 1, Fall 1986, pp. 44-74.

Messier, W.F., Jr., and J.V. Hansen. "A Case Study and Field Evaluation of EDP-XPERT." *Symposium on Audit Judgment*. University of Southern California, Los Angeles, California, February 1988.

_____, et al. "Expert Systems in Accounting and Auditing: A Framework and Review." *Proceedings of the University of Oklahoma Behavioral Research Conference*. Norman, Oklahoma, August 1983, pp. 182-202.

Meyer, P.L. *Introductory Probability and Statistical Applications*. Reading, MA: Addison-Wesley, 1970.

Michie, D. "A Prototype Knowledge Refinery." In *Intelligent Systems: The Unprecedented Opportunity*. Ed. J.E. Hayes and D.Michie. New York: John Wiley, 1984, pp. 57-69.

_____, and R. Johnston. *The Creative Computer*. Harmondsworth, Middlesex, England: Penguin Books, 1984.

Miller, A.C., M.W. Merkhofer, and R.A. Howard. *Development of Automated Aids for Decision Analysis*. Menlo Park, CA: Stanford Research Institute, 1976.

Miller,P.L. *A Critiquing Approach to Expert Computer Advice: ATTENDING*. Marshfield, M.A.: Pitman, 1984.

Minsky, M.L. "A Framework for Representing Knowledge." In *The Psychology of Computer Vision*. Ed. P. Winston. New York: McGraw Hill, 1975, pp. 211-277.

Mishler, E.G. *Research Interviewing: Context and Narrative*. Cambridge, MA: Harvard University Press, 1986.

Mock, T.J. *Measurement and Accounting Information Criteria*. Studies in Accounting Research No. 13, American Accounting Association, 1976.

_____, and A. Wright. "Evaluating the Effectiveness of Audit Procedures." *Auditing: A Journal of Practice and Theory*, Fall 1982, pp. 33-44.

_____, and A. Wright. "An Investigation of a Measurement Based Approach to the evaluation of Audit Evidence." *Audit Symposium V*. University of Kansas, Lawrence, KA, 1980, pp. 61-76.

Morris, N.M., and W.B. Rouse. "The Effects of Type of Knowledge upon Human Problem Solving in a Process Control Task." *IEEE Transactions on Systems, Man and Cybernetics*, vol. SMC-15, no. 6, November/December 1985, pp. 698-707.

_____, et al. "On Looking into the Black Box: Prospects and Limits in the Search for Mental Models." *Psychological Bulletin*, 100, no. 3, 1986, pp. 349-363.

Moulin, B., and D. Rousseau. "Automated Knowledge Acquisition from Regulatory Texts." *IEEE Expert,* vol. 7, no. 5, October 1992, pp. 27-35.

Mullarkey, J. "The Case for the Structured Audit." *Research on Auditing Symposium VII.* The University of Kansas, Lawrence, KA, 1984, pp. 75-84.

Myers, C.D., J. Fox, S.M. Pegram, and M.F. Greaves. "Knowledge acquisition for expert systems: Experience using EMYCIN for leukemia diagnosis." In *Proceedings of the Third BCS Conference on Expert Systems.* Ed. J. Fox, London, 1983, pp. 277-283.

Mylopulos, J., and H. Levesque. "An Overview of Knowledge Representation." *7th. German Workshop on Artificial Intelligence*, New York: Springer Verlag, 1983, pp. 143-157.

Nachmias, D. and C. Nachmias. *Research Methods in the Social Sciences.* New York: St. Martin's Press, 1981.

Nathan, N.M.L. *Evidence and Assurance.* Cambridge: Cambridge University Press, 1980.

Naumann, J.D., and A.M. Jenkins. "Prototyping: The New Paradigm for Systems Development". *MIS Quarterly*, September 1982, pp. 29-44.

Neches, R., W.R. Swartout, and J.D. Moore. "Enhanced maintenance and explanation of expert systems through explicit modeling of their development." *IEEE Transactions on Software Engineering,* vol. SE-4, no. 11, November 1985, pp. 1337-51.

Negotia, C.V., and D. Ralescu. *Simulation, Knowledge-based Computing, and Fuzzy Statistics.* New York: Van Nostrand Reinhold, 1987.

Newell, A., and H.A. Simon. *Human Problem Solving.* Englewood Cliffs, NJ: Prentice-Hall, 1972.

Nguyen, T.A., W.A. Perkins, T.J. Laffey, and D. Pecora. "Knowledge Base Verification." *The AI Magazine*, vol. 8, no. 2, Summer 1987, pp. 69-75.

Nilsson, N.J. "Probabilistic Logic." *Artificial Intelligence*, 28, 1986, pp. 71-87.

Nisbett, R.E. and L. Ross. *Human Inference: Strategies and Shortcomings of Social Judgment.* Englewood Cliffs, NJ: Prentice-Hall, 1980.

Nisbett, R.E., and T.D.Wilson. "Telling more than we can know: verbal reports of mental processes." *Psychological Review*, 84, 1977, pp. 231-259.

Oatley, K. "Inference, navigation and cognitive maps." In *Thinking.* Ed. P.N. Johnson-Laird and P.C. Watson. Cambridge: Cambridge University Press, 1977, pp. 537-547.

O'Keefe, R.M. "Expert Systems and Operational Research - Mutual Benefits." *Journal of the Operational Research Society*, vol. 36, no. 2, 1985, pp. 125-129.

O'Leary, D. "Methods of Validating Expert Systems." *Interfaces*, 18, no. 6, November-December 1988, pp. 72-79.

_____. "Validation of Expert Systems." *Decision Sciences*, vol. 18, no. 3, Summer, 1987a, pp. 468-486.

_____. "Is Prototyping of ES Audit Models Research." *Audit Judgement Symposium* . University of Southern California, Los Angeles, CA, February, 1987b.

_____. "Validation of Business Expert Systems." *Audit Judgement Symposium* . University of Southern California, Los Angeles, February, 1986.

Ornstein, R. *Multimind: A new way of looking at human behavior.* Boston: Houghton Mifflin, 1986.

Ould, M.A., and C. Unwin. *Testing in Software Development.* Cambridge: Cambridge University Press, 1986.

Owen, D.L. "The concept of influence and its use in structuring complex decision problems." Ph.D. Dissertation. Stanford University, 1979.

Pearl, J. "On Evidential Reasoning in a Hierarchy of Hypotheses." *Artificial Intelligence,* 28, 1986a, pp. 9-15.

_____. "Fusion, Propagation and Structure in Belief Networks." *Artificial Intelligence,* 29, 1986b, pp. 241-288.

_____. "A Constraint-Propagation Approach to Probabilistic Reasoning." In *Uncertainty in Artificial Intelligence.* Ed. L.N. Kanal and J.F. Lemmer. New York: Elsevier North-Holland, 1986c, pp. 167-196.

_____. "Reverend Bayes on Inference Engines: A Distributed Hierarchical Approach." *Proceedings of the National Conference on Artificial Intelligence.* Pittsburg, 1982, pp. 133-136.

Phillips, L., and J. Boxall. "A problem structuring analysis of heuristics and biases." *Decision Analysis Unit, Technical Report 83-1.* London: London School of Economics and Political Science, 1983.

Piaget, J. *The Development of Thought: Equilibriation of Cognitive Structures.* Oxford: Basil Blackwell, 1977.

_____. *To Understand is to Invent.* New York: Grossman, 1973.

_____. *The Principles of Genetic Epistemology.* London: Routledge and Kegan Paul, 1972.

Polanyi, M. *The Tacit Dimension.* New York: Doubleday, 1967.

Politakis, P.G. *Empirical Analysis for Expert Systems.* London: Pitman, 1985.

Pollack, M.E., J. Hirschberg, and B.Webber. "User Participation in the Reasoning Processes of Expert Systems." *AAAI-82,* Pittsburg, PA, 1982, pp. 358-361.

Pople, H. "Heuristic Methods for Imposing Structure on Ill-Structured Problems: The Structuring of Medical Diagnosis." In *Artificial Intelligence in Medicine.* Ed. P. Szolovits. Boulder, Colorado: Westview Press, 1982, pp. 119-190.

Porter, M.E., and V.E. Millar. "How Information Gives You Competitive Advantage." *Harvard Business Review*, vol. 63, no. 4, July-August 1985, pp. 149-160.

Prerau, D.S. "Knowledge Acquisition in Expert Systems Development." *The AI Magazine*, vol. 8, no. 2, Summer 1987, pp. 43-51.

Pressman, R.S. *Software Engineering: A Practitioner's Approach.* New York: McGraw-Hill, 1987.

Quinlan, J.R. "INFERNO: A Cautious Approach to Uncertain Inference." *The Computer Journal*, 26 (3), 1983a, pp. 255-268.

_____. "Consistency and Plausible Reasoning." *Proceedings of the 8th International Joint Conference on Artificial Intelligence.* Karlsruhe, West Germany, 1983b, pp. 137-144.

Ramaprasad, A. "Cognitive process as a basis for MIS and DSS design." *Management Science*, vol. 33, no. 2, February 1987, pp. 139-148.

Rappaport, A., ed. *Information for Decision Making.* Englewood Cliffs, NJ: Prentice-Hall, 1970.

Raufels, P. "Expert Systems: State of the Art and Future Prospects." *Proceedings of the German Workshop on Artificial Intelligence.* New York: Springer Verlag, January 1981, pp. 98-111.

Ravinder, H.V., D.N. Kleinmuntz, and J.S. Dyer. "The Reliability of Subjective Probabilities Obtained Through Decompositions." *Management Science*, vol. 34, no. 2, February 1988, pp. 186-199.

Reboh, R. "Extracting Useful Advice from Conflicting Expertise." *Proceedings of the International Joint Conference on Artificial Intelligence.* IJCAI, Karlsruhe, West Germany, 1983. pp. 146-150.

Reimann, P., and M.T.H. Chi. "Human Expertise." *Human and Machine Problem Solving.* New York: Plenum Press, 1989, pp. 161-191.

Rennels, G.D., E.H. Shortliffe, F.E. Stockdale, and P.L. Miller. "A Computational Model of Reasoning from the Clinical Literature." *AI Magazine*, vol 10, no.1, Spring 1989, pp. 49-57.

Rescher, N. *Cognitive Systematization.* Oxford, England: Basil Blackwell, 1979.

_____. *Plausible Reasoning.* Assen, The Netherlands: Van Gorcum, 1976.

Reynolds, G., D. Strahman, N. Lehrer, and L. Kitchen. "Plausible Reasoning and the Theory of Evidence." Technical Report 86-11. Computer and Information Science Department, University of Massachusetts at Amherst, 1986.

Rich, E. *Artificial Intelligence.* New York: McGraw Hill, 1983.

Riesbeck, C.K. "Knowledge Reorganization and Reasoning Style." In *Developments in Expert Systems.* Ed. M.J. Coombs. London: Academic Press, 1984, pp. 159-175.

Robinson, J.A. "A Machine-oriented Logic Based on the Resolution Principle." *Journal of the ACM*, 12, 1965, pp. 23-41.

Robinson, P., and D. Foster. *Experimental Psychology: A Small-N Approach.* New York: Harper and Row, 1979.

Saaty, T.J. *The Analytic Hierarchy Process*. New York: McGraw Hill, 1980.

_____. "Modeling Unstructured Decision Problems - The Theory of Analytic Hierarchies." *Mathematics and Computers in Simulation*, September 1978, pp. 147-158.

_____. "A Scaling Method for Priorities in Hierarchical Structures." *Journal of Mathematical Psychology*, June 1977, pp. 234-281.

_____, and K.P. Kerns. *Analytical Planning*. New York: Pergammon Press, 1985.

Salmon,W.C. *Logic*. Englewood Cliffs, N.J.: Prentice-Hall, 1984.

Samnet, M.G. "Critique on 'Procedures for the Communication of Uncertainty in Auditor's Working Papers'." In *Behavioral Experiments in Accounting II*. Ed. T.J. Burns. Columbus, Ohio: The Ohio State University, 1979, pp. 158-168.

Schank, R.C. and R.P. Abelson. *Scripts, Plans, Goals and Understanding*. Hillsdale, NJ: Lawrence Erlbaum, 1977.

_____, and S. Slade. "Advisory Systems." In *Artificial Intelligence Applications in Business*. Ed. W. Reitman. Norwood, NJ: Ablex, 1984.

Schepanski, A. "Tests of Information Processing Behavior in Credit Judgement." *The Accounting Review*, Fall 1983a, pp. 503-512.

Schmalhofer, F. "Expert Systems as Cognitive Tools for Human Decision Making." In *Expert Judgment and Expert Systems*. Ed. J. Mumpower, *et al.* New York: Springer Verlag, 1987, pp. 269-288.

Schmucker, K.J. *Fuzzy Sets, Natural Language Computations, and Risk Analysis*. Rockville, MD: Computer Science Press, 1984.

Schoemaker, P.J.H. "The Expected Utility Model: Its Variants, Purposes, Evidence and Limitations." *Journal of Economic Literature*, June 1982, pp. 529-563.

Schon, D. *The Reflective Practitioner: How Professionals Think in Action*. New York: Basic Books, 1983.

Schum, D.A., and A.W. Martin. "Formal and Empirical Research on Cascaded Inference in Jurisprudence." *Law and Society Review*, vol. 17, 1982, pp. 105-157.

_____. "Assessing the Probative Value of Evidence in Various Inference Structures." Technical Report number 81-02. Houston, TX: Rice University, Department of Psychology, 1981.

_____. "Empirical Studies of Cascaded Inference in Jurisprudence." Technical Report number 80-01. Houston, TX: Rice University, Department of Psychology, 1980.

Selfridge, M., and S.F. Biggs. "GCX, A computational Model of the Auditor's Going-Concern Judgement." *Symposium on Audit Judgment*. University of Southern California, Los Angeles, California, February 1988.

_____, and G.R. Krupka. "GCX - A Cognitive Expert System for Making Going Concern Judgments." CSE/CARC Technical Report #86-20, University of Connecticut, Storrs, Connecticut, Department of Computer Science and Engineering, 1986.

Sen, A., and G. Biswas. "Decision Support Systems: An Expert Systems Approach." *Decision Support Systems*, vol.1, no. 3, 1985, pp. 197-204.

Sergot, M. "A Query-the-User Facility for Logic Programming." In *Proceedings of the European Conference on Integrated Interactive Computing Systems*. Ed. P. Degano and E. Sandewall. New York: Elsevier North-Holland, 1983, pp. 27-41.

Shacter, R.D. "Evaluating Influence Diagrams." *Operations Research*, 34, 1986, pp. 871-882.

Shafer, G. "Probability Judgment in Artificial Intelligence." In *Uncertainty in Artificial Intelligence*. Ed. L.N. Kanal and J.F. Lemmer. New York: Elsevier North-Holland, 1986, pp. 127-136.

_____. "Constructive Probability." *Synthese*, 48, 1981, pp. 1-61.

_____. *A Mathematical Theory of Evidence*. Princeton, NJ: Princeton University Press, 1976.

_____, and R. Srivastava. "The Bayesian and Belief-Function Formalisms I. A General Perspective for Auditing." *Symposium on Research on Auditing*. School of Accountancy, University of Waterloo, Waterloo, Ontario, Canada, November 1987.

_____. "Managing Uncertainty in Expert Systems: A Perspective for Auditing." *Symposium on Expert Systems and Audit Judgment*, University of Southern California, Los Angeles, CA, February 1986.

_____, and A.Tversky. "Languages and Designs for Probability Judgment." *Cognitive Science*, 9 ,1985, pp. 309-339.

_____, P.P. Shenoy, and K. Mellouli. "Propagating Belief Functions in Qualitative Markov Trees." *International Journal of Approximate Reasoning*, vol. 1, no. 4, October 1987, pp. 349-400.

Shannon, R.E. *Systems Simulation: The Art and the Science*. Englewood Cliffs, NJ: Prentice Hall, 1975.

Shanteau, J. "Psychological Characteristics of Expert Decision Makers." In *Expert Judgment and Expert Systems*. Ed. J. Mumpower, *et al.* New York: Springer Verlag, 1987a, pp. 289-304.

_____. "Psychological Characteristics of Expert Decision Makers." *Symposium on Expert Systems and Audit Judgment*, University of Southern California, Los Angeles, CA, February 1986.

_____. "Some Unasked Questions about the Psychology of Expert Decision Makers." *Proceedings of the 1984 IEEE Conference on Systems, Man and Cybernetics*. Halifax, Nova Scotia, 1984, pp. 408-413.

_____, and R.H. Phelps. "Judgment and Swine: Approaches and Issues in Applied Judgement Analysis." In *Human judgment and decision processes in applied settings*. Ed. M.F. Kaplan and S. Schwartz. New York: Academic Press, 1977, pp. 255-272.

Shaw, M.L.G., and B.R. Gaines. "An Interactive Knowledge-Elicitation Technique Using

Personal Construct Technology." In *Knowledge Acquisition for Expert Systems: A Practical Handbook.* Ed. A.L. Kidd. New York: Plenum, 1987, pp. 109-136.

Shen, H.C., and K.C.C. Chan. "An Aid for Knowledge Acquisition in Knowledge-Based Systems." Unpublished Manuscript. Department of Systems Design, University of Waterloo, Waterloo, Ontario, Canada, 1986.

Shooman, M.L. *Software Engineering.* New York: McGraw Hill, 1983.

Shope, R.K. *The Analysis of Knowing.* Princeton, NJ: Princeton University Press, 1983.

Shortliffe, E.H. *Computer-Based Medical Consultations: MYCIN.* New York: Elsevier, 1976.

_____, and B.G.Buchanan. "A Model of Inexact Reasoning in Medicine." *Mathematical Biosciences*, vol. 23, 1975, pp. 351-379.

Shpilberg, D., and L.E. Graham. "Developing ExperTAX: An Expert System for Corporate Tax Accrual and Planning." *Auditing: A Journal of Practice and Theory*, vol. 6, no. 1, Fall 1986, pp. 75-94.

Silva, A.H., and D.C.Regan. "Using Cognitive Psychology Techniques for Knowledge Acquisition." *Proceedings of the IEEE International Conference on Systems, Man and Cybernetics.* Atlanta, GA, 1986, pp. 530-535.

Simon, D.P., and H.A. Simon. "Individual differences in solving physics problems." In *Childrens' Thinking: What Develops?* Ed. R.S. Seigler. Hillsdale, NJ: Lawrence Erlbaum Associates, 1978.

Simon, H.A. *The Sciences of the Artificial.* 2nd ed. Cambridge: MIT Press, 1981.

Sims, D., C. Eden, and S. Jones. "Facilitating Problem Definition in Teams." *European Journal of Operations Research*, 6, 1981, pp. 360-6.

Slatter, P.E. *Building Expert Systems: Cognitive Emulation.* London: Ellis Horwood, 1987.

Sloman, A. "Why We Need Many Knowledge Representation Formalisms." In *Research and Development in Expert Systems.* Ed. M.A. Bramer. Cambridge: Cambridge University Press, 1985, pp. 163-183.

Slovic, P., B. Fischhoff, and S.Lichtenstein. "Behavioral Decision Theory." *Annual Review of Psychology*, 28, 1977, pp. 1-39.

Smets, P. "Subjective Probability and Fuzzy Measures." In *Fuzzy Information and Decision Processes.* Ed. M.M. Gupta and E. Sanchez. New York: Elsevier North-Holland, 1982, pp. 87-91.

_____. "Medical Diagnosis: Fuzzy Sets and Degrees of Belief." *Fuzzy Sets and Systems*, 5, 1981, pp. 259-266.

Smith, D.G. *Analytical Review.* CICA Research Study, Canadian Institute of Chartered Accountants, 1983.

Sommerville, I. *Software Engineering.* Reading, MA: Addison-Wesley, 1985.

Sperber, D. *On Anthropological Knowledge.* Cambridge: Cambridge University Press, 1985.

_____, and D.Wilson. *Relevance.* Cambridge, MA: Harvard University Press, 1986.

Spiegelhalter, D. "A Statistical View of Uncertainty in Expert Systems." In *Artificial Intelligence and Statistics.* Ed. W.A. Gale. Reading, MA: Addison Wesley, 1986, pp. 17-55.

Spires, E.E "Combinations of Audit Evidence: Model and Test of Model." *Symposium on Audit Judgement.* University of Southern California, Los Angeles, California, 1989.

Srivastava, R. "A Note on Internal Control Systems with Control Components in Series." *The Accounting Review*, vol. LX, no. 3, 1985, pp. 504-507.

Stamper, R. "Management Epistemology: Garbage In, Garbage Out." *IFIP Working Group 8.3. Knowledge Representation for Decision Support Systems.* July 1984.

Stefik, M., J. Aikins, R. Balzar, J. Benoit, L. Birnbaum, F. Hayes-Roth, and E. Sacerdoti. "Basic Concepts for Building Expert Systems." In *Building Expert Systems.* Ed. F. Hayes-Roth, D.A. Waterman, and D.B. Lenat. Reading, MA: Addison-Wesley Inc., 1983, pp. 241-280.

Steinbart, P. "Materiality: A Case Study Using Expert Systems." *The Accounting Review*, vol. LXII, no. 1, January 1987, pp. 97-116.

_____. "The Construction of an Expert System to Make Materiality Judgments." Ph.D. Dissertation. Michigan State University, East Lansing, MI, 1984.

Steiner, G. "Comprehensive Managerial Planning." In *Strategic Planning for MIS.* Ed. E.R.Mclean and J.V.Sodden. New York: Wiley, 1977, pp. 31-63.

Steiner, G.A. *Strategic Planning.* New York: The Free Press, 1979.

Sterling, L. "Logical Levels of Problem Solving." *Logic Programming*, vol. 2, 1984, pp. 151-163.

Stevens, R.G. "An Investigation of the Descriptiveness of the General Theory of Evidence and Auditing." *Auditing: A Journal of Practice and Theory*, vol. 3, no. 1, Fall 1983, pp. 55-74.

Stewart, T.R., and C. McMillan, Jr. "Descriptive and Prescriptive Models for Judgment and Decision Making: Implications for Knowledge Engineering." In *Expert Judgment and Expert Systems.* Ed. J. Mumpower, *et al.* New York: Springer Verlag, 1987, pp. 305-320.

Strat, T.M. "Continuous Belief Functions for Evidential Reasoning." *Proceedings of the National Conference on Artificial Intelligence.* Austin, TX, 1984, pp. 308-313.

Stringer, K.W., and T.R. Stewart. *Statistical Techniques for Analytical Review in Auditing.* New York: John Wiley, 1986.

Suchman, L.A. *Plans and Situated Actions: The Problem of Human-Machine Interaction.* New York: Cambridge University Press, 1987.

Sufrin, B.A., I.H. Sorensen, C.C. Morgan, and I.J. Hayes, "Notes for a Z Handbook." *Oxford University Programming Group Internal Report.* 1985.

Sugeno, M. "Theory of Fuzzy Integrals and Its Applications." Ph. D. Thesis. Tokyo Institute of Technology, 1974.

Sullivan, J.D. "The Case for the Unstructured Audit Approach." *Research on Auditing Symposium VII.* The University of Kansas, Lawrence, KA, 1984, pp. 61-68.

Sviokla, J.J. "Business Implications of Knowledge-based Systems. Part I." *Database*, vol. 17, no. 4, Summer 1986, pp. 5-19.

_____. "Business Implications of Knowledge-based Systems. Part II." *Database*, vol. 18, no. 1, Fall 1986b, pp. 5-16.

Swanson, D.B., P.J. Feltovich, and P.E. Johnson. "Analysis of Physician Expertise: Implications for the Design of Decision Support Systems." In *Medinfo77*. Ed. D.B. Shires and H.Wolf. Amsterdam: North-Holland, 1977.

Swartout, W.R. "XPLAIN: A System for Creating and Explaining Expert Consulting Systems." *Artificial Intelligence*, vol. 21, no. 3, September 1983, pp. 285-325.

_____. *Producing Explanations and Justifications of Expert Consulting Systems.* Cambridge: MIT, Report 251, 1981.

Swinburne, R. *An Introduction to Confirmation Theory.* London: Methuen, 1973.

Szolovits, P. and S.G. Pauker. "Categorical and Probabilistic Reasoning in Medical Diagnosis." *Artificial Intelligence*, 11, 1978, pp. 115-144.

Toba, Y. "A Semantic Meaning Analysis of the Ultimate Proposition to be Verified by Independent Auditors." *The Accounting Review*, vol. LV, no. 4, October 1980, pp. 604-619.

_____. "A General Theory of Evidence as the Conceptual Foundation in Auditing Theory." *The Accounting Review*, January 1975, pp. 7-24.

Torasso, P., and Console, L. *Diagnostic Problem Solving*." London, UK: Kogan Page, 1989.

Turban, E., and P.R.Watkins. "Integrating Expert Systems and Decision Support Systems." *MIS Quarterly*, vol. 10, no. 2, June 1986, pp. 121-136.

Tversky, A. "Elimination by Aspects: A theory of Choice." *Psychological Review*, 79(4), 1972a, pp. 281-299.

Vandamme, F. "Knowledge Extraction from Experts in View of the Construction of Expert Systems." In *Expert Judgment and Expert Systems.* Ed. J. Mumpower, *et al.* New York: Springer Verlag, 1987, pp. 321-338.

van Melle, W., A.C. Scott, J.S. Bennett, and M.A. Peairs. "The EMYCIN Manual." Technical Report, Heuristic Programming Project, Stanford University, California, 1981.

Veasey, P.W., and S.J. Pollard. "Preparing the Organization for IPSE." *The ICL Technical Journal*, vol 5, issue 2, November 1986, pp. 253-273.

Vinze, A.S., Karan, V., and U.S. Murthy. "A Generalizable Knowledge-based Framework for Audit Planning Expert Systems." *The Journal of Information Systems*, vol. 5, no. 2, 1991, pp. 78-91.

Vitale, M., B. Ives, and C. Beath. "Identifying Strategic Information Systems." *Proceedings of the Seventh International Conference on Information Systems*. San Diego, 1986, pp. 265-276.

von Fraassen, B.C. *The Scientific Image*. Oxford: The Clarendon Press, 1980.

von Winterfeld, D. "Structuring Decision Problems for Decision Analysis." *Acta Psychologica*, 45, 1981, pp. 77-94.

Waddington, C.H. *Tools for Thought*. St. Albans, England: Paladin, 1977.

Warren, C. "Confirmation Reliability - The Evidence." *The Journal of Accountancy*, February 1975, pp. 85-89.

Washington, M.T. "Incorporating Internal Control System Reliability in Audit Evidence Evaluation Using Cascaded Inference Theory." *Symposium on Audit Judgment*. University of Southern California, Los Angeles, California, February 1988.

Wasil, E., B. Golden, and A. Assad. "Using the Analytical Hierarchy Process to Rank Heuristics on the Basis of Accuracy." Working Paper MS/S 83-023, Department of Management Science and Statistics, University of Maryland, 1983.

Watkins, P.R. "Judgmental Support Systems (JSS): A Proposal for Integrating Auditor Judgment and Judgement Support Research." *Conference on Audit Judgment*. University of Southern California, Los Angeles, California, February 1987.

Watson, S.R., and D.M. Buende. *Decision synthesis: The principles and practice of decision analysis*. Cambridge: Cambridge University Press, 1987.

Watson, S., and A.Freeling. "Assessing Attribute Weights." *Omega*, 10, 1983a, pp. 582-583.

_____. "Comment on: Assessing Attribute Weights by Ratios." *Omega*, 11, 1983b, p. 13.

Wensley, A.K.P. "Research Directions in Expert Systems." In *Knowledge-based Management Support Systems*. Ed. G. Dukidis, F. Land, and G. Miller. London: Ellis Horwood, 1989, pp. 248-275.

_____. "User-Interface Design for Expert Systems." Paper presented at IFIP Working Group 8.3, Durham, England, July 1984a.

_____. "User-Interfaces: Major Issues." Unpublished Paper. 1984b.

Wessells, M.G. *Cognitive Psychology*. New York: Harper and Row, 1982.

Wetter, T. "Common Sense Knowledge in Expert Systems." In *Expert Judgment and Expert Systems*. Ed. J. Mumpower, *et al.* New York: Springer Verlag, 1987, pp. 339-358.

White, A.P. "Inference Deficiencies in Rule-Based Expert Systems." In *Research and Development in Expert Systems*. Ed. M.A. Bramer. Cambridge, England: Cambridge University Press, 1985, pp. 39-50.

Wierzchon, S.T. "On Fuzzy Measure and Fuzzy Integral." In *Fuzzy Information and Decision Processes*. Ed. M.M. Gupta and E. Sanchez. New York: Elsevier North-Holland, 1982, pp. 79-86.

Wilensky, R. *Planning and Understanding*. Reading, MA: Addison-Wesley, 1983.

Wisudha, A. "Design of Decision-Aiding Systems." In *Behavioral Decision Making*. Ed. G. Wright. London: Plenum Press, Chapter 11, 1985, pp. 235-256.

Woods, D.D. "Graphical Representation of Complex Worlds." *Proceedings of the IEEE Conference on Systems, Man and Cybernetics*. Atlanta, GA, 1986, pp. 259-261.

Wright, A. "Behavioral Research in Auditing: The State-of-the-Art." *The Auditor's Report*. Auditing Section, American Accounting Association, vol. 11, no. 2, Winter 1988, pp. 1-5.

Wright, G. *Behavioral Decision Theory*. Harmondsworth, Middlesex, UK: Penguin Books, 1984.

_____, and P. Ayton. "Eliciting and Modelling Expert Knowledge." *Decision Support Systems*, vol. 3, no. 1, 1987, pp. 13-26.

Yazdani, M. "Knowledge engineering in PROLOG." In *Expert Systems: Principles and Case Studies*. Ed. R. Forsyth. London: Chapman and Hall, 1984, 175-183.

Yu, V.L., L. Fagan, S. Wraith, W. Clancey, A. Scott, J. Hannigan, R. Blum, B. Buchanan, and S. Cohen. "Evaluation of the Performance of a Computer-based Consultant." *Computer Programming in Biomedicine*, vol. 9, 1979a, pp. 95-102.

_____. "Antimicrobial Selection by Computer: A Blinded Evaluation by Infectious Disease Experts." *Journal of the American Medical Association*, 1979b, pp. 1279-1282.

Zadeh, L. "Review of 'A Mathematical Theory of Evidence - by G.Shafer'." *AI Magazine*, Fall 1984, pp. 81-83.

_____. "Fuzzy as a Basis for a Theory of Possibility." *Fuzzy Sets and Systems*, 1, 1978, pp. 3-28.

ISBN 1-55876-056-3
90000>
9 781558 760561